CURRENT PRACTICES IN HIGH-TECH HOME CARE

About the Authors

Lenard W. Kaye, D.S.W., is Professor of Social Work & Social Research and Director of the Ph.D. Program at the Graduate School of Social Work & Social Research at Bryn Mawr College, Bryn Mawr, Pennsylvania. Dr. Kaye has published approximately 100 journal articles and book chapters on specialized topics in gerontology and health care and 10 books including *New Developments in Home Care Services for the Elderly: Innovations in Policy, Program, and Practice* (1995); *Home Health Care* (1992); *Elderly Men: Special Problems and Professional Challenges* (1997); *Part-Time Employment for the Lower Income Elderly: Experiences From the Field* (1997); *Controversial Issues in Aging* (1997); and *Self-Help Support Groups for Older Women: Rebuilding Elder Networks Through Personal Empowerment* (1997); and *Men as Caregivers to the Elderly* (1990). Dr. Kaye sits on the editorial boards of the *Journal of Gerontological Social Work* and *Geriatric Care Management Journal* and is a Fellow of the Gerontological Society of America.

Joan K. Davitt, M.S.S., M.L.S.P., is Instructor and Research Associate at Bryn Mawr College Graduate School of Social Work and Social Research. Ms. Davitt holds two master's degrees, the Master's of Social Service and the Master's of Law and Social Policy from Bryn Mawr College Graduate School of Social Work and Social Research. Ms. Davitt is editor of *A Guide to Nursing Homes in Philadelphia* and author of a book chapter The Importation of High Technology Services into the Home in *New Developments in Home Care Services for the Elderly*. She has published numerous articles on home health care, advance care planning and life-sustaining treatment issues, and housing options for older adults. She is currently completing her doctorate in social work and social research at Bryn Mawr College.

About the Contributor

Raymond L. Albert, J.D., M.S.W., is Associate Professor and Director, Law and Social Policy Program at Bryn Mawr College Graduate School of Social Work and Social Research. He is the author of the text *Law and Social Work Practice* (Springer Publishing Company), which he is currently revising for a second edition.

CURRENT PRACTICES IN HIGH-TECH HOME CARE

Lenard W. Kaye, DSW
Joan K. Davitt, MSS, MLSP

SPRINGER PUBLISHING COMPANY

Springer Publishing Company, Inc.
536 Broadway
New York, NY   10012-3955

Cover design by Janet Joachim
Acquisitions Editor: Bill Tucker
Production Editor: J. Hurkin-Torres

99 00 01 02 03 / 5 4 3 2 1

Library of Congress Cataloging-in-Publication Data

Kaye, Lenard W.
    Current practice in high-tech home care / Lenard W. Kaye, Joan K. Davitt ; with a chapter by Raymond L. Albert.
        p.   cm.
    Includes bibliographical references and index.
    ISBN 0-8261-1256-0 (hardcover)
    1. Home care services—Technological innovations.   2. Medical technology.   I. Davitt, Joan K.   II. Albert, Raymond.   III. Title.
    [DNLM: 1. Home Care Services—organization & administration—United States.   2. Home Care Agencies—organization & administration—United States.   3. Technology, Medical. WY 115 K23c 1999]
    RA645.3.K387 1999
    362.1′4—dc21
    DNLM/DLC
                                                            98-48398
                                                                CIP

We are dedicating this book to our mothers, Harriet and Annabelle. Their love, support, and wisdom have never faltered and never failed to enrich our lives.

L.W.K. AND J.K.D.

Contents

List of Tables

Acknowledgments

The authors wish to acknowledge the support of those individuals and organizations whose contributions served to make this project a success. We thank Dr. Ursula Springer, President, and Bill Tucker, Managing Editor at Springer Publishing Company, for expressing initial interest and providing ongoing support for the preparation of this manuscript. Jean Hurkin-Torres, our Production Editor, was most skillful in moving the manuscript to publication with minimal delay.

We are most grateful for the financial support and encouragement of the AARP Andrus Foundation's Board of Trustees; their former Administrator, Dr. Kenneth G. Cook; and Project Officer, Dr. Pamela B. Kerin. The support of the Andrus Foundation made possible the performance of the initial research on which this book is based.

Raymond L. Albert, a faculty member at the Bryn Mawr Graduate School of Social Work and Social Research and the research project's Legal Consultant, provided insightful analyses of the broad legal implications of high-tech service delivery for vulnerable populations. His chapter in this volume is an important contribution to this analysis.

Susan Reisman Kaye edited earlier versions of the professional and consumer guides to high-tech home health care that chapters 11 and 12 are based on. Susan also assumed lead responsibility for researching and updating the literature review presented in chapter 2. Her work, as always, is first rate.

Our original team of field interviewers, coders, data entry personnel, and transcribers performed in yeoman-like fashion throughout the course of the original research project. They included Paulette Canuso, Julie Chippendale, Janis Edwards, Dr. Keivan Fatolomi, Alison Garside, Dorothy Gibbons, Eileen Gildea, Lisa Layne, Sonya Lindgren, Susan Reisman Kaye, Shipra Sinha, and Naomi Wilansky. Tembeka Ntusi and Patricia Schumann deserve special mention for the significant contributions they made in performing selected in-person and telephone data collection and data processing tasks. Mary Katherine Kraft provided helpful consultation in statistical processing during the course of the original research.

Our thanks extend to various individuals within the Bryn Mawr College and Graduate School of Social Work and Social Research community who assisted in the administrative, budgetary, and technical execution of the project. Included here are Ruth W. Mayden, Dean; Marcia Martin, Associate Dean; Nona Smith, Faculty Grants Officer; Thomas Warger, former Director of Academic Computing; Diane Craw, Assistant to the Dean; Adrienne D'Amato, former Secretary to the Dean; Josiane Allen, former Secretary to the Dean; and Peg McConnell and Lorraine Wright, Faculty Secretaries.

Val J. Halamandaris, President of the National Association for Home Care (NAHC) in Washington, DC, was most cooperative in providing formal endorsement for the national survey of home health care agency executive directors. His staff also participated in reviewing drafts of the survey questionnaire used in conducting the research reported in this book.

We extend our sincere thanks to the cooperating executive directors and coordinating site staff at the participating Pennsylvania and Delaware home health care agencies. They are Timothy Cousounis, President and CEO, and Mary Jo Leyden and Sue Donovan, agency staff, Community Health Affiliates, Ardmore, PA; Mahlon Fiscel, Executive Director, and Eleanor Rhinier, agency staff, Neighborhood Visiting Nurse Association, Westchester, PA; Terry Miller, Executive Director, and Beverly Starkes, agency staff, Jefferson Home Health Services, Philadelphia, PA; and J. Mark Baiada, President, Bayada Nurses, Inc., Morristown, NJ; Carole Shaw, Executive Director, Bayada Media, Media, PA; Hiram Torres, Executive Director, Bayada Willow Grove, Willow Grove, PA; and Ginny Gotides, Executive Director, and Karen Foggin, agency staff, Bayada Wilmington, Wilmington, DE.

The willing participation of the staff and patients at the local agency sites and the executive directors comprising the national sample of home health care agencies in this investigation was, of course, of crucial importance in carrying out this analysis. Their capacity to give of themselves and share their organizational, professional, and personal experiences in home health care was pivotal in bringing our research to a successful conclusion.

I

Setting the Scene

CHAPTER 1

Introduction

THE SURGE IN HOME HEALTH CARE

Regardless of what now appears to be a long-term state of resource scarcity in the public sector, one specialized field of the health and human services, home health care, has seemingly proven that it is not only able to survive but even thrive. The home care industry is considered to be both the fastest growing (Freeman, 1995) and most diverse (Kane, Kane, Illston, & Eustis, 1994) sector of health care. A cost containment philosophy and patient desire for improved access to alternative forms of health care, especially community-based, noninstitutional health and social services, are certainly contributing factors to the home care expansion phenomenon (Hudson, 1996) and provide a rather compelling explanation for why home care has now eclipsed hospital care (Blumenthal & Haynes, 1995). However, the simple fact that home care is such an attractive health care option may have proven to be as influential as any factor, including its cost savings qualities, in the ultimate decision to expand in-home care (Applebaum, 1997).

As the health care system continues down the path toward a capitated, prospective payment system, home health care is likely to be the commonly preferred route not only for patients but also for those who are expected to foot the bill. By the year 2000, it is estimated that 85% of all health care will be delivered either in the home or in an ambulatory setting, a situation that escalates existent pressure on health care providers to discover cost effective strategies for health delivery (Warner, 1998).

Reflective of the current popularity of home care, the number of organizations providing in-home services to functionally impaired individuals continues to increase at an impressive rate. The home care service industry has grown from a mere 1,100 such programs in 1963 to more than 20,000 currently. In the context of a home care boom, the structure, auspice, and service repertoire of those organizations delivering in-home services remains diverse, with help provided to millions of individuals confronted by chronic health conditions, acute illness, terminal illness, and permanent disabilities each year. The fastest growing segments of the industry are hospital-based and freestanding proprietary agencies comprising 26% and 47% of all Medicare-certified agencies, respectively. However, of the 20,000 operating organizations, more than 8,000 home care agencies are noncertified and include home care aide organizations and hospices (National Association for Home Care, 1997). These programs remain outside Medicare for various reasons, including the likelihood that they do not provide the kinds of services that Medicare covers or do not provide skilled nursing care, which is required for reimbursement of home care services under Title XVIII of the Social Security Act.

Just as home care organizations have proliferated in recent years, so have hospices. Hospice programs provide palliative rather than curative care for the terminally ill and their families including medical, social, emotional, and spiritual services. The outlook for growth in hospice care, like home care, is strong given increases in the aging population, the increasing number of persons with AIDS, rising health care costs, and the attractiveness of the hospice care philosophy, which emphasizes holistic, patient-family, in-home centered health care delivery. Between 1984 and 1996 the total number of hospices participating in Medicare increased from a mere 31 to 2,154. In 1996, an additional 746 hospices were operating but were noncertified (Hospice Association of America, 1997). The proportion of hospices that are Medicare-certified is increasing, while the proportion of noncertified hospices is decreasing. Given the focus of this volume on the evolving profile of in-home care, it is important to note that the majority of Medicare-certified hospice programs are home care agency based.

HIGH-TECH HOME CARE

Among the categories of in-home services that have witnessed particularly active growth in recent years is that of high-tech care. Indeed, in-home services that reflect the use of high-technology equipment and techniques represent one of the newest and most challenging developments in this expanding area of service delivery. This dimension of home care is, in fact, projected to expand at an especially rapid pace in the years ahead. As reported by the Hastings Center:

> The high-tech home care industry has rapidly and relentlessly erased, for increasing numbers of families, the boundary between hospital and home, between the intensive care unit and the living room. More and more patients now receive in the privacy of their homes highly sophisticated medical treatments—ventilator therapy and artificial nutrition channeled through infusion pumps—that 20 years ago would only have been available in special care units (Hastings Center, 1994, p. 1).

THE CHANGING ENVIRONMENT OF HOME CARE

As the kinds of services comprising the home health care delivery package continue to evolve and reflect increasing measures of technology-enhanced components, it is important to recognize that a dramatic revolution in the complexity and industry positioning of home health care services is underway as well. Twenty years ago home care was depicted in exceedingly simplistic terms. This service category had little status in the professional community. Considered an ancillary service of low priority, workers occupied positions of exceedingly limited status in the health services sector. Home care's reputation as a stepchild to hospital and even nursing home care was reinforced by those who considered in-home services to consist largely of a supportive-maintenance component without therapeutic, preventive, and remedial elements. Home care's less esteemed standing expressed itself in terms of its limited availability and use, limited career opportunities for its front-line staff, and few opportunities for these workers to develop positive occupational identities (Kaye, 1985).

Today, the rapid expansion in the range of available in-home technologies has served to alter both the home environment and the nature of treatment provided to the functionally impaired older person. Home care workers are not only continuing to be challenged by the multiple needs associated with the home-based client's personal, familial, and emotional worlds, but also by a whole new set of technological advances, treatment modalities, and client conditions. These developments appear destined to alter substantially the landscape of gerontological home care and, in particular, the legal, technical, and ethical organizational and training regimens to which home care personnel and their elderly patients are exposed.

EMERGENT ROADBLOCKS TO EXPANSION

Of course, the home care revolution is not proceeding without its inevitable challenges and roadblocks. First, the home health care sector should not be interpreted as being totally immune to cuts in funding. More than a few politicians remain very concerned that the uncontrolled expansion of home care will ultimately translate into a whole new set of unanticipated and unmanageable costs accruing to tax-dependent programs like Medicare and Medicaid. While data indicate that the number of nursing home residents 85 years of age and over (per 1,000 population) actually decreased by 10% during the 10-year period 1985 to 1995 (U.S. Census Bureau, 1995), cost containment enthusiasts remain unconvinced that increased use of in-home care will be accompanied in the long run by declining utilization patterns of other forms of health care and in particular long-term institutional care. It is undeniable that home health care costs are increasing rapidly, from $3 billion in 1990 to $17 billion in 1996.

Congress, concerned by the escalating costs, included a number of measures in the 1997 Balanced Budget Act meant to curtail expenditures, including an interim payment system that places a cap, or ceiling, on the amount Medicare will reimburse each home care agency. This provision in the Act runs the risk of rolling back home health care reimbursement rates by lowering the per-patient cap at agencies to fiscal year 1994 levels minus 2%.

Another action taken by Congress by means of the Balanced Budget Act seeks to correct the tendency by some home care agencies to routinely provide clients with personal care services (e.g., assistance with eating, bathing, and dressing) beyond what Medicare law intended. Government officials maintain that the new laws will serve to return home health care to the original intent of the program—the provision of relatively short-term services for patients in medical need of skilled nursing and therapy services. The changes outlined above are expected to cut an estimated $16.2 billion from the home health outlays over the next 5 years (McLeod,

1998). However, spokespersons for home health care organizations and consumers warn that such policies run the risk of harming the most vulnerable of patients—those who are very ill and in need of the most intense and costly services.

Legislative proposals are being presented to hold the tide on the anticipated home health care cuts brought on by Balanced Budget Act changes in Medicare. The drama, which has potentially powerful consequences for the well being of home care organizations and their consumers, has not yet played itself out (NASW News, April 1998).

There are also cries that home health care is not adequately regulated so as to insure that quality, responsible care is going to be delivered in consistent fashion. Concerned observers point to the proliferating number of proprietary home care agencies that have entered the market obviously thinking that reimbursements for services rendered are lucrative. Akin to the nursing home scandals of the sixties and seventies, these critics predict the widespread occurrence of horrendous accounts of misuse of government funds and negligent care of vulnerable homebound older persons by greedy, profit-seeking home care organizations and their uncaring, poorly trained staff. In similar fashion, the quality of hospice care, a field of specialty introduced only 25 years ago, can vary, it is argued, considerably from one program to the next. Uniform, quality standards do remain less than fully developed, especially for home health care organizations offering end-of-life care. The absence of such standards led in part to the passage of the sections of the Balanced Budget Act impacting Medicare. While Medicare pays for much of the home care and hospice care in this country, being a Medicare certified agency does not, in and of itself, assure quality. And, while approval by such national bodies as the Joint Commission on Accreditation of Healthcare Organizations or the Community Health Accreditation Program would promote high standards in home care and hospice organizations, it is not required at this time (Crowley & Glasheen, 1998). Government officials continue to argue that the problems of fraud and abuse in home health care are significant, including improper charges to Medicare by home care organizations and, more recently, exaggerated threats to patients by organizations of reduced and discontinued benefits in the near future.

Still other difficulties challenge the trend toward home care expansion. Both home care and hospice coverage, while expanding through Medicaid, Medicare, and private insurance, can be difficult to access, negotiate, and subsequently secure by the novice consumer. The requirements and rules of eligibility may be complex and difficult to interpret and comprehend. Uninformed consumers without personal advocates but instead with a tendency toward passivity and confusion when dealing with formal community programs, government entitlements and benefits, and the ever present small print, may become demoralized and withdraw from the process of securing needed services.

THE CHOICE ACCORDING TO ELDERS IS CLEAR

Amidst the concurrent warnings of the nonbelievers and skeptics and the unfaltering expansion in the availability of in-home care throughout the country one fact remains patently clear. The vast majority of older adults, regardless of their potentially falteringly health, prefer, if they had the choice, to remain in the familiar environs of their own homes rather than being relocated to nursing homes, homes for aged persons, or even the residences of their relatives. Public opinion polls and health care service utilization research have repeatedly confirmed that individuals with disabilities wish to receive care at home if it is possible (Applebaum, 1997). Home care responds to the apparent basic human need during periods of vulnerability and decline to remain in one's own home setting. More than ever before, technology-enhanced services and equipment make it possible for even the most incapacitated older adult to do just that.

RATIONALE AND PURPOSE OF THE BOOK

The pronounced demographic shift in the profile of the population in this country requires innovative measures to satisfy increasing demands for widespread access to quality health care. By the year 2000, it is estimated that the 65 and older population will comprise 35.4 million persons. The number of those aged 65 or older could double between 1995 and 2025 (Health Care Financing Administration, 1996). In January of 1997, 32.3 million of the 261.6 million civilian noninstitutional population in the United States (12%) was 65 years of age or older. The Census Bureau has projected by the year 2050 as many as one in five Americans could be over 65 (U. S. Department of Labor, 1998).

State and federal payors, the private insurance sector, and those citizens who pay for substantial portions of their health care out-of-pocket will continue to exert cost containment pressure on the health care industry. At the same time consumers want high quality care and convenient access to the latest in health care innovation including technological advances in home-based service delivery. We argue that the technological revolution in home-delivered services, while progressing extremely rapidly, is proceeding without adequate systematic analysis of the comparative experiences of high-tech providers and their consumers. Nor do we think such analyses, even when they are performed, are figuring in prominent enough fashion in the development of best-practice approaches to planning, implementing, and operating high-tech home health care programs.

Information, which reflects current practice in high-tech home care, is critically needed to help inform the growing number of multidisciplinary professional personnel engaged in the planning, administration and delivery of this category of service. Unfortunately, the knowledge base on this topic remains underdeveloped, rarely drawing on applied research depicting current high-tech home care practice. This volume was designed to contribute in part to filling this very gap in the professional and multidisciplinary long-term care and in-home service delivery literature.

The primary purpose of this volume is to offer the reader convenient access to much needed information about the unique benefits, drawbacks, and challenges of importing high technology into the homes of older persons and the disabled. We believe this book is unique in its purposeful combination of both a descriptive report of research-based observations from the front-lines of home health agency operation and interpretive analyses of major issues, policies, and practices informing the delivery of high-tech home health services. Its unique quality is further reinforced by the fact that it proceeds to translate or reframe the research and analysis into concrete guidelines and recommendations for professional practice in home health care. The prescriptions for practice contained within this volume are intended to be of particular value to a wide range of home health care personnel. Content will be relevant to those agency planners and administrators, managers, and supervisors who are considering engaging in or have recently implemented a high-tech service program in their organization as well as in-home direct service providers such as occupational, speech, and physical therapists; nurses; social workers; and home health aides that are likely to work with patients receiving high-tech care.

ORGANIZATION OF THE BOOK

This book has been organized into three major sections. Section I introduces the reader to the field of high-tech home health care. It scans the historic and contemporary literature in home health care and aging and highlights significant developments and factors expected to influence the manner in which the home health service sector is likely to evolve in the context of the technology boom in health care.

Section II of the book reports on two streams of home health research conducted by the authors. Findings from both a national survey of home health care executives and an intensive local field study of direct service providers and older consumers of home health care are presented. Chapter 3 presents dominant profiles of both providers and consumers of traditional and high-tech home health care. Chapter 4 describes the experience of providing high-tech in-home services. In chapter 5 the experience of receiving high-tech home care is considered by providers and by older consumers themselves. Chapter 6 addresses issues pertaining to the rights of the home health patient. Finally, chapter 7 explores the impact that the introduction of high technology methods, services, and equipment is having on the structure and function of the home care organization.

It should be noted that the research reported in Section II and content presented elsewhere in the volume focus on the experience of providing home health services for primarily older adults. Indeed, the home health industry predominantly serves an aging population of individuals experiencing declining health. The emphasis of our research was on the intersection of high-tech home care and the older adult population. We realize, however, that other populations of consumers need and benefit from home health care services including the developmentally disabled, individuals with AIDS, pregnant women, sick children, accident victims, and others. The reader should realize that much of what is said herein, while referring to older adults, will have direct relevance and application value to other age groups who are beneficiaries of the interventions offered by home care organizations.

Section III introduces the reader to in-depth discussions of a series of crucial professional practice topics and issues in high-tech home health care. This section considers the legal (chapter 8), ethical (chapter 9), and financial reimbursement (chapter 10) dimensions of service. Section III also presents concrete professional practice guidelines for organizing and delivering high-tech care (chapter 11) and effectively informing consumers of the availability of such services (chapter 12). This section concludes by considering future trends and directions in the high-tech home health care field. Recommendations growing out of the authors' research are also presented (chapter 13).

The book's appendix contains technical details concerning the methodologic and statistical procedures adhered to in the performance of the research reported on in section II as well as the authors' recommendations for performing research of this type successfully (appendix A). That discussion will be of particular interest to those readers who are methodologically oriented and interested in the research strategies employed by the authors. The appendix also contains a guide to a wide variety of resources for those seeking more information about high-tech home health care services (appendix B), including references to government offices, professional and consumer organizations and associations, professional and scholarly journals and periodicals, and advocacy and special interest groups. Finally, a listing and description of selected categories of high-tech home health care service offered by organizations and available to the consumer in need of assistance is provided (appendix C).

THE RESEARCH REPORTED ON IN THIS BOOK

The research findings presented in section II (chapters 3–7) and from which practice guidelines, recommendations, and projections are offered in section III (chapters 8–13) represent a two-tiered inquiry into the experience of delivering and receiving traditional and high-tech in-home services. Specifically, it consisted of: a national survey and analysis of technology-enhanced service provision by both Medicare-certified and noncertified home care agencies; and an intensive local assessment of technology-enhanced home care service provision and consumption in the greater Philadelphia metropolitan area according to actual service providers and service consumers.

Both inquiries focused on a series of issues, all of which centered on a pivotal concern for this research: What role does technology play in the organization and delivery of home health care services? The following specific questions formed the conceptual foundation for the research project and guided the analysis of information collected.

1. What are the range and type of technology-enhanced home care services and equipment provided to the functionally impaired aged?
2. What are the organizational characteristics of home care agencies that engage in the delivery of technology-enhanced services and equipment?
3. What are the characteristic profiles of persons receiving technology-enhanced home care?
4. What influence does the provision of technology-enhanced home care have on home health care organizational structure and function?
5. To what degree are home care agencies confronted with various legal, moral, and ethical issues that have arisen during the course of delivering technology-enhanced home care?
6. To what extent are home care personnel equipped to respond to the technological and accompanying legal/ethical dimensions of contemporary home care service delivery?
7. What formal mechanisms have been established to address the legal, informational, and ethical demands of high-tech home care?
8. What is the relationship between type of home care services provided and provider and consumer perceptions of service quality and adequacy?

Answers to these questions were intended precisely to give direction to the development of a series of practical guidelines that would assist both agency providers in developing and older consumers in evaluating technology-enhanced home care services. Those practice guidelines (see chapters 11 and 12) are intended for both home care agency providers considering or engaged in the provision of high-tech home health care and the prospective consumers (older adults and their relatives) of such services.

DEFINING HIGH-TECH CARE

Throughout this book, technology-enhanced home care or high-tech home care is defined as those in-home methods of diagnosis, treatment, and rehabilitation that are physically embodied in specialized equipment and related supplies and services. Conversely, traditional home care services are defined as those interventions not requiring specialized equipment, treatment, or supplies to be performed. Given this definition, such intravenous (IV) therapies as antibiotic, chemotherapy, diuretic, hydration, enteral and total parenteral nutrition, pain control, steroid, chelation, respiratory, phlebotomy, and growth hormones would be clearly categorized as high-tech care. In fact, infusion therapy services have emerged as the most widely available high-tech service through home care organizations. Other high-tech interventions include the use of such respiratory therapy equipment as oxygen systems, nebulizers, apnea monitoring, suction equipment and tracheostomy supplies, and transtracheal oxygen supplies. Still other high-tech services to be considered in this volume include personal emergency response systems, "smart house" applications, computer-assisted interventions such as telehealth and telemedicine technology, and even the use of robotics.

CHAPTER 2

The Evolution of In-Home Technologies

INTRODUCTION

Expected increases in the older population have been widely documented in the literature. According to the World Health Organization, the world population increased by 80 million during 1996 with a total in excess of 5,800 million. Whereas the population of children and adolescents grew by 0.7%, the older population increased by 2.4%. Between 1990 and 1995, the number of persons 65 years of age and older increased by 14% globally, and it is projected that this population will grow by 82% between 1996 and 2020 (World Health Organization, 1997). In the United States alone, the Congressional Budget Office (1991) estimated that the over 65 age group will more than double by 2030.

In response to the projected increase in the aged population, Eastaugh (1981), more than 15 years ago predicted that elder care would be "the biggest future growth market for most health care providers." Indeed, the Institute for Health and Aging, between 1985 and 1988, found that all types of agencies experienced increases in the number of clients served who were over 65 years of age. Of particular relevance to this discussion, the Institute reported that over half of the home health agencies reported increases in clients served who were aged 85 and over during the years 1984 through 1986 (Institute for Health and Aging, 1986). Current home care statistics confirm these projections. In 1997, the National Association for Home Care reported over 20,000 home care organizations in the United States and its territories serving some 7 million persons (National Association for Home Care, 1997). The rapid growth of home care as compared to institutional services is additionally documented by health industry employment statistics. Between 1988 and 1995, home care employment more than doubled while, concurrently, hospital employment increased by just 10% and total health care industry employment grew 31% (National Association for Home Care, 1997).

Projections that the costs associated with nursing home care will double by the year 2005, while home health care costs will increase by only 70%, should further fuel the demand for both skilled and unskilled in-home services in the years ahead (Rivlin & Wiener, 1988). In 1997, the National Association for Home Care confirmed the cost-effectiveness of providing care in the home as well as the significantly lower annual increase in cost as compared to that of hospitalization or skilled nursing home care. During the period of 1994 through 1996, home health charges per visit increased 3.6%, whereas daily charges for hospital and skilled nursing facility care increased 12% and 16%, respectively (National Association for Home Care, 1997). The argument that community-based care is more cost efficient, humane, and compassionate than institutional care can only add further impetus to this trend of utilizing noninstitutional services such as home health care. Finally, the fact that opinion polls and surveys have repeatedly confirmed the powerful preference shown by older adults for noninstitutional, community-based service supports during times of need will insure that home-based services become increasingly the intervention of choice (Collopy, 1990a).

THE EXPANSION OF HOME HEALTH CARE

In modern times home care has been viewed as a service that is provided after other care has been delivered; something that was needed because mainstream medical services were unable to resolve the problem (Benjamin, 1993). Indeed, throughout most of the eighteenth and nineteenth centuries most people were cared for in the home by family. The first home care program, the Boston Dispensary, was created in 1796. The first hospital-based home care program, credited to Boston University Home Medical Service, was founded in 1885 (Keenan & Fanale, 1989).

As the provision of formal medical care progressed, the focus of service intervention remained on the home. The number of physicians practicing after the turn of the century began to increase along with the number of house calls.

By the late nineteenth century, modern science, industrialization, and urbanization began to shift the locus of medical care from the home to hospitals and doctors' offices. Changes in the social climate combined with economic factors contributed to a change in the nature of home care. Emphasis was increasingly being placed on public health and teaching families about prevention and hygiene, rather than on the actual delivery of services in the home (Reverby, 1987).

With improvements in public health, the health care system began to see increasing numbers of chronically ill patients. By the early 1900s, care of the chronically ill became an increasing problem for both physicians and voluntary hospitals (Benjamin, 1993). Beginning in the 1920s re-newed interest in home care was sparked by those interested in treating the chronically ill (Fox, 1992). Health care providers agreed that the chronically ill should not be occupying needed space in acute care hospi-tals. Where they disagreed was around which alternative, in-home care or institutional care, was best for such treatment. Opponents of home care favored the "specialized chronic disease hospital" as the appropriate site for caring for chronically ill persons (Boas & Michelsohn, 1929; Jarrett, 1933a; Jarrett, 1933b). The concerns related to home care centered around the capabilities of families to learn to care for a chronically ill relative and the limitations imposed by the home environment (e.g., poor lighting, ventilation, etc.). The debate around home care continued through the 1930s and 1940s, concluding in a study by the Commission on Chronic Illness (1956). This report suggested the need for "organized home care programs" that could offer a full range of services and would be coor-dinated by a single agency or institution (U.S. Public Health Service, 1955). "These programs should be centralized, with coordinated care planning, and a team approach to service provision" (Commission on Chronic Illness, 1956).

As time progressed, the financial benefits accruing to home care began to be emphasized. Blue Cross plans began to experiment with home care services, seeing home care as a way to reduce costly hospitalization (Foll-mann, 1963). Blue Cross plans established a direct link between hospital-ization and home care, even limiting, in some cases, the number of days of home care to the number of unused hospital days. At the same time, the debate around a federal role in health care ensued. The Social Security

Administration reviewed existing home care programs and the many Blue Cross plans. This research culminated in the creation of Medicare and Medicaid, which contained provisions for home care services. Within the Medicare system, the inclusion of limited home care coverage was believed to be one way to control the potentially rapid progression of medical costs in such a federal program. Planners reasoned that by offering home care (limited to certain types of services, of course) they were offering a strategy to reduce expenditures, while still providing adequate medical care to those who needed it. Specific services were limited, with emphasis on highly skilled, medically oriented services that would be covered if, and only if, the person had a hospital stay immediately prior to requesting home care.

Medicaid, on the other hand, did not view home care in the same way. Emphasis under Medicaid was on institutional care as opposed to home care. Medicaid (Title XIX) provided incentives for states to subsidize institutional care (Stevens & Stevens, 1974). States were not forced to fund in-home services even at minimal levels. Simply mentioning them in legislation or regulations was deemed sufficient. It was not until 1967 that amendments to Social Security made home health care mandatory rather than optional under Medicaid. Amendments to Medicare in 1972 extended coverage to the nonelderly disabled and persons with chronic renal disease and eliminated coinsurance requirements for home health care. Creation of the social services block grant (Title XX) in 1974 further extended home care services to older people and adult chronically ill persons.

In the mid 1970s to early 1980s, concerns mounted about the increased amount of public money being spent on nursing home care that may have been unnecessary (Benjamin, 1993). Proponents of home care pushed for expanded coverage as a cost-saving measure. Amendments under the Omnibus Budget Reconciliation Act of 1980 (OBRA 1980) eliminated limits on the number of allowable home visits, the prior hospitalization requirement, and the deductible under Part B. These regulatory changes fueled the expanded use of home health care services. Finally, amendments to Medicare in 1982 expanded the benefit to include hospice care for the terminally ill.

In the early 1980s the home care market experienced a great influx of proprietary providers. This was further encouraged by Medicare amendments under the OBRA 1980, which allowed all for-profit agencies to be Medicare certified regardless of their state licensure status. Eventually the number of proprietary agencies would grow to one third of all Medicare-certified agencies (Benjamin, 1993).

The next phase of policy development brought about a change in the way hospitals were reimbursed for service. This change was destined to impact all health care providers. The Prospective Payment System (PPS) created an additional surge of activity in the home care arena. "The PPS, implemented between 1983 and 1985, is a single policy change with as impressive an impact on health care provision as the initial implementation of Medicare and Medicaid in 1965" (Estes et al., 1993).

This policy dramatically shifted the locus of care provision to the home and community and away from the hospital. The increased demand and need for services for patients who were being discharged "quicker and sicker" from the hospital propelled the expansion of home health care even more dramatically (Kaye, 1988). An Institute for Health and Aging (IHA) study found that community-based agencies, including home health care providers, were seeing an increased intensity of need. There was a greater demand for services provided immediately upon discharge, an increased need for multiple services, greater need for services on a daily basis, more total hours of care, and more high-tech services (Estes et al., 1993). As a result, many services that were typically delivered in the hospital were adapted to be provided in the home, including physical, occupational, and speech therapy; pulmonary therapy; postsurgical nursing and rehabilitation; and many high-tech services. An indicator of this shift in care can be seen in the growth in hospital-based, Medicare-certified home health agencies (an increase of 77% between 1990 and 1996) (National Association for Home Care, 1997). Hospitals began to see a new market for health care: "the hospital at home." The trend toward care in the home helped spur the transition of case management from an institutional focus to an emphasis on the continuum of care in the community and was indeed a boon to private, publicly funded, and not-for-profit geriatric care managers alike (Quinn, 1995).

The expansion of Medicare and Medicaid has led to a boom in the home care industry. Medicare annual home health care expenditures have grown steadily as the number of Medicare-certified home care agencies has reached an all time high. As of 1996 there were 10,027 certified home health agencies counted among an estimated total of 20,215 home care agencies of all types. It is estimated that approximately 3.9 million Medicare enrollees received home care services through Medicare in fiscal year 1997 at a cost of nearly $20.5 billion. Medicaid home health expenditures for 1995 are estimated at $9.4 billion and growing (National Association for Home Care, 1997). It is noteworthy that Medicaid home care subsidies reduce the likelihood of nursing home admission for at-risk older persons using home care services. Simultaneously, it results in the substitution of formal home care for informal care provided by family members. Thus, it can be seen that the availability of Medicaid subsidies for home care can reduce nursing home expenditures while also reducing the amount of family care provided without charge (Ettner, 1994).

Although home care has grown at a rapid pace during the past 20 years, it still represents a small proportion of spending for all personal health care services. Only about 9% of Medicare and 8% of Medicaid benefit expenditures were for home care services in 1997 and 1995, respectively. Even so, the home care industry continues to expand at a rapid pace (National Association for Home Care, 1997). The estimated total spending on home care services in 1995 was approximately $35.2 billion. Medicare paid for 48.7%, Medicaid payments totaled 24.2%, and out-of-pocket expenditures accounted for 22.8%. Private insurance and all other sources of funding paid the remainder (Agency for Health Care Policy and Research, 1997).

THE ORGANIZATION OF HOME HEALTH CARE

Home health agencies have very diverse organizational configurations (Schmid & Hasenfeld, 1993). Agencies can be hospital-based, skilled nursing facility-based, freestanding, or part of a larger social or health service agency. They may be for-profit, public, or nonprofit. They can offer a wide array of services all delivered directly by agency staff (the generalist approach), or can specialize in certain types of services and subcontract all other services to other providers (the specialist strategy). They may offer only health care, limiting themselves to medical, nursing, or therapy services (Collopy, Dubler, & Zuckerman, 1990). Others may offer a broader range of services, including personal care services. Still others may merely provide coordination of service delivery, such as nurse registries.

According to Schmid and Hasenfeld (1993), a generalist strategy enables the organization to provide a more comprehensive system of care, to reach a broader target population, and to be responsive to changes in the demand for and supply of services. However, this approach is more costly, increases administrative demands, may be less efficient, and requires additional quality control. A specialist strategy enables an agency to target a special population or service. Specialization reduces administrative demands (quality control issues become less burdensome) within the agency and increases efficiency. However, specialization can lead to fragmentation of the service network, thereby reducing consumer access to services and increasing service coordination costs (Schmid & Hasenfeld, 1993). Also, specialist agencies can be slow to respond to market changes. Likewise, specialization can require "complex referral, subcontracting, and special vendor relations between agencies" (Collopy, Dubler, & Zuckerman, 1990).

Home health care agencies operate in highly competitive markets with an ever-rising demand for service. However, the mere fact that more services are being provided does not assure that these services are effective. Reimbursement for such services has become increasingly restricted while regulations governing the actual provision of service and the quality of such services have not kept pace with this changing industry. A number of factors impact the ability of the long-term care system to ensure high quality. These include consumer and provider characteristics, fiscal constraints, inadequate regulation, lack of quality assurance methods, and lack of a coherent social policy for home care. The continual creation and disbanding of agencies attests to the difficult nature of providing home health services in an efficient and effective manner. The lack of institutionalized rules and regulations regarding organizational structure promotes instability within the industry, which can erode quality (Schmid & Hasenfeld, 1993).

Estes et al. (1993) describe three main trends in the health care arena, which have impacted on traditional organizational structure and access to services—isomorphism, medicalization, and informalization. Isomorphism is a process of homogenization where individual types of organizations begin to look and act more and more alike (Estes et al., 1993). Government policies that gave greater access to for-profit home care providers and cutbacks in reimbursement and availability of government subsidies have pushed nonprofit agencies into an increasingly competitive market. According to Estes et al. (1993) most agencies in 1986 and 1987 were adding highly medical services to their program, and there was very little variation between nonprofit and for-profit agencies. However, research found that in 1984 through 1986 for-profit agencies were more likely to add highly medical services while nonprofits were more likely to add nonmedical services (Binney & Estes, 1990). Also, Medicare-certified agencies were more likely to add highly medical services than uncertified agencies (Binney & Estes, 1990). This has impacted the broad spectrum of services typically offered by nonprofit agencies. This factor, coupled with increased emphasis (by reimbursement sources) on medical or highly skilled services (medicalization), has focused service provision on those services that are most profitable—medically based, postacute, high-tech services.

Informalization refers to the increased shift to the informal sector to provide chronic care and supportive services. A high value may be attached to the role of informal care giver—family member, neighbor, clergy, among others—as is the case among many rural older people for whom independence is a key component of their culture (Magilvy, Congdon, & Martinez, 1994). This "warring dualism" of medicalization and informalization, fueled by public policy and technological advances, has decreased the comprehensive nature of home care services provided by home health care agencies, resulting in greater emphasis on high-tech services and less emphasis on custodial, supportive services.

TECHNOLOGY AND IN-HOME SERVICES

Accompanying the expansion of home care has been the continuous expansion in the range of high-tech medical care that can be accessed by the older adult (National Center for Health Services Research and Health Care Technology Assessment, 1988; Office of Technology Assessment, 1984, 1987). Medical and communications technologies have been successfully miniaturized and made portable so as to enable their availability in the home of the older adult. No longer are such devices and techniques restricted to the confines of more traditional institutional settings such as hospitals. Halamandaris (1986/87) points out that "the same technology that has allowed us to save lives is now being employed to help us care for survivors." And, ever more frequently, this process is being played out within the natural and familiar surroundings of the home.

The taxonomy of technology is subject, according to Haber (1986), to a binary classification system that distinguishes between health care technology and ecologic technology. Presently available home environmental enhancement devices include communications equipment such as automatic alarms signaling the need for help; automatic telephone dialing systems; electronic safety systems and monitors; in-home computers for self-instruction on taking medication, maintaining proper nutrition, and promoting self-care; and even robotics. Treatment-related high-tech services available in the home include artificial nutrition and hydration; mechanical ventilation; intravenous therapy; apnea monitors; bone growth stimulators; home dialysis; chemotherapy; platelet infusions; morphine drips;

IV infusion of fluids and medication; antibiotic therapy; and computerized health monitoring equipment (Kaye & Reisman, 1991b). In addition to applications directly supporting home care patients, computer networks offer caregivers access to a broad array of services. Caregivers can and do utilize computer technology in the home for services including communication, information, and decision support, all of which assist with the delivery of nursing care (Brennan, Moore, & Smyth, 1991).

When the above technologies are combined with some of the more straightforward devices now benefitting the homebound such as adaptive devices on tubs, beds, and stairs, and assistive devices that aid in dressing, bathing, grooming, and cooking, a complex and, in some sense, perplexing home environment begins to take shape. The use of such technologies in conjunction with the appropriate design of the older person's dwelling can enhance the individual's "environmental fit," "competence," safety, and communications capability, all of which enable greater control over the environment (Office of Technology Assessment, 1984).

While few home care settings reflect the utilization of more than one or two of the health, medical, and electronic technologies outlined above, home care services can expect to witness the increased likelihood that greater numbers of these new procedures and devices will be found in any given patient's home. In fact, the offering of high technology products and services represents the segment of the home care industry with the greatest projected rate of compound growth (Kane, 1989).

The emergence of technology-enhanced service in the home can be expected to have both positive and negative features. Haddad (1992) has highlighted the advantages and disadvantages of these interventions. The advantages include:

> . . . 1) the presence of family and familiar surroundings; 2) less opportunity to contract infectious diseases; 3) generally less expensive; and 4) greater opportunity for activity and participation in family life. The disadvantages include: 1) the increased burden on the family; 2) the invasion of family privacy; 3) the potential out-of-pocket costs for client and family; and 4) the absence of immediate professional care in case of an emergency.

Expansion of medical technology in the homes of older adults has, not unexpectedly, generated concerns about the appropriate use of such technology. On the one hand, it can be seen as replacing expensive hospitalization with a less costly and less restrictive alternative. However, opponents have argued that there are costs and liabilities to this expansion. According to Estes et al. (1993) those liabilities include: increased demands on informal caregivers; increased need for highly skilled, specially trained staff; changes in organizational structure; increased potential for agency liability; and increased risk to patients. Other drawbacks to the importation of health and medical treatment technologies into the home include reductions in patient autonomy, independence, and privacy. Zola (1987) suggests that "to make the home a mirror image of the hospital might make it no longer a home but a private hospital room and thereby defeat the very purpose of the shift." Ruddick (1994) takes this a step further suggesting that transferring hospital technology into the home not only causes a physical transformation of the environment, but also a social and emotional transformation of family members and their roles. The impact of altered family roles may result in strained and even damaging relationships. Under such circumstances, hospital care can help preserve crucial family relationships and actually provide greater patient autonomy. Yet others contend that further research is in order to assess more accurately the frequently sited costs and benefits of high-tech home care. Several studies, which have concluded that such in-home alternatives can help contain health care expenditures, have focused on antibiotic therapics, which are typically less expensive to administer than nutrition therapies, leading to a call for further systematic investigation of cost effectiveness (Arno, 1994).

While critics may focus on the shortcomings of high-tech home care as compared to available alternatives, it must be noted that there are situations where no equally good alternative exists locally. Take, for example, the experience of many rural older persons who reside in areas where little or no aging expertise exists or where institutional alternatives may not be available. Williams (1995) stresses the importance of a telecommunications system for such rural settings that would connect patients, local health care professionals, regional hospitals, referral centers, medical schools, and both state and federal agencies. In the case of rural America, a gap in services could be successfully filled.

THE CHANGING PROFILE
OF THE HOME CARE PATIENT

Paralleling the expansion in available home care technology is the changing profile of the home care population. Home care staff are providing service to individuals who are older, more deteriorated, and increasingly dependent on others for life maintenance. This appears to be due in no small part to the current economic incentive to discharge hospital patients sooner than had been the case in the past. Many are convinced that Medicare's Prospective Payment System for hospital care has not only led to an expansion of home health care, but has also altered the very profile of the home care population. This has added to the burden of home care programs and their staff to address the needs of an increasingly infirm aged population (Kaye, 1991). Fifteen years ago, the Office of Technology Assessment (1984) predicted that diagnostic-related groups would broaden the home use of medical care technologies. At the same time, they cautioned that the lack of reimbursement and available skilled providers of care would limit access to life-sustaining technologies as well as compromise their quality and safety.

While the profile of the typical home care recipient reflects an older, more deteriorated individual, the subset of high-tech home care patients are, in general, more likely to be younger, male, married, White, and living with others (Kaye & Davitt, 1995b). This distinction may very well point to differential access to certain categories of in-home care.

While empirical investigations confirm similarities among the majority of aged recipients of home care, in the realm of practical applications it is imperative to recognize the diversity among this population as well. Subgroups' cultural norms regarding informal and formal social support, barriers to accessing services, and service expectations and the resultant satisfaction or lack thereof must be taken into careful consideration to assure quality care across the board. For example, among Latino older persons, level of disability and availability of social supports influence the probability of utilizing paid in-home care. These predictors of usage, however, differ for non-Latino Whites (Wallace, Levy-Storms, & Ferguson, 1995). Additionally, significant income barriers to community-based care for Latino older persons have been documented (Wallace, Campbell, & Chih-Yin, 1994). Similarly, differences have been uncovered between African Americans and Whites in the respective emphasis placed on formal and informal care in the home. A comparison of older people entering home care following hospital discharge revealed that African Americans received significantly fewer hours of formal home care per week and significantly more hours of informal care per week, specifically from the primary care giver (Chadiha, Proctor, & Morrow-Howell, 1995).

Subpopulations of current or potential home care recipients may be identified not only by race or ethnicity, but also by any of a number of attributes.

Even the likelihood of accessing home care varies based on factors such as marital status, total number of activities of daily living, number of medical conditions, age, race, and gender (Mauser & Miller, 1994). Proper attention to the impact of these attributes will help insure equal access and quality service provision.

ORGANIZATIONAL RESPONSIBILITY AND HIGH-TECH HOME CARE

Quality Assurance and Staff Training

Used in the traditional sense of the phrase, quality assurance refers to measures directed at assuring appropriate, safe, and effective care. Such measures will ideally include establishing standards of care, monitoring care routinely to assess whether standards are being observed, taking action in the event that standards are not being met, and conducting assessments at regularly scheduled intervals. Assessments may be of three types: structural assessments that include a review of material and human resources and the organization of the agency or service; process assessments to evaluate the activities by caregivers done to, for, or with clients; and outcome assessments that address the effects of care on the clients' status (Weber et al., 1997).

The increased use of technology and highly skilled services in the home only emphasizes the need for expanded quality assurance strategies in each home health care agency. Quality assurance encompasses various aspects of service delivery. Agency administrators can look to federal and state regulations, accreditation, and certification standards for guidance in establishing policies and procedures to promote quality in service delivery (Mehlman & Younger, 1991). Procedural standards for many specific treatments have been established by various professional groups. Generally these standards provide definitions, describe appropriate provider types, and provide strategies for program implementation and ongoing service delivery, including patient selection criteria, care plan development, patient monitoring, and termination of service (Mehlman & Younger, 1991). Standards have also been developed for various aspects of professional behavior related to client interaction and service delivery. These standards cover various types of professional and paraprofessional personnel.

Hughes (1995) contends that, over time, home care providers will more frequently be required by regulators and payers to document the quality and effectiveness of their services and prove that they are offering a good value for the necessary expenditures. To do so will require that agencies have the requisite skills to conduct, or subcontract, thorough and meaningful evaluations of their offerings and consumer preferences.

Personnel issues impact directly on the provision of high-quality services. Although it is essential in any discipline or service to have well-trained staff, there is an especially great need for additional training and skill on the part of staff who are providing high-tech services. Many of these services are new to the home care arena. They may require highly technical or complicated equipment or very detailed and sensitive treatment modalities. "Home care nursing has evolved to a sophisticated array of technical skills reminiscent of hospital intensive care nursing" (Keenan & Fanale, 1989). This need for more highly trained and specially skilled staff will exacerbate already difficult recruitment measures and may require modification of recruitment strategies. Therefore, recruitment strategies may vary for high-tech agencies or programs.

In the search for technically qualified home care nurses, agencies will logically seek out those professionals with appropriate experience within institutional settings. While this strategy yields recruits with the requisite skill set—infusion therapy, for example—there remains an often-unrecognized training need. Such training must focus on the transition from hospital to home. The passage between health care settings may be fraught with frustration and stress, which, if left unresolved, will necessarily impact the quality of patient care (Coulter, 1997).

The agency's role for ensuring quality does not end once staff has been hired. Lindeman (1992) speaks to the need for training in high-tech service delivery as a basic component of nursing education. According to Lindeman, nurses need training on the use of equipment; the use of monitoring and recording devices; patient education; making clinical decisions in conditions of ambiguity; and dealing with ethical dilemmas and conflict. "One goal of nursing education is to prepare practitioners who can combine safe high-tech with meaningful high touch" (Lindeman, 1992). This, however, does not mean that nurses will no longer need continuing education. High-tech treatment is an expanding and dynamic arena. New innovations arise that must be passed on to staff. Staff will need continuing education and training related to equipment and treatment changes.

Training is essential for both those staff who are actually delivering high-tech services and for paraprofessional staff who provide ancillary assistance. Overall, home health aides provide more hours of service to patients than any other category of home health care staff. Therefore, it is more likely that they will be in the home when something goes wrong (e.g., equipment failure). Likewise, they provide much ancillary support to patients who may be receiving high-tech services. Home health aides provide many services, including monitoring temperature, pulse, and respiration; irrigating foley catheters; assisting with self-administered medications; and so forth (Mehlman & Younger, 1991). At a minimum, they will need training on emergency procedures, equipment use, and symptom recognition, as well as training on specific treatments that they may be involved in providing (Liebig, 1988; Collopy, Dubler, & Zuckerman, 1990; Kaye, 1992; Lindeman, 1992).

Staff Turnover, Burnout, and Exploitation in Home Care

The nature of home care and the profile of the typical home care recipient create significant opportunities for employee discontent and stress, which may be expressed adversely in employee attitude, conduct, and retention. Typically, burnout refers to the emotional exhaustion and frustration experienced by human service professionals as the result of the excessive demands on their resources. Burnout among human service workers may be attributed to a number of specific factors. When working with an aged or frail population, there are transferential issues that force employees to confront their own aging, potential dependency, and mortality. Additionally, there is often a sense of being unable to do enough to assist a client with a seemingly endless barrage of problems. And, finally, there is the devaluation of older people and those who are chronically dependent in our society, which carries over to care providers who themselves bear the stigma through association (Poulin & Thomas, 1998).

Ultimately, burnout may lead a worker to leave the job or the profession altogether. Staff turnover has been a major problem in the home care industry for many years. Costly and frequent turnover among paraprofessionals, such as home care aides, and the related issue of worker shortage is well documented in the research literature (Crown, MacAdam, & Sadowsky, 1992; de Savorgnani, Haring, & Davis, 1992). In addition to ensuring high-quality care, training can reduce staff burnout by enhancing staff skills, acknowledging the professional nature of staff and the valuable role they play and preparing staff for advancement in their careers and in the organization (Kaye, 1992). Programs to minimize turnover rates among front-line workers in long-term care are increasingly multifaceted, including staff support groups and improvements to the work environment in addition to skill enhancement efforts ("Frontline Workers," 1994). Research has also confirmed that improved benefits, systematic training, supportive supervision, job enrichment/growth, and guaranteed hours contribute to job satisfaction and reduce turnover (Schmid & Hasenfeld, 1993). Recognition of good staff performance has been touted as a way to reduce staff stress and burnout (Brent, 1992). Building an opportunity to communicate with other staff and to participate in program planning and agency policy are also helpful strategies for promoting staff allegiance and commitment to the agency and patient.

The nature of home care additionally increases the potential for exploitation for both workers and consumers. Agencies must closely monitor the worker-client relationship to ensure that neither party is being exploited (Friedman & Kaye, 1979; Schmid & Hasenfeld, 1993). Frequent communication with the consumer and family members of those receiving services along with close supervision and education and training for staff is essential to the provision of quality care. Agency administrators must develop thorough strategies for monitoring staff performance, including frequent on-site inspections, close supervision, and involvement of staff in ongoing evaluation. "QA results should not only be used to improve patient outcomes but to assist staff in upgrading their performance" (Larkins & Hellige, 1992).

Admissions Criteria, Reimbursement, and Liability Issues

As previously noted, the vast majority of home health care expenditures in the United States can be attributed to Medicare, Medicaid, and private insurance companies. Each of these third-party payors has its own unique set of eligibility requirements designed to identify qualifying patients. In the case of Medicare, the largest public payor for home care, there are five qualifying criteria as well as coverage criteria. In addition, services must be deemed medically reasonable and necessary. Initial determination of eligibility must be made by a Medicare-certified home health agency. In contrast to Medicare, Medicaid is designed to provide coverage for those with low income and resources. Although federal legislation stipulates the general requirements of eligibility, states have latitude with regard to the nonmandatory regulations and waivered services (Rosenzweig, 1995). Similarly, the array of eligibility requirements across private insurers is vast and cannot be easily classified.

Providers of home health services, depending on auspice, may play a role in this eligibility determination process. Regardless, each agency must establish organization-specific admissions criteria. Development of admissions criteria is particularly essential to the success of any high-tech program. According to Larkins and Hellige (1992), in developing admissions criteria for high-tech services, the agency should focus on agency resources, available caregivers, environmental resources, and reimbursement. The pivotal aspect to all admissions, however, is conducting a complete patient assessment. Patient assessment consists of determinations of: (a) the staff's ability to handle patient needs; (b) the availability and capability of a caregiver; (c) the suitability of the home environment; and (d) adequate reimbursement sources or ability to pay for service (Larkins & Hellige, 1992).

Reimbursement issues are especially important in high-tech care, due to the novelty of many treatments. Agencies are, in many cases, at the mercy of either public or private insurance providers for financial reimbursement. Denial of coverage has been frequently documented in the literature as one of the major barriers to quality, comprehensive home health care (Collopy, Dubler, & Zuckerman, 1990; Dombi, 1992; Kaye, 1992; Larkins & Hellige; 1992; Mehlman & Youngner, 1991). If Medicare or other third-party payors deny reimbursement, the agency must then make a choice. The agency can discharge the patient, or "continue care without reimbursement—at its own fiscal peril" (Collopy, Dubler, & Zuckerman, 1990). Insurers can deny coverage all together, deny coverage for professional services, or dispute the duration and frequency of care (Dombi, 1992). These decisions can raise ethical, legal, and liability dilemmas for the agency.

Concerns about liability extend beyond reimbursement issues. Although there have been relatively few malpractice suits against home care agencies or individual providers, the risk remains, particularly in the case of high-tech home care. Three major sources of liability have been identified. Contractual liability refers to a breach of contract or failure to fulfill express or implied promises to patients. Tort liability results from negligence in patient care, a situation in which the agency or staff are subject to a malpractice action. In the case of high-tech home care, in particular, there is the risk of products liability when harm is inflicted as a result of defective or improperly installed equipment (Kapp, 1995a). (See chapter 8 for a more detailed discussion of liability.)

Patient and Caregiver Education

Another important factor in preventing agency liability is patient understanding of treatment or informed consent (Larkins & Hellige, 1992). Patients must be informed about the purpose of their treatment, any risks or negative side effects, and the benefits and alternatives to the treatment. Specific risks to receiving the treatment at home must also be explained along with the limitations of the service, expectations for self-care, and patient liability for payment.

An essential component of responsible staff performance is the provision of adequate patient education. Patient education should consist of knowledge of the disease process, understanding of self-care tasks and regimen, explanation of proper procedures during emergencies (including appropriate emergency contact numbers, equipment use, preventive activities), and recognizing signs and symptoms of problems (Grieco, 1991; Liebig, 1988; Smith, 1992; Worcester, 1990). Family members and other caregivers must be included in this educational process. In many cases they will be responsible for providing the self-care needs of patients and will be in the home much more frequently than most staff.

Patient and caregiver education is not simple. Patients and their caregivers need to be assessed for their learning potential and motivation to complete self-care tasks. Providers should consider the physical and psychosocial status of the patient (e.g., are they in pain, depressed, anxious, fatigued?). All of these factors will impact the patient's ability to learn. Also, staff should consider the patient's physical ability to carry out the necessary self-care tasks. Performance of each task should be demonstrated by patients or their caregivers prior to discharge to home. Staff should also be aware of various educational techniques to enhance the teaching environment (Worcester, 1990). Not everyone learns in the same way or at the same pace. Also, patients may have very obvious barriers to learning, such as vision or hearing impairments, mobility and dexterity problems, and cognitive deficits, that will require staff to develop creative strategies to teach self-care.

Worcester (1990) suggests the following strategies when teaching older adults:

1. Allow the patient to control the pace of learning.
2. Begin with what the patient knows—clear-up misconceptions.
3. Use repetition.
4. Check understanding before changing topics.
5. Limit amount of material presented.
6. Use large print, pictures, contrasting colors, magnifying aides.
7. Use audio aides, eliminate background noise.
8. Have patient demonstrate by performing task or repeating steps.
9. Provide adaptive devices to enhance patient abilities.

The need for documentation of patient teaching is just as important as direct care documentation (McAbee, Grupp, & Horn, 1991). Agencies will need to demonstrate that they provided the proper instruction in the event the patient or family later questions the patient's treatment or services.

THE CHALLENGE OF HIGH-TECH CARE

The most common type of high-tech treatment is infusion therapy. "Providing IV therapy in the home setting is one of the most rapidly growing trends in the home care industry" (McAbee, 1991). High-tech infusion therapy includes artificial nutrition and hydration, administration of IV antibiotics, IV chemotherapy, IV pain management, and blood component infusion. The advantages of home IV treatment include reduction in the risk of infection, ability of the patient to receive care in a less restrictive and more pleasant environment, involvement of patient in care, and cost savings to the system. While the advantages of in-home infusion therapy are considerable, there are potential drawbacks or at least special challenges that the agency is likely to confront. They include the need for round-the-clock coverage by the agency, assurances that nursing education and skills remain current, potential complications associated with reimbursement for services rendered, and possible difficulties in working with physicians. According to McAbee, Grupp, and Horn (1991) "safe home intravenous services require appropriate discharge planning, client admission criteria, and client/caregiver education."

Problems with IV therapies range from difficulty with storage space for supplies and equipment to dealing with emergencies during nonworking hours. For many of these treatments, agencies may require that a caregiver be available, that the patient receives the treatment in the hospital first, or that the home environment be adequate to support the treatment.

THE ETHICS OF HOME HEALTH CARE

Technology importation to the home has also served to raise a range of exceedingly complex ethical concerns for staff of community home care agencies (Coile, 1990; Macklin & Callahan, 1990). Traditionally, issues of medical and bioethics have been of primary concern to acute care and long-term care facilities (Besdine, 1985). Such matters are now filtering down to the home care network at an increasingly rapid pace. The initial charge of high-tech home care appears to be the development of guide-lines for dealing with potential ethical issues or conflicts, to determine appropriate staff roles in such cases, to identify the organization's stance on specific ethical issues, and to be available to respond to individual cases as they arise. In this regard, home care agencies, in similar fashion to long-term care institutions, may need to consider using ethics commit-tees or similar governing bodies in addressing issues of medical ethics, life prolongation technologies, and determination of agency policy (Reamer, 1987). Kapp (1995a) argues that ethical and legal issues sur-rounding in-home life-sustaining medical treatment, physical or chemi-cal restraints as behavior management tools, and contractual liability between agency and consumer, among others, should be identified, anticipated, and prepared for proactively. Opportunities for agency liabil-ity in these areas are more numerous now than in the past. This is due, in part, to patients and caregivers with higher consumer expectations and the increased use of independent contractors to fill highly specialized roles in scattered locations, thereby diluting the extent of direct control over service and product provision.

Since enactment of the Patient Self-Determination Act in 1991, agen-cies are required to develop written policies and procedures on advance directives and to understand the state law related to advance directives and life-sustaining treatment decisions. They are also required to communi-cate this information to new patients at the time of admission. Research has shown that patients are interested in discussions on advance planning for treatment decisions should they become incapacitated, but they expect health care workers (doctors, nurses, social workers) to initiate these discussions (Emanuel, Barry, Stoeckle, Ettelson, & Emanual, 1991). Yet, many health care providers have not developed adequate policies or pro-cedures for dealing with these difficult ethical issues (Davitt, 1992). Such policies and procedures are essential to promote patient autonomy and thereby increase service quality and reduce agency liability.

This raises another issue that is yet to be resolved—assessing patient competence. Staff will be asked increasingly to determine whether pa-tients are able to make certain decisions for themselves. Such questions as how to assess decision-making capacity; when to defer to family members or caregivers on treatment decisions; or which family member to defer to, can be very perplexing and frustrating for staff. Issues related to patient autonomy and self-determination, conflicts between patient and family, and conflicts between patient and staff arise daily in home health care. Staff will also experience similar dilemmas related to the rights of caregivers (Collopy, Dubler, & Zuckerman, 1990).

Ethical concerns extend beyond patient care and patient rights. From the perspective of home care providers, two of the most common types of ethical issues relate to problems with payer regulations and coworker competency (Haddad, 1992). As can be expected, home care personnel will find themselves increasingly caught in the middle of these numerous complex matters. Therefore, it is essential for agencies to develop specific policies, procedures, and guidelines for dealing with these and other ethical dimensions of service delivery.

SUMMARY

Questions that arise out of the recent developments in home care deserve serious attention. They suggest a clear and compelling agenda for observers of the field of in-home service delivery. The willingness of providers and observers to test the waters in high-tech home care will hopefully result in improved programs for the growing number of functionally impaired older people who want their needs to be satisfied within the familiar surroundings of their own homes.

II

Observations from the Field: National and Local Perspectives

T he chapters in this section present findings arising from the two stages of research that constitute the basis of this volume: a national survey of the current status of high technology applications in a sample of 153 home health care organizations situated throughout the United States and a local field study of 92 home health care staff and 67 older recipients of service associated with four home care organizations located in the greater Philadelphia metropolitan area (southeastern Pennsylvania and northern Delaware). Together, the four local agencies represent a wide range of organizational auspices of such programs, including hospital based, Visiting Nurses Association, freestanding proprietary, and freestanding nonprofit. All agencies in the local survey are Medicare certified.

Whereas the national survey focused on the opinions and experiences of executive directors of home health care programs, the local study compiled data on the personalized views of agency staff and older home health care clients. The local study provides the opportunity to compare perspectives concerning the delivery and consumption of both traditional and high-tech home care services. Local data were collected during a series of face-to-face interviews with staff and patients. The national study was performed by means of mail questionnaires. A subset of the national survey questions were adapted for use in the local interviews. In general, staff interviewed in the local study were asked to discuss the challenges associated with delivering home care services and serving high-tech patients in particular. Patients in the local study were asked to comment on their personal experience receiving home health care services. A full review of the methods of data collection for both stages of the research are found in appendix A. As a rule, the chapters below first present the results of the national survey followed by findings from the local survey. Rather than presenting individual summaries of findings at the end of each chapter, a complete summary and discussion of findings from both the national and local surveys will be found in the initial section of chapter 13.

CHAPTER 3

Profiling the Providers and Consumers of High-Tech Home Health Care

T his initial chapter of findings presents a descriptive profile of the participating organizations in the national survey of home health care agency executive directors as well as the staff employed by those organizations and the consumers they serve. Descriptions are also provided of the staff and consumers studied in the local analysis. Taken together, these profiles should provide the reader with a useful barometer of the more typical characteristics of organizations, personnel, and consumers engaged in the home care experience.

PARTICIPATING AGENCY PROFILES IN THE NATIONAL SURVEY

Structural Characteristics

Table 3.1 summarizes data reflective of the national sample of home care organizations. As shown, approximately half of the 153 agencies that were studied are not-for-profit. Almost three in 10 are for profit, and the remainder are public or governmental agencies. The largest proportion

TABLE 3.1   Profile Characteristics of Home Health Care Agencies (National Survey)

Profile variable	Frequency	Percent	Mean
Corporate status			
Not-for-profit	76	49.7	
For-profit	44	28.8	
Public	33	21.6	
Auspice			
Hospital	46	31.1	
Proprietary	40	27.0	
Official	22	14.9	
Voluntary	19	12.8	
Other	21	14.2	
Community service area			
Mostly rural	65	42.2	
Mostly urban	12	7.8	
Mostly suburban	14	9.1	
Some mix of the above	63	40.9	
Provision of hospice services			
Yes (certified)	39	25.3	
Yes (not certified)	33	21.4	
No	82	53.2	
How long providing home care services			17.3 years
Number of home visits in last fiscal year			36,902 visits
Sources of funding/reimbursement			
Medicaid	135	87.7	
Private insurance	132	85.7	
Medicare	129	83.8	
Patient fees	110	71.4	
Veterans benefits	75	48.7	
Donations	56	36.4	
Title XX homemaker/chore service	45	29.2	
Other	39	25.3	

TABLE 3.1 (*Continued*)

Profile variable	Frequency	Percent	Mean
Total agency operating budget for last fiscal year			
$0–999,999	61	41.8	
$1 million–1,999,999	24	16.4	
$2 million–2,999,999	14	9.6	
$3 million–3,999,999	7	4.8	
$4 million–4,999,999	8	5.5	
$5 million +	32	21.9	
Home health care operating budget for last fiscal year			
$0–999,999	84	57.5	
$1 million–1,999,999	22	15.1	
$2 million–2,999,999	14	9.6	
$3 million–3,999,999	8	5.5	
$4 million–4,999,999	3	2.1	
$5 million +	15	10.3	
Most frequent referral sources			
Hospitals	74	48.1	
Physicians	41	26.6	
Social service agencies	14	9.1	
Family/friends	12	7.8	
Self-referrals	5	3.2	
Other	8	5.1	

identifies themselves as being under hospital auspices, with a slightly smaller group indicating a proprietary auspice. The remainders are divided among voluntary, official (public/governmental) and other auspices (e.g., skilled nursing facility, health maintenance organization (HMO), health-related facility). Hospital-based programs are evenly distributed in terms of their corporate status and auspice. Participating agencies are evenly representative of mostly rural or a mixture of rural, urban, and suburban community service areas. A slight majority does not provide either certified or noncertified hospice services.

While more than 40% of the agencies had a total agency operating budget during the immediate past fiscal year of less than $1 million, a substantial proportion (almost 22%) report total agency operating budgets to be in excess of $5 million. When the home health care operating budgets alone are considered, almost three quarters of the agencies report their most recent fiscal budgets to be less than $2 million per annum. Only one in every 10 agencies reported home health care budgets in excess of $5 million. Medicare, Medicaid, private insurance (e.g., long-term care, general health, automobile), and patient fees constitute the most common sources of funding and reimbursement for services rendered across all agencies. Less common funding sources include special grants from public and private sources such as township authorities and private foundations, local tax levies, charity funds, state subsidies, and Medicaid waiver demonstration funds. Medicare is easily the most frequent payment source for the vast majority of the agencies, followed by Medicaid, patient fees, and private insurance.

Participating agencies report providing home care services an average of 17.3 years. The average number of home visits made to patients during the most recently completed fiscal year is 36,902. It should be noted, however, that the median number of annual home visits is 11,870 with agencies reporting as few as 30 and as many as 509,900 visits completed over a 12-month period. The extreme range in figures reported for home visits highlights the fact that agencies surveyed for the purposes of this investigation differ dramatically in size.

Sources of Referral

The home health care agencies in our national sample easily receive the largest proportion of their referrals from hospitals. This represents the most frequent referral source for almost half of the agencies. Physician referrals represent the second most frequent referral source (identified as such by almost a quarter of the executive directors). Far less frequently utilized sources (in descending order) include social service agencies, family and friends, and self-referrals. Other, extremely infrequent sources of referral, include clergy and religious groups, home infusion pharmacies, rehabilitation and skilled nursing facilities, private geriatric case managers, insurance companies, and other home health care agencies.

Approaches to Marketing

A final dimension along which the profiles of participating agencies in the national survey are considered is that of marketing techniques used.

All responding executive directors were asked to indicate which techniques and approaches to marketing are employed by their agencies. Executive directors were also asked to assess the relative effectiveness of the varying techniques employed for purposes of marketing their home health care services. Table 3.2 summarizes these data. The most frequently used techniques of marketing agency services in descending frequency are printed brochures and flyers, directory listings, presentations and speeches, and in-person outreach. Newspaper and magazine ads and special promotions are used less often but still are employed by a slight majority of agencies. Marketing approaches employed by fewer than 50% of the surveyed agencies include (in descending popularity) focus groups, direct mailings, public service messages, written or telephone surveys, and television or radio commercials.

In-person outreach stands out as the most effective marketing technique as specified by agency executive directors. Other techniques with relatively high effectiveness ratings (mean scores of 3.0 or higher on a 4-point scale), are presentations and speeches, focus groups, and directory listings. Directors are least confident in the effectiveness of television or radio commercials and written or telephone surveys. These data, which parallel

TABLE 3.2   Types and Effectiveness of Marketing Techniques Used in Recruiting Clients (National Survey)

Marketing technique	Percentage of agencies using technique	Effectiveness level*	
		Mean	S.D.
Printed brochure/flyer	94.6	2.9	0.7
Directory listing	89.0	3.0	0.7
Presentation/speech	87.0	3.1	0.7
In-person outreach	78.2	3.4	0.6
Newspaper/magazine ad	63.7	2.7	0.7
Special promotion	61.2	2.9	0.7
Focus group	48.5	3.0	0.6
Direct mailing	47.8	2.7	0.8
Public service message	43.7	2.7	0.7
Written/telephone survey	39.5	2.6	0.8
TV/radio commercial	33.3	2.5	0.7

*Effectiveness level: potential range in scores from 1–4 where 1 = very ineffective, 2 = somewhat ineffective, 3 = somewhat effective, and 4 = very effective.

S.D., standard deviation.

findings reported earlier in a six-city survey of marketing strategies in health and social services for older people (Kaye, 1995; Kaye, 1996; Kaye & Reisman, 1991a), highlight the relatively greater efficaciousness of more personalized, face-to-face forms of marketing communication by human service programs serving older and vulnerable service populations.

Staffing Profiles

Table 3.3 presents data on the size and category of staff at participating agencies in the national survey including the extent to which they participate in skills training programs. Agencies employ an average of 35.7 full-time and 49.8 part-time staff. As expected, a clear majority of agency staff are classified as being stationed in the field (an average of 73.3 per agency), while an average of 14.9 staff are assigned primarily office-based tasks to perform. The mean sizes of the home health care work force stipulated above notwithstanding, it should be noted that there is considerable range in the sizes of the varying home health care programs. Full-time staff range from as few as zero to as many as 700. Part-time staff also range from as few as zero to as many as 700. Field staff range

TABLE 3.3   Profile Characteristics of Staff at Participating Home Health Care Agencies (National Survey)

Profile variable	Mean	S.D.	Percent
Number full-time staff	35.7	76.1	
Number part-time staff	49.8	98.4	
Number field staff	73.3	126.2	
Number office staff	14.9	23.0	
Agency staff required to participate in ongoing training			
Nurses			91.9
Home health aides			90.5
Administration			81.9
Social workers			54.8
Therapists (OT, PT, ST)			54.4
Support staff			52.3
Homemakers			47.5
Other			11.5

S.D., standard deviation; OT, occupational therapy; PT, physical therapy; ST, speech therapy.

from as few as zero to as many as 900, whereas office staff number as few as one to as many as 149.

The vast majority of agencies require one or more categories of staff to participate in ongoing training for the purposes of skills upgrading. This requirement for staff training is consistently strong across all categories of agencies regardless of their corporate status, auspice, or community area served. Nurses, home health aides, and administrative personnel can easily be separated out as representing those staff most likely to be required to participate in ongoing training by their employers. These categories of staff have mandatory training requirements established by large majorities of the participating agencies. Such an in-service training requirement is considerably less commonplace for social workers; occupational, physical, and speech therapists; support staff; and homemakers. (The implications of these divergent training policies for different categories of home health care personnel for the delivery of home care services generally, and high-tech services in particular, will be further considered in chapter 4). Other individuals engaged in agency training programs on an even less frequent basis include volunteers, board members, nutrition staff, and chaplains.

Patient Profiles

Data were also collected that reflect the demographic profile of patients receiving service from the national sample of home care agencies over the course of the last fiscal year (see Table 3.4). An average of 699.4 patients were served during the past fiscal year, with individuals served ranging from a low of 11 at one agency to a high of 6,095 at another (median = 376).

Survey data highlight the dominant focus of home health care programs on serving older adults (data on patient profiles were provided by approximately two thirds of participating agencies and should therefore be treated with a degree of cautiousness). Well over twice as many 55 to 74 year olds are served on the average (249) than are those who are less than 55 years of age (104). More striking is the fact that more than three times as many 75 years old and older patients are served on the average (321) than are those who are less than 55 years of age. Given these data, the advanced age of the population cannot be overstated. Home health care appears heavily colored by a geriatric focus to service provision.

The patient population served is also dominated by women (an average of 423 served in the last year compared to 276 men), persons who are

TABLE 3.4   Profile Characteristics of Patients at Participating Home Health Care Agencies (National Survey)

Profile variable	Mean	S.D.
Total number patients served in last fiscal year	699.4	960.7
Age		
0–54 years	104.4	188.1
55–74 years	249.0	367.9
75+ years	321.2	449.2
Gender		
Female	423.5	573.4
Male	276.0	393.3
Marital status		
Not married	397.3	796.6
Married	289.6	484.8
Race		
White	488.8	575.5
People of color	127.2	291.4
Living arrangements		
Living alone	176.6	299.8
Living with others	382.1	677.2

S.D., standard deviation.

not married (an average of 397 compared to 290 married persons), Whites (an average of 489 compared to 127 persons of color), and those who live with others (an average of 382 compared to 177 persons who live alone).

Summary Profile Differences

Summarized below are differences among participating agencies across certain major profile variables when considering these agencies' corporate status, auspice, community service area, availability of high-tech services, and provision of hospice service. Corporate status, auspice, and community service area prove to be particularly useful variables to consider in uncovering potential differences within the survey sample. Subgroup differences are significant when considering an agency's corporate status on three profile variables (length of time providing home health care services, number of patients served, and number of office staff) and for an agency's community service area on three profile variables (number of part-time staff, number of patients served, and number of office staff). Most telling, however, is that significant differences emerge on all seven profile variables when considering auspice. And these differences tend to be more powerful than differences in corporate status and community service area.

Voluntary (not-for-profit) auspice agencies have been providing home health care significantly longer than any other type of agency. Official or public agencies have been doing so for a significantly shorter period of time than voluntaries, but significantly longer than hospital-based or proprietary agencies. Voluntary agencies also serve significantly greater numbers of patients, have significantly more full-time staff, and significantly more office staff than any other category of agency. Furthermore, voluntaries make significantly more home visits than hospital-based and public programs (but not proprietaries), have significantly more part-time staff than hospital-based programs (proprietary programs do as well), and have significantly more field staff than hospital and official programs.

Whether high-tech services are provided proves not to be a useful variable to consider when trying to uncover differences in agencies on the above delineated profile variables. Nor is hospice service provision particularly helpful in distinguishing differences in agency profiles. (Hospice providers do emerge as employing significantly more part-time staff than their nonhospice counterparts).

This analysis suggests that voluntary, not-for-profit programs stand out in differentiating ways from agencies under other auspices. They can lay claim to the longest period of time having been engaged in home health care service provision (44 years on average), having larger staffs (especially office staff), making more home visits, and serving more patients than any other category of provider. On the other hand, while proprietary programs have been engaged in service delivery for a relatively brief period of time (12 years on average), their volume of service and expanse of operation has grown at an apparently faster, more aggressive pace than either hospital or official (public) programs. Given the length of time that public programs have been operating (between 21 and 26 years on average), it would appear that their growth rate is the slowest or, put differently, has remained the most stable of all agency types.

THE LOCAL SURVEY

Staff Profiles

Table 3.5 presents data on the size and type of staff participating in the local study interviews. The largest number of staff are direct-care nurses—either registered nurses (most commonly) or licensed practical nurses. The second largest group of staff interviewed is home health aides or homemakers. The remaining groups interviewed, in descending order, are supervisory/management staff; therapists (including physical, speech, and occupational); and social workers. The average age of agency staff is 39 years. The youngest staff person is 23, while the oldest is 63. An overwhelming majority of staff are women. A large majority of staff are White. Only 12% of staff are African American. More staff are married than not. Of the nonmarried staff, the largest proportion are single, followed by those who are divorced, and then those who are separated.

Staff were asked several questions about their education and work status. The majority of respondents are well educated with 52% completing 13 to 16 years of school, and 25% completing more than 16 years. Almost 21% of staff completed 9 to 12 years of school, and only a small number (2%) did not attend school beyond the eighth grade.

Two thirds of local staff work full time. Staff were asked to indicate how long they had been working at their present employing agency and how long they had been working in home health care in general. The average period of time staff have been working in their current agency is 2.8 years, with employment ranging from as little as 1 month to as much as 29 years. The average period of time staff report working in home health care in general is 6.5 years, with a range from 1 month to 29 years. The vast majority of staff interviewed (nine of every 10) provide direct services to patients. Staff serve an average caseload of 14.9 patients, with a minimum caseload of 0 and a maximum of 80.

Patient Profiles

Table 3.6 summarizes sociodemographic data for patients interviewed. The average age of patients is 76 years with a minimum age of 51 and a maximum of 104. As was observed in the national data, the patient population is dominated by women (67%), Whites (81%), and patients who live with others (80%). However, the local data differ in terms of marital status. More of the local interviewees are married (52%) than not married.

TABLE 3.5   Profile Characteristics of Home Health Care Agency Staff (Local Survey)

Profile variable	Frequency	Percent	Mean	S.D.
Staff type				
Registered nurse	43	46.7		
Home health aide	22	23.9		
Supervisor/administrator	10	10.9		
Licensed practical nurse	5	5.4		
Therapist	5	5.4		
Social worker	5	5.4		
Other	2	2.2		
Gender				
Female	90	97.8		
Male	2	2.2		
Race				
White	78	84.8		
African American	11	12.0		
Asian American	1	1.1		
Other	2	2.2		
Marital status				
Married	63	68.5		
Single	16	17.4		
Divorced	10	10.9		
Separated	3	3.3		
Education level				
5–8 years	2	2.2		
9–12 years	19	20.7		
13–16 years	48	52.2		
16+ years	23	25.0		
Work status				
Full-time	61	67.8		
Part-time	29	32.2		
Age in years			39.21	10.49
Number of months at agency			34.15	44.00
Number of months in home care			77.84	104.71
Caseload			14.87	13.18

S.D., standard deviation.

TABLE 3.6   Profile Characteristics of Home Health Care Agency Patients (Local Survey)

Profile variable	Frequency	Percent	Mean	S.D.
Age			76	12.10
Gender				
Female	45	67.2		
Male	22	32.8		
Race				
White	52	81.3		
African American	12	18.7		
Marital status				
Married	32	51.6		
Widowed	20	32.3		
Single	7	10.4		
Divorced	3	4.5		
Living arrangements				
Lives with spouse	31	47.0		
Lives with other relative	20	30.3		
Lives alone	13	19.7		
Lives with non-relative	2	3.0		
Education				
0–4 years	2	3.0		
5–8 years	8	12.1		
9–12 years	34	51.5		
13–16 years	18	27.3		
16+ years	4	6.1		

S.D., standard deviation.

Of the not married patients, more are widowed than single or divorced. Most of the patients are high school graduates, with a slight majority completing 9 to 12 years of school. An additional 27% completed some postgraduate education, and 6% completed 16+ years of school.

Medicare proves to be the predominate reimbursement source for patients and agencies. Almost 68% of the patients have their home health care covered by Medicare. Medicaid, on the other hand, is used by only 3% of patients. Private insurance accounts for 31% of patient reimbursements, while 9% of patients pay privately for services. A very small number of patients benefit from Title XX block grant funds, while no patients are covered under the Veterans Administration home care benefit.

Patient Diagnosis

Approximately one quarter of the recipients of home care suffer from some type of cardiovascular problem including stroke, congestive heart failure, and arteriosclerosis. Another one in five patients suffer from neuromuscular or bone disease including paralysis, gait dysfunction, arthritis, and fractures. Approximately 13% are receiving assistance for wounds or pressure sores, and 13% have some type of cancer. Many of the patients have more than one medical diagnosis. Just over one quarter (26%) of patients have a secondary diagnosis of cardiovascular problems, while 24% suffer from some type of neuromuscular or bone disease. The secondary diagnoses of diabetes, respiratory problems, and bowel or bladder problems occur equally as often (9% for each).

According to their medical charts, the majority of patients have a prognosis of fair, guarded, or poor. Only 24% have a good prognosis. However, a large majority of patients (87%) are viewed by staff as being oriented in terms of mental status. Only 6% are viewed as forgetful, and even fewer are considered to be disoriented.

Patients were asked to rate their own health. Overall, patients tended to be more positive than staff about their health. Almost 40% of patients rate their health as good and an additional 7% feel they are in excellent health. However, no patients were given an excellent prognosis by staff. In contrast to the positive perspective of patients related to their prognosis or health status, fewer patients are comfortable with their ability to provide their own care when no one else is around. A majority of patients (58%) are uncomfortable with providing their own care while alone. Patients are mainly concerned with emergencies that may arise while they are alone.

Home Care Services Received by Patients

It is not surprising that a clear majority (85%) of patients is receiving skilled nursing services. Given the high degree of reimbursement through Medicare (which only pays for skilled care needs) and private insurers (which predominantly pay for skilled nursing care), it can be expected that a large number of patients would be receiving skilled nursing care. The second most frequently received service is the assistance of a home health aide (58%). Physical therapy services are received by approximately one quarter of the patients (keep in mind that patients may receive more than one service concurrently). In the case of patients interviewed in the local survey, the receipt of occupational and speech therapies and social work services was rare.

Medicare reimbursement also impacts the amount of time a patient receives home health care service. Almost three quarters of the patients interviewed had been receiving services for 1 year or less. Slightly less than one quarter of the patients had been receiving services for 13 months to 2 years and less than 5% of patients had been receiving services for more than 2 years. Clearly, third-party reimbursement restrictions on the length of service are impacting these patients.

Only six of the patients interviewed were receiving high-tech services. Of those, one half receive artificial nutrition and hydration. All of the patients receiving high-tech services were only receiving one high-tech service.

Circumstances Leading to Home Care

More than three quarters of the patients in this study (76.1%) were seen in a hospital prior to receiving home care benefits. Hospitals play a key role in referring patients to home health care. The majority of patients (58%) in this research were informed of home health care through hospital staff. Physicians referred an additional 13% of patients, and 15% were informed of the service by friends or family. Hospital staff also play a key role in arranging for home health care services. Almost 40% of the patients had assistance from hospital staff in arranging for home health care. Another 25% of patients' say that the doctor arranged such services, and almost 20% of patients depended on family to arrange services.

Having profiled the central characteristics of home health care's organizational entities, service personnel, and service beneficiaries, we now proceed to characterizing the service delivery experience. The next chapter focuses in particular on the various components of the service package and the ways in which traditional and high-tech interventions are differentiated from each other.

CHAPTER 4

The Experience of Providing High-Tech Home Care

This chapter presents data reflecting the range, frequency, methods of payment, and structure of general and high-tech services provided by home health care agencies in the national survey. In addition, findings are offered that document directors' views of which interventions constitute high-tech care and the plans agencies have for providing high-tech services in the future. Similar data are presented reflecting the experiences and views of local personnel as well.

THE NATIONAL ANALYSIS

Services Provided Directly

Executive directors were first asked about the types of general services that their agencies provide directly. Table 4.1 summarizes these data. As shown, the most common interventions, provided by more than 90% of agencies surveyed, are skilled nursing and home health aide services. These services, which have traditionally represented the core interventions in home health care, are followed by social work and physical therapy, offered by more than 60% of the agencies. A third group of services, offered by between 50% and 60% of agencies, are

TABLE 4.1   Types of Services Provided by Home Health Care Agencies (National Survey)

| | Yes | | No | |
Service	Frequency	Percent	Frequency	Percent
Home health aide	142	93.4	10	6.6
Skilled nursing	140	92.1	12	7.9
Physical therapy	102	67.1	50	32.9
Social work	98	64.5	54	35.5
Speech therapy	86	56.6	66	43.4
Occupational therapy	79	52.0	73	48.0
Durable medical equipment	20	13.2	132	86.8
Pharmacy	12	7.9	140	92.1
Other	36	23.7	116	76.3

speech therapy and occupational therapy. Considerably less common interventions include durable medical equipment and pharmacy services. Other services, each provided less frequently, include chaplain, preventive medicine, nutrition or dietitian, home delivered meals, psychiatric, and groundskeeping services.

A number of profile variables are useful in understanding who is more and less likely to offer particular home health care interventions. Auspice and corporate status prove to be particularly helpful in underscoring differences in agency service packages. Public or official home care agencies are considerably less likely to offer social work, physical therapy, speech therapy, and occupational therapy services. Those programs serving primarily rural populations also reflect a tendency to offer a more narrow range of home health care services. Voluntary, not-for-profit agencies appear to offer the greatest variety of services. Hospital-based and proprietary programs fall somewhere in between those agencies offering a narrower range of services and those offering a more comprehensive selection of services. Those agencies that do and don't provide high-tech care do not differ significantly in terms of the range of general home health care services offered. Hospice programs also do not appear to differ dramatically from their nonhospice counterparts except for the fact that the former (as you would expect) are significantly more likely to have available in-house pharmacy services.

DIRECTORS' VIEWS OF WHAT
CONSTITUTES HIGH-TECH CARE

Directors were given the opportunity to offer their opinions as to whether a range of specific interventive procedures constituted technologically enhanced care for the patient. Table 4.2 summarizes these data both for separate service and equipment items and all such services and equipment in the aggregate. Items in the aggregate comprise a Technological Services Index (TSI), the development of which is described in greater detail in appendix A. As shown, those services perceived to be high tech by more than 50% of directors are parenteral and enteral nutrition or hydration, chemotherapy (infusion), antibiotics (infusion), pain control and palliative measures, renal dialysis, blood component infusion, ventilator care, and cardiac telemetry. Those services and equipment least likely to be viewed as technologically enhanced include incontinence care, ostomy care, pressure sore care, personal emergency response systems, electronic monitoring and recording of vital signs, and transcutaneous electronic nerve stimulators. The mean number of services and equipment classified as high-tech is 9.3 of the 21 items. Taken together, the various infusion therapies clearly dominate the directors' list of high-tech home care services.

Directors' views of what constitutes high-tech care did not vary significantly when considering differences in their agencies' corporate status, auspice, geographic area served, and whether hospice and high-tech services are offered. Interestingly, a relatively weak, but nevertheless statistically significant, correlation emerged between scores on the TSI and the Legal-Ethical Issues Index (LEII) (development of this index is described in greater detail in appendix A and considered more fully in chapter 6). Thus, more frequent experiences with a range of legal and ethical issues in home care are accompanied by more broad or multifaceted views of what services and equipment entail technologically enhanced care.

High-Tech Services Provided by Agencies

Based on the study definition of high-tech care ("those in-home methods of diagnosis, treatment, and rehabilitation that are physically embodied in specialized equipment/supplies or highly technical services"), 115, or 76%, of agencies surveyed engage in the provision of such interventions.

TABLE 4.2   Directors' Views on Whether a Range of Services/Equipment Are High Tech (National Survey)

	Viewed as high tech		Not viewed as high tech	
Service/Equipment	*Frequency*	*Percent*	*Frequency*	*Percent*
Chemotherapy (infusion)	133	88.1	18	11.9
Antibiotics (infusion)	123	81.5	28	18.5
Blood component infusion	121	80.1	30	19.9
Ventilator care	118	78.1	33	21.9
Parenteral/enteral nutrition or hydration	116	76.8	35	23.2
Renal dialysis	114	75.5	37	24.5
Pain control/palliative measures	104	68.9	47	31.1
Cardiac telemetry	94	62.3	57	37.7
Bone growth stimulation	74	49.0	77	51.0
Apnea monitors	60	39.7	91	60.3
Robotics	59	39.1	92	60.9
Tracheostomy care	54	35.8	97	64.2
Self-instruction computer	49	32.5	102	67.5
Telecommunications/closed circuit television	46	30.5	105	69.5
Transcutaneous electronic nerve stimulators	32	21.2	119	78.8
Electronic monitoring/recording of vital signs	30	19.9	121	80.1
Oxygen patient care	21	13.9	130	86.1
Personal emergency response systems	21	13.9	130	86.1
Pressure sore care	16	10.6	135	89.4
Ostomy care	12	7.9	139	92.1
Incontinence care	6	4.0	145	96.0
Summary Index Score	Mean = 9.3		S.D. = 4.6	

Summary index score range: 0–21 where higher score indicates more services and equipment are viewed as being high tech.
S.D., standard deviation.

The likelihood that an agency provides high-tech care does not differ significantly when considering their corporate status, auspice, geographic community served, or whether hospice services are available.

Agencies not providing high-tech care have apparently chosen not to for several reasons. Most commonly, noninvolvement is due to a poor fit between the type of agency in question and the organizational structure required to deliver high-tech services; an agency having other, higher ranking priorities; and low demand or need for such services in an agency's delivery area. A fourth, less common, reason was that the size of the agency and the current staffing pattern did not allow for the provision of high-tech services. The following reasons offered by two agency directors are illustrative:

"Our agency does not provide this kind of care due to reimbursement issues and lack of referrals."

"As a small agency we try to provide only those services we can adequately supervise. Our service is not available 24 hours a day."

Table 4.3 summarizes the frequency with which a range of possible high-tech services and equipment is offered (either in-house or externally contracted for) by participating agencies in the survey. The most commonly available services (provided by 90% or more of agencies surveyed) are incontinence, ostomy, and pressure sore care (note: these are services not considered technologically enhanced by the vast majority of directors). Next most common (provided by between 80% and 90% of agencies) are nutrition and hydration, antibiotic, pain control and palliative, tracheostomy, and oxygen care therapies. Services provided by slight majorities of respondents (50% to 65% of agencies) include chemotherapy, apnea monitors, and transcutaneous electronic nerve stimulation. Services rarely provided by home health care agencies (available less than 10% of the time) include renal dialysis, bone growth stimulation, telecommunications/ closed circuit television, self-instruction computers, and robotics.

Special analyses were performed to determine possible differences in the pattern of service offerings by different categories of agencies. These analyses reveal that hospice providers are more likely to have available (either directly or through a contractor) a wider range of high-tech services than nonhospice providers, especially in the case of pain control and palliative therapies, blood component infusion therapies, and the availability of personal emergency response systems. A tendency also emerges for urban, public, and hospital-based agencies to provide a more narrow range of high-tech services.

Within agency analysis of high-tech services provided most frequently reveals that antibiotic, nutrition and hydration, pain control and palliative, and infusion therapies generally stand out as being most commonly provided followed by blood component infusion, chemotherapy, tracheostomy,

TABLE 4.3   High-Tech Services/Equipment Provided Directly, Contracted, and Not Provided by Home Health Care Agencies (National Survey)

Service/Equipment	Provided directly		Contracted		Provided directly or contracted	
	Frequency	Percent	Frequency	Percent	Frequency	Percent
Incontinence care	130	92.9	1	.7	131	93.6
Pressure sore care	129	92.1	1	.6	130	92.9
Ostomy care	125	89.9	2	1.4	127	91.4
Tracheostomy care	115	82.1	4	2.9	119	85.0
Pain control/palliative measures	110	77.5	11	7.7	121	85.2
Oxygen patient care	102	72.9	18	12.9	120	85.7
Antibiotics (infusion)	101	72.1	15	10.7	116	82.9
Parenteral/enteral nutrition or hydration	97	67.8	21	14.7	118	82.5
Apnea monitors	70	49.6	18	12.8	88	62.4
Chemotherapy (infusion)	59	41.8	22	15.6	81	57.4
Ventilator care	58	40.8	10	7.0	68	47.9
Transcutaneous electronic nerve stimulators	54	38.3	18	12.8	72	51.1
Electronic monitoring and recording of vital signs	51	36.7	3	2.2	54	38.8
Personal emergency response systems	28	20.3	24	17.4	52	37.7
Blood component infusion	27	19.3	9	6.4	36	25.7
Cardiac telemetry	15	11.1	7	5.2	22	16.3
Bone growth stimulation	9	6.5	3	2.2	12	8.7
Renal dialysis	7	5.0	3	2.1	10	7.1
Self-instruction computer	4	2.9	1	.7	5	3.6
Telecommunications/ closed circuit television	2	1.5	3	2.2	5	3.7
Robotics	1	.7	1	.7	2	1.5

oxygen, pressure sore, incontinence, and ostomy care in that order. Such services are most commonly paid for with private insurance and Medicare followed by Medicaid and out-of-pocket patient payments.

High-Tech Services Planned for the Future

What high-tech services do home health care agencies already engaged in high-tech service provision plan to offer in the future? Thirty-one, or 20%, of the survey participants indicate that they plan to provide one or more additional high-tech services in the future. Varying kinds of infusion therapies dominate the planned provision scenarios of these agencies including general infusion, chemotherapy, nutrition and hydration, antibiotics, pain control, and blood component (product) therapies. Other less frequently mentioned services planned for the future include home phototherapy, ventilator care, and apnea and uterine monitoring. It is noteworthy that more than a quarter of the agencies studied (28%) who are not currently engaged in high-tech service provision plan to do so in the immediate years ahead. (Of course, these intentions may be impacted by the changes in reimbursement brought on by the Balanced Budget Act of 1997.)

THE LOCAL ANALYSIS

The Meaning of Home Health Care

Data were collected in the local survey on staff perceptions of the goal or objective of home health care and the meaning and factors that serve to define high-tech services. Both open-ended and forced-choice questions were employed to collect these data. Content analysis was carried out on open-ended, written staff responses to a question that asked staff to complete the following sentence: "The primary goal or objective of providing home health care is . . ." These data reveal that the primary goal of home health care is perceived to be that of maintaining the client in the home setting, which affords greater involvement of family and loved ones, enhances patient comfort, and promotes patient autonomy and self-determination. As one staff person put it, the goal of home health care is: "to enable a patient to remain in a comfortable environment with family and loved ones, which allows for the greatest amount of independence."

Staff were also asked to define in open-ended fashion what high tech means to them. Analysis of these comments reveal that two thirds of staff view high-tech services as those that use new or highly specialized equipment or services. A smaller proportion of staff (12%) see high-tech interventions as needing highly skilled, specially trained personnel to provide such services. Interestingly, 6% of the staff respondents did not know what makes a service high tech. Of the staff that are unclear about high-tech services, the vast majority (67%) are home health aides. The remaining 33% of those staff who are unclear as to what defines a service as high-tech identified themselves as nurses. No therapists or social workers indicated that they felt confused about what characterized high-tech service. It should be noted that within group analysis revealed that 30.8% of home health aides are unclear as to what makes a service high-tech compared to only 4% of nurses. Of the nurses (both registered nurses (RNs) and licensed practical nurses (LPNs)) that responded to this question, 75% feel that high-tech services are those that use new or specialized equipment or services. Only 12% of nurses feel that the need for service provision by highly skilled, specially trained personnel make a service high tech in and of itself, and 8% feel that a greater need for patient and family education makes a service high tech.

Local staff were given the opportunity to indicate a range of factors that, in their opinion, make a service high tech. These responses confirm that high tech incorporates multiple defining factors. More than nine of every 10 staff (93%) consider high-tech services to be embodied in specialized equipment. A clear majority of staff (83%) also indicates that the intensity of skilled nursing provided to a patient can impact their view of a service being "technology rich." Sixty percent feel that the novelty of the specific treatment makes a service high-tech, while 54% feel the amount of skilled nursing time is important in defining high-tech services. Finally, almost half of staff feel that the degree of difficulty in teaching patients and family self-care for a particular treatment is an important factor in defining a service as high tech.

The Extent of Engagement in High-Tech Care

Most staff (76%) perceive that their involvement in the provision of high-tech services has increased over the past 5 years. Of those that feel requests for high-tech service have increased, 53% are nurses, 21% are home health aides, and 26% are therapists or social workers. Staff report that on average 22% of their patients are receiving high-tech services, although the range in proportions of staff case loads receiving high-tech services varies dramatically, ranging from 0% to 100%.

Many staff assist with or directly provide high-tech services: 23% indicate they do it often, 36% assist sometimes, 27% rarely assist, and 14% never assist in the delivery of high-tech services. The data reflecting the extent to which various staff categories are engaged in high-tech care are noteworthy. Of the staff who report assisting with delivery often, 45% are nurses, 32% are therapists or social workers, and 23% are home health aides. Within staff group analysis revealed that 20% of nurses are often engaged in high-tech care, 35% of therapists or social workers are often involved, and 24% of home health aides are often involved. If those staff who indicate they are sometimes involved in high-tech care are combined with those who indicate they are often involved, the proportion of nurses, therapists and social workers, and home health aides who are involved in high-tech care rises to 67%, 40%, and 62%, respectively.

Staff were asked to indicate up to five high-tech services that they had been involved in providing. The most commonly cited high-tech service is infusion therapy (this includes IV nutrition and hydration, chemotherapy, antibiotics, and pain management). (See Table 4.4 for a more detailed list of high-tech services provided).

Training and Personnel Issues

Based on the local survey of home care staff, it seems clear that not all service providers are required to participate in ongoing training related to the delivery of high-tech services. Two thirds of the staff interviewed, however, are required. Of those who report they are required to participate, 63% are nurses (RNs and LPNs), 25% are home health aides, and 12% are therapists or social workers. Within group analysis of various staff categories reveals that 78% of nurses interviewed are required to participate compared to 71% of home health aides and 37% of therapists and social workers.

Staff receive training more often for performing specialized services or procedures than specifically for the use of specialized equipment. Staff are nearly unanimous in feeling that the provision of high-tech services requires more training than traditional home health services. Most staff are satisfied with the intensity and quality of high-tech training in their agencies.

While almost 86% of staff feel that the agency provides adequate staff coverage for high-tech patients, it should be noted that only one in five staff report being consulted by agency administration during the initial planning of specific high-tech services. Professional staff are more likely to be consulted on planning decisions related to high-tech services. Almost half of staff who report being consulted are nurses and slightly more than one third are therapists and social workers. Only 16% of all staff who are consulted are home health aides. It is noteworthy that 35% of therapists and social workers maintain that they are consulted about high-tech service provision compared to only 18% of nurses and 14% of home health aides.

TABLE 4.4   Characteristics of High-Tech Service Delivery (Local Survey)

Profile variable	Frequency	Percent	Mean	S.D.
Percent of caseload receiving high-tech service			22	27.4
Staff provision of high-tech service				
Often	21	22.8		
Sometimes	33	35.9		
Rarely	25	27.2		
Never	13	14.1		
High-tech service				
Nutrition/hydration	36	17.7		
Infusion therapy	28	13.8		
Pain management	21	10.3		
Antibiotics	17	8.4		
Mobility assistance	15	7.4		
Decubitus care	12	6.0		
Tracheostomy care	11	5.4		
Incontinence care	10	5.0		
Oxygen care	9	4.4		
Chemotherapy	6	2.9		
Ventilator care	6	2.9		
Electronic monitor	6	2.9		
Ostomy care	5	2.5		
Blood component infusion	2	1.0		
Apnea monitor	2	1.0		
Transcutaneous electronic nerve stimulation	2	1.0		
Renal dialysis	1	.5		
Cardiac telemetry	1	.5		
Computer	1	.5		
Other	12	6.0		

S.D., standard deviation.

The Challenge of High-Tech Care

Table 4.5 summarizes data on staff perspectives related to the provision of high-tech services. Staff were asked to list up to three benefits of high-tech service provision. Slightly less than half of staff indicate that the greatest benefit to receiving high-tech services is that patients are allowed to "age in place" in their own homes. This is the most frequently cited

TABLE 4.5 Benefits, Drawbacks, and Challenges of Providing High-Tech Home Health Care Services (Local Survey)

Profile variable	Frequency	Percent
Benefits		
Aging in place	55	46.2
Increased patient comfort	17	14.2
Cost savings	16	13.4
Patient improvement	12	10.1
Availability of more comprehensive services	9	7.6
Patient/family involved in care	8	6.7
Other	2	1.7
Drawbacks		
Stress on family/patient	37	36.3
Unsuitable home environment	14	13.7
Reimbursement/cost factors	12	11.8
Lack of quick response in emergency	9	8.8
Lack of adequate number of trained staff	7	6.9
Increased risk to patient	6	5.9
Scheduling adequate coverage	5	4.9
Difficulty accessing physician	3	2.9
Coordinating multiple agencies	2	2.0
Increased agency liability	1	1.0
Other	6	5.9
Challenges		
Stress on family/patient	62	31.8
Lack of adequate number of trained staff	39	20.0
Unsuitable home environment	17	8.7
Scheduling adequate coverage	16	8.2
Coordinating multiple agencies	11	5.6
Lack of quick response in an emergency	7	3.6
Reimbursement/cost factors	6	3.1
Increased risk to patient	4	2.0
Difficulty accessing physician	2	1.0

benefit. As one staff person noted: "there is a value to being in familiar surroundings—it helps emotional and physical recovery."

Increased patient comfort and reduced stress is the second most frequently cited benefit by staff. According to one staff member: "care at home decreases anxiety, secondary to a less threatening environment."

Staff also mention cost savings (although less frequently) as a benefit to high-tech home care. Other benefits, even less frequently cited, include patient improvement, availability of more comprehensive services, and patient and family involvement in care.

There are also drawbacks to providing high-tech care in the home. Again, staff were given the opportunity to list up to three choices. The number one drawback is the stress placed on families and caregivers. The second most frequently cited drawback is the unsuitable nature of the home environment. Staff also feel that reimbursement and cost factors are major drawbacks to such services. One staff person stated this shortcoming quite succinctly: "Insurance determines how many hours per year a patient needs home health care—this may not adequately meet the clinical needs of the patient." Staff also indicate they are concerned about the lack of immediate response in an emergency and the lack of adequate numbers of trained staff at the agency.

These drawbacks inevitably present challenges to staff providing high-tech services. Table 4.5 also presents a comparison of these two variables (drawbacks and challenges) based on staff responses. Paralleling the drawbacks cited above, stress on family, patient, and caregivers is the most often cited challenge. One staff member put the challenge this way: "More home health care services which are covered by insurance would increase family participation in patient care and the family's willingness to keep the patient at home—the family needs a support system."

Lack of adequate numbers of trained staff is also high on the list of challenges cited. The unsuitability of the home environment is a challenge in the eyes of some staff as well. Scheduling adequate staff coverage also seems to be a concern of significance for staff.

The Effectiveness of High-Tech Care

According to the local analysis of the service delivery experience, the most effective services appear to be in the area of infusion therapies. Staff report general infusion therapy most often to be the most successfully delivered service, followed by IV pain management, nutrition and hydration, and IV antibiotics. Finally, decubitus care is mentioned as the most successfully delivered high-tech service by a lesser number of staff.

As was the case in the national survey of agency executives, staff in the local survey appeared to be hesitant to indicate that their agency might have problems delivering certain high-tech services. In fact, 68 staff (74%) were not willing to say which services their agency delivers least effectively. Of the staff that did identify services that they feel are delivered least effectively, ventilator care was the most frequent response.

Ironically, infusion therapy is also high on this list. Nutrition and hydration therapy is the third most frequently cited service in the least effective category.

The Role of Patients in High-Tech Care

Staff were also asked to discuss their impressions of their patients' participation in their own care. The majority of staff feel that patients are informed about their legal rights as patients. Staff were asked to indicate how their agencies encourage patient participation. The most frequent procedure is providing an explanation of patient rights at admission (this is provided by virtually all agencies). The second most frequent procedure is that staff actively seek patient feedback and input (also performed by virtually all agencies). Staff also indicate, in descending order, that they provide education and information to patients and conduct regular care plan conferences.

Staff indicate that there is no difference in terms of decision-making capacity between high-tech patients and traditional service patients. The majority of staff feel that high-tech patients are just as likely to lack decisional capacity as traditional home care patients.

A large majority of staff feel that high-tech services enhance the quality of life for older home care patients. Overall, staff feel that patients are satisfied with the high-tech services they receive. Of course, as with more traditional home care, problems can be expected to arise during the course of high-tech service provision. Staff were asked to identify those areas where it is most difficult to please high-tech patients. The most frequent response category voiced by staff is that of reducing patients' anxiety about their health status and the use of equipment in their treatment. One staff person noted that: "Patients are frightened of the technology; this impairs their ability to learn."

One in every four staff feel that it is most difficult to provide adequate service hours to the patient. This includes coverage during both emergencies and off-hours. A slightly smaller proportion of staff indicate that they struggle with a lack of fit between client expectations and the care plan. Finally, one in 10 staff feel that reducing the patient's sense of isolation and providing an opportunity for social interaction is the most difficult aspect of high-tech service provision in terms of pleasing patients (see Table 4.6).

Two thirds of the local staff interviewed feel that it is more difficult to teach high-tech patients and their families self-care tasks as compared

TABLE 4.6   Most Difficult Areas in Which to Please High-Tech Patients (Local Survey)

Profile variable	Frequency	Percent
Reducing anxiety about health & treatment	28	37.3
Providing adequate service hours	19	25.3
Lack of fit between client expectations & care plan	16	21.3
Reducing sense of isolation	8	10.7
Other	4	5.3

to general home care patients and their families. Slightly more than one quarter of the staff think the teaching difficulty level is about the same. A limited number of staff feel teaching is less difficult with high-tech patients.

Staff are largely in agreement that the use of highly technical equipment impacts the patient or family's ability to do self-care. The most anxiety-producing services for patients and family members appear to be infusion therapy. This is followed by ventilator care, mobility assistance, and pain management.

Staff most often identify the patient's daughter as performing the necessary self-care tasks for high-tech patients. Daughters are followed in descending order of frequency by the spouses of patients, their sons, the patients themselves, and other relatives. Other relatives involved to lesser degrees in patient self-care tasks include nephews, nieces, aunts, uncles, and in-laws.

Whereas this chapter considered staff views of how the service delivery experience gets played out from the perspective of the provider, the next chapter considers both the patient and family response to service delivery. Indeed, high-tech home health care is conceptualized as the integration of both formal (provider) and informal (patient and family) support elements in the promotion of service efficacy. Such a perspective requires that we now proceed to a consideration of the remaining two components in the relational triad.

CHAPTER 5

The Experience of Receiving High-Tech Home Care

T his chapter presents data on the characteristic profile of high-tech home health care patients. This profile is compared against the profile of home health care patients generally. The admissions criteria for high-tech patients are also considered. Data are drawn from both the national and local surveys.

THE NATIONAL PERSPECTIVE

Profiling the High-Tech Patient

Agency directors were asked to provide data on the demographic profiles of those patients receiving high-tech services in the most recently completed fiscal year. Specifically, data were sought reflecting the age, gender, marital status, race, and living arrangements of these persons. These demographic variables paralleled those considered in profiling the general population of home health care service recipients. Table 5.1 summarizes this information and compares high-tech profile data against data on all patients in the national survey. These data should be considered with caution given that a substantial proportion of director's chose not to respond to this section of the survey instrument. Forty of 115 agencies (35%) delivering

TABLE 5.1   Profile Characteristics of All Patients and High-Tech Patients at Participating Home Health Care Agencies (National Survey)

Profile variable	High-tech patients Mean	S.D.	All patients Mean	S.D.
Total number of patients served in last fiscal year	76.9	128.6	699.4	960.7
Age				
0–54 years	26.4	53.5	104.4	188.1
55–74 years	33.2	71.0	249.0	367.9
75+ years	12.9	29.5	321.2	449.2
Gender				
Male	38.8	71.2	276.0	393.3
Female	34.7	59.3	423.5	573.4
Marital status				
Married	46.3	87.8	289.6	484.8
Not married	36.8	70.4	397.3	796.6
Race				
White	61.0	98.1	488.8	575.5
People of color	14.1	32.3	127.2	291.4
Living arrangements				
Living with others	67.1	119.8	382.1	677.2
Living alone	6.3	16.2	176.6	299.8

S.D., standard deviation.

high-tech services provided client profile data. As shown, an average of 76.9 high-tech patients was served during the past fiscal year, representing 11% of the total patient population served. The median number of high-tech patients served was 20, with agencies ranging from serving as few as one to as many as 513 high-tech patients. Hospice provider agencies served considerably more high-tech patients on the average (93) compared to non-hospice providers (61). The numbers of high-tech patients served by agencies varying in terms of corporate status, auspice, or geographic area served did not differ significantly.

The largest proportion of high-tech patients is situated in the 55 to 74 year age range, whereas the largest proportion of all patients served resides in the 75 and older age range. It appears clear that high-tech patients tend to be younger than patients are generally. Furthermore, high-tech recipients of service are also considerably more likely than home care patients generally to be male than female, married than not married, and living with others than living alone. Finally, a slightly greater proportion of high-tech patients are White compared to home health care patients generally.

Admissions Criteria for High-Tech Patients

Agency directors were asked whether they use special admissions criteria for high-tech patients. A slight majority (54%) indicated that they do. The likelihood that agencies have special admissions criteria for high-tech patients does not vary significantly when considering corporate status, auspice, or geographic community served. On the other hand, nonhospice agencies display a greater likelihood of having established special admissions criteria as compared to their hospice-providing counterparts (63% compared to 45%). Agencies registering higher numbers of home visits are also significantly more likely to have such special policies in place.

Agencies were also asked to describe their special high-tech admissions criteria. Of the agencies that have criteria, 51 provided descriptions of them. The most frequently cited criterion is that there be an available informal caregiver in the home (cited by 33.3% of respondents), followed by the need for a safe home environment (22%). While 14% of the agencies indicate that the patient must be able to be taught self-care, 8% accept high-tech patients only if they have the staff expertise to handle the patient's treatment needs. Finally, 6% of directors cite the requirement that the patient must be seen in the hospital prior to initiating the treatment at home. The same percentage of agencies (6%) requires prior physician approval for home health care. A large majority of agencies have multiple criteria (37 or 72%) for admission of high-tech patients. However, even for these agencies, having an available caregiver remains the most frequently cited criterion. Other responses include a safe home environment, teaching self-care, physician approval, and necessary staff expertise.

Caregiver Involvement in High-Tech Care

Given the importance of an available relative or friend to serve as the patient's informal caregiver, the ways in which patients or their caregivers are involved in the delivery of high-tech care takes on added significance. The direct, hands-on, participation of patients themselves and their significant others in care far exceeds any other form of involvement. Direct forms of assistance by caregivers are mentioned almost 60% of the time. Descriptions of this assistance highlight the pivotal importance of staff involvement early on in the education and teaching of informal caregivers. Descriptions go on to reflect considerable functional specificity as well as high levels of personal responsibility assigned to family caregivers. The following descriptions offered by directors are illustrative:

> [Patients and caregivers are] taught procedures, discussion of treatment options, taught disease process/pathophysiology and sight/sounds to observe and actions to take to manage care.

> Patients and/or caregivers are taught—Pumps, IV care and troubleshooting.

> They are directly involved in the mixing of additives in the bag or of starting and disconnecting the bag of the prescribed solution.

> Patients/families are taught to set-up and administer treatments, recognize problems, and seek help appropriately.

> [They are involved in the] operation and maintenance of computerized programmable pumps; being aware of adverse signs and symptoms of medications/computer pump problems/disease process; maintaining potency of IV accessibility; complying with directions.

One director made the distinction between different levels of family involvement depending on the service time frame:

> If the care is long term, they must learn to handle it themselves. If short term, they must be taught adverse reactions and when to seek help.

Direct involvement in care by patients and their informal supports appears crucial in many instances for containing costs, providing coverage during those times that agency staff are not available, and insuring the ultimate success of the agency plan of care and the well-being of the patient. Consider the following remarks:

> [They are] extremely involved—patients/caregivers are automatically trained to be as independent as they are willing to be.

> [They] must be able, willing, and available to learn independent management of procedures.

> Caregivers must be available and responsible for backup since we cannot always guarantee service.

> They are taught to manage as much of the direct care as possible.

Less frequent forms of patient/caregiver involvement include the monitoring of agency staff and more broad-based oversight responsibilities related to the formulation, maintenance, and reformulation of the plan of care.

Agency directors were finally probed as to whether high-tech patients are more likely to lack decisional capacity than those receiving traditional home health care services. It is interesting to note that more than seven of every 10 directors feel that high-tech patients are no more or less likely to lack decision-making capacity than traditional patients. In fact, for those respondents leaning in one direction or the other on the question, the clear majority feels that high-tech patients are less likely to lack capacity in the area of decision-making compared to other patients.

THE LOCAL PERSPECTIVE

The Experience of Service Receipt

Questions were included in the local survey that probed the level of service patients receive including the number of visits per week. The majority of patients receive visits three to four times per week or less (63%). Slightly more than one third of the patients receive five or more visits per week. Some patients also receive assistance from individuals other than agency staff. Over two thirds of the patients receive help from others including daughters (mentioned by 28% of patients), spouses (mentioned by 24% of patients), nonagency paid caregivers (mentioned by 15% of patients), and sons or sisters (mentioned in each case by 13% of patients). The types of services that others generally provide most commonly include personal care, help with chores/errands, and assistance with medical care. Assistance from informal helpers appears to be fairly nonconfrontational for patients. That is, the large majority of patients report little or no disagreement with informal caregivers.

Satisfaction with Care

This section presents data on patient satisfaction with formal home health care agency services. Patients were asked to rate their satisfaction level for services they are currently receiving. The large majority of patients (70%) are very satisfied with received services. Virtually all remaining patients were somewhat satisfied. Patients are also pleased with the quality of the services they are receiving. Likewise, the large majority of patients feel their requests for assistance are responded to promptly.

Overall, patients have not experienced problems with obtaining medical supplies. Over three quarters of the patients report no problems with securing medical supplies. For those that do have problems, the difficulties tend to be related to cost. One elderly patient noted: "I got someone to donate a bed and chair because I couldn't afford the monthly payment."

High levels of documented satisfaction with agency services are also reflected in patient views as to their need for additional services. The majority of patients do not desire to have additional services. Of those that would like additional services, most want more hours of the same service. Finally, patients seem to be in general agreement with agency staff when it comes to their plan of care. Less than one in 10 patients feel their wishes related to their care have differed from staff.

Views of Specialized Services

Each patient was asked a series of questions pertaining to each service received. These questions were asked more than once depending on the number of services each patient was receiving. Services were divided into three groups: skilled nursing; home health aide; and other professional services including physical, speech, and occupational therapy and medical social work.

Patients appear quite pleased with the various services they are receiving. Of the patients receiving skilled nursing services, 83% feel that this service has helped to improve their health. Similarly, 78% of the patients receiving home health aide services feel it has improved their health, while almost 95% of the patients receiving other professional services agree that it has improved their health. Patients receiving skilled nursing services seem to be more content with the amount of service they are receiving than patients receiving other professional services or home health aide services. In all three categories, patients are pleased with staff knowledge of service provision. It is interesting to note that in some cases patients believe staff provide services in disciplines other than their own. For example, according to one patient, RNs or LPNs may provide physical therapy, while home health aides assist with skilled nursing care.

Patients were asked to indicate whether anyone other than agency staff help with a particular service. As expected, more patients receive informal assistance with home health aide services (58% of patients) and other professional services (47% of patients) than with skilled nursing services (29%). Spouses and daughters are the two most frequently listed informal helpers substituting for nurses in the provision of skilled nursing services

(40% and 27% of the interviewees cited spouses and daughters, respectively) and substituting for home health aide services (20% and 32% of the interviewees cited spouses and daughters, respectively). In the case of the provision of professional therapy and social work services, other hired staff (mentioned 33% of the time) is the number one cited alternative provider rather than relatives or family members.

Patients are also generally pleased with the quality of the service they are receiving. A majority of patients ranked the quality of skilled nursing services as excellent (64%), of home health aide services as excellent (57%), and of other professional services as excellent (68%). Increased patient comfort is viewed as the greatest benefit to skilled nursing and home health aide services. Interestingly, a majority of patients feel that actual improvement in their health status is the greatest benefit accruing from other professional services.

Relatively few patients' report experiencing any problems with the services they are receiving. Only 12% of patients have experienced problems with skilled nursing services, 29% with home health aide services, and 11% with other professional services. Of those who experienced problems, most attribute this to changes in staff or new staff or to lack of staff knowledge. One patient's comments are illustrative: "When the regular aide was sick or on vacation, the substitute aides would not come or they would come at the wrong time."

For those patients receiving skilled nursing services, more than one third feel that the stress placed on the patient and family is the greatest drawback to receiving such services at home. One patient was worried, in particular, about the burden placed on her primary caregiver in carrying out the self-care instructions of the nurse: "My sister needs relief; she already has enough to do."

For patients receiving home health aide services, almost half feel that scheduling adequate coverage is the greatest drawback to receiving such services. As one client stated: "The aide has to leave at a certain time to get to the next patient even if they were late or I'm not ready for them to go."

Finally, patients who are receiving other professional services feel that scheduling adequate coverage and the increased risk to the patient in the area of self-care responsibilities are the greatest drawbacks to receiving these services at home.

The next chapter maintains a focus on direct patient issues. However, the emphasis turns from patient perceptions of service quality and efficacy to issues related to their individual rights as service consumers.

CHAPTER 6

The Rights of Patients

T his chapter of findings considers a series of issues pertaining to the individual rights of home health care consumers. Executive directors in the national survey as well as local personnel were queried as to: the range and frequency of ethical and legal issues confronted by agency personnel; whether their agencies have policies to deal with decisions surrounding life sustaining treatment and patients with questionable decision-making capacity; the extent to which patients are informed about their legal rights; and agency procedures for encouraging patient participation in treatment decisions.

NATIONAL PERSPECTIVES

Ethical and Legal Issues in Home Health Care

Table 6.1 presents the frequency with which home health care agencies in the national survey have faced a range of ethical and legal issues during the past year. The 12 legal and ethical issues listed in Table 6.1 together comprise a Legal-Ethical Issues Index (LEII), which was constructed especially for this analysis. The development of the LEII is described in appendix A. As shown, the most common issue has been the use of living wills. Other issues lying on the higher end of the scale's midpoint include decisions by patients to forego life-sustaining treatment, use of durable powers of attorney for health care, interaction with guardians, and conflicts between the family's wishes and the patient's wishes. Least frequently dealt with are issues pertaining to conflicts between the surrogate's and the patient's wishes, problems with obtaining informed consent, and surrogate decision making and substituted judgment.

The mean score on the LEII indicates such issues, taken together, are dealt with only rarely to sometimes. Factor analytic procedures performed on the items in the LEII (a statistical procedure described in greater detail in appendix A) identified three dimensions within which these legal-ethical issues fall—those pertaining to patient rights (designated factor I), those pertaining to a patient's right to die (designated factor II), and those pertaining to the delegation of patient authority (designated factor III). As illustrated in the paired *t* values in Table 6.1, right to die issues are faced

TABLE 6.1 Frequency with Which Home Health Care Agencies Have Faced a Range of Ethical and Legal Issues During the Past Year (National Survey)

Issues	Mean†	S.D.
Use of living wills (c)	2.1	1.0
Use of durable powers of attorney for health care (d)	1.8	.9
Decisions by patients to forego life-sustaining treatment (a)	1.6	1.0
Interaction with guardians (public or private) (e)	1.6	.8
Conflicts between family's wishes and patient's wishes (k)	1.6	.8
Decisions determining patient competence (h)	1.5	.9
Decisions by families to forego life-sustaining treatment (b)	1.4	1.0
Issues of patient's right to privacy and confidentiality (j)	1.3	1.1
Limited guardianships/conservatorships (f)	1.1	.8
Surrogate decision making/substituted judgments (i)	.9	.9
Problems with obtaining informed consent (g)	.8	.7
Conflicts between surrogate's (guardian or durable power of attorney) and patient's wishes (l)	.8	.8
Summary Index Score	1.4	.5

				t values	
Factors	*Mean*	*S.D.*	*I × II*	*I × III*	*II × III*
I. Patient rights	1.1	.6	−7.6**	−6.7**	2.7*
II. Right to die	1.7	.8			
III. Delegation of authority	1.5	.6			

Factor I = issues g, h, i, j, k, l; factor II = issues a, b, c; factor III = issues d, e, f.

†Item, index, and factor score range: 0–3 where 0 = never, 1 = rarely, 2 = sometimes, and 3 = often.

*p < .01   **p < .001   S.D., standard deviation.

significantly more often than either patient rights or delegation of authority issues. Furthermore, patient rights issues are dealt with least often, significantly less so than delegation of authority issues.

Several interesting differences emerge across home health care agency types in terms of their experience in dealing with various legal-ethical issues. Perhaps unexpectedly, high-tech home health care programs emerge as dealing significantly less often with legal-ethical issues generally than those agencies not engaged in providing high-tech services. Specifically, the high-tech agencies have significantly less frequent involvement in issues pertaining to patient rights and delegation of authority. As might be expected, hospice providers report significantly more involvement in right to die issues but equivalent levels of involvement in other categories of legal-ethical issues compared to nonhospice providers. Finally, proprietary home health care programs stand out as dealing less often with legal-ethical issues generally and in particular with issues pertaining to the rights of patients.

Other analyses confirm that the length of time agencies have been engaged in home health care is not associated with the frequency with which they deal with legal-ethical issues during service provision. On the other hand, increases in the number of patients served and the number of home visits made is positively associated with increases in the full range of legal and ethical issues confronted as gauged by the LEII and in patient rights (factor I) issues in particular.

Special Agency Policies:
Advance Directives and Decision-Making Capacity

Agency executive directors in the national analysis were posed two questions about formalized policies meant to help guide staff in the decision making process: one pertaining to policies regarding the handling of decisions about life-sustaining treatment and one dealing with policies for patients having questionable decision-making capacity.

Life-Sustaining Treatment Policy

More than two thirds of the agencies surveyed (100 or 68%) have internal policies regarding how staff should handle decisions about life-sustaining treatments. The proportion of agencies having such formalized policies did not vary significantly when considering agencies differing in their corporate status, auspice, geographic area served, high-tech status, or whether hospice patients are served.

Agencies that have such policies were asked to send to the authors a copy of those guidelines. Seventeen agencies sent copies of their internal policies related to life-sustaining treatment and advance directives. The written policies of the 17 agencies were reviewed to identify possible observable trends in developing and implementing policies on advance directives.

It was discovered that almost half the respondents distribute written materials on advance directives to new clients. Of the respondents who indicated when this process is initiated, 100% provide this information during the initial home visit. Less than half provide a verbal explanation of a patient's rights and agency policy in addition to the written materials. The most popular form for distributing written information to the consumer is a brochure, which in most cases is structured in a question and answer format.

Most agencies delegate the responsibility of distributing information or initiating discussions to nursing staff. Only one agency indicated that the physician would handle this. Although the physician is not the key staff person involved in these discussions, many agencies were discovered to have policies in place that allow for referrals to the physician for more detailed discussions or case review. Other professionals that agencies refer home care consumers to include lawyers and social workers.

Agencies have a wide range of policies and procedures for dealing with life-sustaining treatment decisions. Some agencies seem to place more emphasis on do not resuscitate (DNR) orders written by the physician, than advance directives executed by the client. Reference to DNR orders was found in almost a third of the descriptions provided. Approximately half of the agencies have incorporated requirements of the Patient Self-Determination Act (42 U.S.C. Medicare and Medicaid, 1990, effective December 1, 1991) in their policies and procedures. Only four of the agencies indicated that they have a system to flag a patient's chart if the patient has an advance directive or DNR order. Staff training on these issues is provided by four of the agencies, and only three agencies offer community education.

Questionable Decision-Making Capacity Policy

A second question was asked of agencies pertaining to the availability of internal policies for dealing with patients having questionable decision-making capacity. Fewer agencies reported such a policy than did those agencies having policies for handling decisions about life-sustaining treatment. Once again, the presence of such an internal policy did not vary significantly when considering the corporate status, auspice, geographic area served, high-tech status, or hospice status of the agencies surveyed in the national analysis. Seventy-five percent of agencies providing high-tech services have such policies, while only 25% of non-high-tech agencies have these policies. Agencies that have policies on decision-making capacity are more likely to have policies on life-sustaining treatment decisions. Agencies that have been in existence longer are more likely to have policies on decision-making capacity of patients. Agencies with larger caseloads are also more likely to have policies on decision-making capacity.

Patient Knowledge of Rights and Participation in Treatment Decisions

A final set of questions in the national survey inquired into executive directors' perceptions of the extent to which patients are informed about their legal rights and the extent to which agencies encourage active patient participation in treatment decisions. The responses of the directors surveyed suggest a relatively well-informed consumer population. Almost three of every 10 directors feel their patients are very informed about their legal rights as patients. An additional 46% maintain that their patients are informed. Approximately one quarter feel their patients are not very informed and only two directors maintain their patients are not informed at all. No significant differences in directors' views emerge when comparing agencies varying in corporate status, auspice, geographic area served, or hospice and high-tech services offered. Interestingly, perceived level of patients' legal rights knowledge is positively associated with a higher frequency of legal-ethical issues addressed by agencies as measured by the LEII and, in particular, a higher frequency of right to die issues (factor II).

Agency directors were finally probed as to the ways in which their agencies encourage patient participation in treatment decisions. It was discovered that four strategies are commonly practiced, with three of the four subscribed to by over 90% of the agencies surveyed. Providing explanations of patient rights upon entry into the program, actively seeking patient feedback and input, and providing information to patients are common practices of more than nine of every 10 agencies. Conducting regular care plan conferences involving staff, family, and the patient is standard policy for almost seven of every 10 agencies. There is no difference in terms of the frequency with which different categories of home health care agencies explain patient rights, seek feedback/input, and provide information to patients. On the other hand, it is interesting to note that public agencies report significantly less frequent involvement in the conduct of staff, family, and patient care plan conferences.

THE LOCAL PERSPECTIVE

This section summarizes local survey data related to patient rights and the agency's ability to support those rights.

Staff Views

Table 6.2 summarizes local data reflective of staff involvement with a variety of ethical and legal issues during the course of their work. It was discovered that more than half of the staff (54%) have some involvement with living wills, but only 39% of staff have experienced the use of durable powers of attorney for health care. What is interesting is that sizable proportions of staff seem to be indicating very little involvement

TABLE 6.2   Staff Involvement in Legal and Ethical Issues (Local Survey)

Profile variable	Often % (frequency)	Sometimes % (frequency)	Rarely % (frequency)	Never % (frequency)
Patient decision to refuse treatment	29.3 (27)	20.7 (19)	16.3 (15)	33.7 (31)
Family decision to forego treatment	25.0 (23)	20.7 (19)	21.7 (20)	32.6 (30)
Living wills	37.4 (34)	16.5 (15)	25.3 (23)	20.9 (19)
Durable power of attorney for health care	18.5 (17)	20.7 (19)	25.0 (23)	35.9 (33)
Guardianship	27.2 (25)	17.4 (16)	22.8 (21)	32.6 (30)
Limited guardian	6.6 (6)	4.4 (4)	29.7 (27)	59.3 (54)
Informed consent	3.3 (3)	6.5 (6)	34.8 (32)	55.4 (51)
Assessing patient competence	15.2 (14)	9.8 (9)	43.5 (40)	31.5 (29)
Surrogate decision making	12.0 (11)	17.4 (16)	23.9 (22)	46.7 (43)
Right to privacy/confidentiality	33.7 (31)	6.5 (6)	28.3 (26)	31.5 (29)
Conflict between patient & family	19.6 (18)	32.6 (30)	28.3 (26)	19.6 (18)
Conflict between surrogate & patient	3.3 (3)	5.6 (5)	26.7 (24)	64.4 (58)

with these issues. Fifty percent of staff are involved with decisions by patients to forego life-sustaining treatment, while 54% of staff have little involvement with such decisions made by family members. Ironically, 45% of staff do interact with guardians, while only 11% interact with limited guardians. Only one in 10 staff experience problems with obtaining informed consent.

Patient Views

Responses from patients in the local survey indicate that they are clearly comfortable with staff explanations of the purpose of various services. Ninety-two percent feel that the purpose of home health care service is explained thoroughly by staff. Far more patients feel they are either very informed or informed (80%) rather than not very informed or not informed at all (20%) about their rights as patients. Such a view by patients is reflected in Table 6.3, where data are reported on whether patients are aware of certain specific rights including the right to informed consent (94% of patients are aware); the right to make treatment decisions (88% are aware); the right to accept, refuse, or discontinue treatment (87% are aware); and the right to formulate an advance directive (64% are aware).

TABLE 6.3   Patient Awareness of Legal and Ethical Rights (Local Survey)

Profile variable	Frequency	Percent
How well informed about rights		
Very informed	26	40.0
Informed	26	40.0
Not very informed	8	12.3
Not informed at all	5	7.7
Awareness of specific rights		
Right to informed consent	61	93.8
Right to decide about treatment	59	88.1
Right to accept/refuse treatment	58	86.6
Right to execute an advance directive	43	64.2
Patients with advance directives		
Durable power of attorney for health care	27	31.8
Living will	21	40.9

It is important to note that although many patients are aware of their rights, they are not necessarily engaging in activities to insure the enhancement of those rights. Only 32% of patients have a living will, and 40% have a durable power of attorney for health care. (While less than half of those interviewed availed themselves of these directives, the proportions are dramatically higher than those found in the general population.) Given the low numbers of executed advance directives, it is interesting to consider the persons that patients consult with in making medical decisions. Physicians are the most frequent choice of patients (mentioned 52% of the time). The person next most frequently approached is the adult child (mentioned 40% of the time), the spouse (mentioned 30% of the time), and other relatives (mentioned 15% of the time).

In the final chapter of findings that follows we return to the organizational dimension of high-tech care, the original point of reference in the service delivery triad. Of immediate interest are the consequences and outcomes that high-tech service delivery is having on the structure and function of the home care agency.

CHAPTER 7

The Impact of High Technology on the Agency

T his chapter considers the various impacts that executive directors in the national survey perceive the importation of high technology to be having on the home health care sector generally and their individual agencies in particular. Inquiries were directed at the relative frequency of requests for high-tech care during the recent past, reasons for any increase in patient requests for high-tech care during the past five years, the evolving issue of agency liability, the range of formal agency mechanisms established to address the legal and ethical aspects of high-tech care, and ways in which high-tech care has changed the home health care agency including expectations concerning staffing and training.

THE NATIONAL PERSPECTIVE

Frequency of Requests for High-Tech Service

The vast majority of national survey directors express conviction that the number of patient requests for high-tech care has increased during the past five years. No differences in directors' viewpoints are discernable when considering variations in an organization's corporate status, auspice, geographic area served, or the availability of hospice services.

Reasons offered by directors for the increase in patient requests for high-tech care highlight the powerful influence of four separate and distinct factors: technological advances, changes in health professionals' attitudes, diagnostic-related groups, and the increased availability of insurance reimbursements. Clear majorities of directors find the convergence of these factors to be extremely influential. Of lesser, but nevertheless substantial influence has been the greater number of frail older adults and the increased emphasis on encouraging older persons to age-in-place (that is, to spend their latter years in the familiar environs of their own homes and communities). Thus, a combination of technological, financial, regulatory, and, to a lesser extent, demographic and value-based factors are influencing high-tech utilization rates according to executives in the home health care field.

Ways High-Tech Care Has Changed Agencies

Agency directors were next asked to identify the ways in which they have found the provision of high-tech home health care to influence agency operations. It is clear that high-tech service provision, more likely than not, is impacting on agency operations. More than nine of 10 directors feel that it has had some degree of influence. However, rather than one single factor dominating the responses of directors, it would seem that a range of factors are playing some role in altering the shape and form of home health care. These include (in descending order of importance): (a) the expansion of staff and services offered; (b) the increase in the skill level of agency staff; (c) an increase in the offering of training and in-service programs for agency staff; (d) increments in the administrative and coordinative demands of office staff; (e) increased capacity to respond to patient referrals; and (f) increased financial demands on agency operations.

For one director, the offering of high-tech care appears to have arrived with mixed consequences:

It has made the quality of the care more important. At the same time it has made the risk and liability much greater.

Organizational growth is a commonly observed consequence:

We receive referrals from infusion therapy companies to provide their skilled nursing. We work closely with three infusion therapy companies. Our census has increased about 300 visits per year.

Offering high-tech services increased the overall growth of the agency tremendously.

The consequences for other directors are clearly training-related:

We have needed better on-call coverage. All nurses have to keep up to date on new technology and techniques, which means relying on agencies for technical assistance that are 80 miles away.

Technological services increased the training and standards set for nursing personnel.

Our agency required more in-servicing of staff and development of tools and procedures.

Recruitment issues are paramount for another executive:

Our organization must have specially trained staff, which are sometimes harder to recruit, especially those with IV skills.

The financial consequences of offering high-tech care dominated the thinking of still other directors:

The cost of providing care has increased drastically, and we are only reimbursed on a per diem basis.

Longer visits, sicker patients requiring more nursing care and more documentation is causing our productivity to be less efficient.

It was not uncommon for agency executives to cite multiple consequences of high-tech service provision:

High-technology services have increased our staff's educational level, and enhanced clinical skills required for RNs, as well as increased the overall number of nursing staff, increased interaction/communication with insurance companies, resulted in the purchase of car phones for better accessibility of on-call nurses, and increased the number of on-call visits.

Service functions are more complex due to the use of complicated equipment which means we have needed to increase professional skills and have more frequent communication with the physician, as well as continuous monitoring of patient treatment. The agency needs more personnel to cover the hours of service required. The reimbursement of these services does not correspond to the agency's investment.

Finally, it is interesting to note that for one agency director the inclusion of high-tech care into the agency's repertoire of services has apparently elevated the status of the program in the eyes of the community:

> Yes, we have added a clinical nurse specialist. This has enhanced our ability to recruit some RNs—but we have lost others. High-tech services serve to reaffirm our mission and this has changed our "dowdy" community image.

Staffing and Training Issues

One question in the national survey questionnaire addressed the degree to which different categories of home health care staff employed by high-tech agency providers are engaged in high-tech service provision from the perspective of directors. Table 7.1 summarizes the extent of involvement of different staff in direct delivery of high-tech care. As shown, and perhaps not unexpectedly, nurses are almost universally involved in high-tech service provision in the opinion of executive directors. Only two agencies report that nurses are not engaged in high-tech care. It is interesting to note that administrators represent the second most common category of personnel involved in high-tech care. Their involvement is commonplace in almost half (47%) of the agencies surveyed compared to physicians, who are engaged in this category of intervention in 46% of agencies.

TABLE 7.1   Extent to Which Staff Are Involved in the Direct Delivery of High-Tech Home Care (National Survey)

Staff category	*Involved in direct delivery of high-tech home care*		*Not involved in direct delivery of high-tech home care*	
	Frequency	*Percent*	*Frequency*	*Percent*
Nurses	112	98.2	2	1.8
Administration	54	47.4	60	52.6
Physicians	52	45.6	62	54.4
Therapists (OT, PT, ST)	36	31.6	78	68.4
Home health aides	20	17.5	94	82.5
Social workers	18	15.8	96	84.2
Support staff	16	14.0	98	86.0
Homemakers	5	4.4	109	95.6

OT, occupational therapy; PT, physical therapy; ST, speech therapy.

Occupational, physical, and speech therapists represent the fourth most common category of personnel providing direct high-tech care, with these professionals engaged in such activities in 32% of agencies. All remaining staff categories (home health aides, social workers, support staff, and homemakers) are each involved in such services, according to directors, in less than 20% of the participating agencies. These perceived staff involvement rates, as specified by agency directors, do not vary significantly when considering agency corporate status, auspice, community served, and hospice status.

Asked to indicate whether staff who are involved in the delivery of high-tech home care receive special agency training, 92% of directors responded in the affirmative. If this figure is compared to the proportion of agencies requiring various staff to participate in ongoing training (see Table 3.3), it becomes clear that the requirements of high-tech home health care carry with them a greater likelihood of agency-mandated training than the requirements of home health care service delivery generally. Even so, it is troubling to note that special training requirements are not required of all high-tech home health care staff providers.

Required agency training tends to focus on preparation specific to the equipment required for a particular intervention. Training is commonly provided in the use of IV access devices, IV antibiotics, IV parenteral nutrition, IV supplies, complicated wound care training, subcutaneous access devices, computerized programmable pumps, ventilator care, and blood transfusions. Many agencies require certification in IV therapy, chemotherapy, and oncology. It is not uncommon for infusion companies to provide the initial training to operate the equipment they rent and then to provide regular inservice technology updates as new equipment is introduced to the market. Training is carried out using multiple formats including staff conferences, in-services, on-site demonstrations, procedural handouts, classes at area hospitals, videotapes, and workshops. Hands-on learning is stressed in many cases.

The Risk of Liability in High-Tech Care

One of the conceivable consequences of providing high-tech care is increased risk of liability for the agency engaged in such an enterprise. When asked, 87 directors, or 81% of respondents, maintained that their risk of liability had increased since they began providing high-tech home care services. While no differences emerge in perceived liability risk levels for hospice service providers as compared to their nonhospice counterparts, there is a strong tendency for proprietary and hospital home health care directors to acknowledge greater increases in the risk of liability as compared to public and voluntary hospital- and nonhospital-based programs.

Factors contributing to this increased risk of liability are specified in Table 7.2. Dominating the responses of agency directors is the resultant need for increased professional skill and expertise and the need to use complicated equipment and monitor and coordinate the activities of multiple service providers. Somewhat less frequently mentioned contributing factors (but still noted by a majority of respondents) are the need for more frequent communication with physicians, the need to monitor high-tech equipment in the home 24 hours a day, and the increased frailty of high-tech patients. Slightly more than one in every three directors cites the use of independent contractors as a liability factor.

TABLE 7.2 Factors Contributing to Increased Risk of Liability Since Agencies Began Providing High-Tech Home Health Care Services (National Survey)

	Yes		*No*	
Contributing factor	*Frequency*	*Percent*	*Frequency*	*Percent*
Need for increased professional skill	75	83.3	15	16.7
Use of complicated equipment	70	78.7	19	21.3
Monitoring and coordinating multiple service providers	70	78.7	19	21.3
Need for more frequent communication with physician	59	66.3	30	33.7
Need for continual (24 hour) monitoring of treatment	54	60.7	35	39.3
Increased frailty/disability of patients	50	56.2	39	43.8
Use of independent contractors	32	36.0	57	64.0

Mechanisms for Addressing the Legal and Ethical
Demands of High-Tech Care

Agency directors were questioned about the various procedures and mechanisms that have been formally established in their agencies to deal with the legal and ethical demands associated with delivering high-tech and other forms of home health care services (see Table 7.3). (The various kinds of legal and ethical issues surfacing during the course of home health care service delivery were considered in chapter 6). Together, these 11 formal mechanisms comprise a Legal-Ethical Mechanisms Index (LEMI), the construction of which is described in appendix A.

TABLE 7.3   **Formal Mechanisms Used by Agencies to Deal with the Legal-Ethical Demands of Delivering High-Tech Home Health Care (National Survey)**

	Yes		No	
Formal mechanism	*Frequency*	*Percent*	*Frequency*	*Percent*
In-service training for staff	107	94.7	6	5.3
External continuing education/ training for staff	103	91.2	10	8.8
Special policies, procedures, or guidelines for high-tech service delivery	101	89.4	12	10.6
Care plan conferences with staff/patients/family	88	77.9	25	22.1
Supervisory sessions	81	71.7	32	28.3
Special-theme staff meetings	64	56.6	49	43.4
Special information/management systems for documenting high-tech delivery	58	51.3	55	48.7
Education programs for patients and their families	52	46.0	61	54.0
Legal counsel/consultants	44	38.9	69	61.1
Ethics committee/ethicists	27	23.9	86	76.1
Use of external resources such as the ombudsman program, etc.	18	15.9	95	84.1
Summary index score*	Mean = 6.6		S.D. = 1.9	

*Summary index score range = 0–11, where high score indicates greater number of formal mechanisms used by agencies.

S.D., standard deviation.

As illustrated in Table 7.3, the directors surveyed have already established a variety of formal agency policies and procedures for dealing with the legal and ethical components of care. The average agency has between six and seven specific mechanisms available to its staff and patients for dealing with legal and ethical challenges. Policies and procedures established by a majority of agencies include (in descending order of frequency): in-service training programs; external continuing education and training programs; special guidelines for high-tech service delivery; care plan conferences for staff, patients, and family; supervisory sessions; special-theme staff meetings; and special information and management systems for documenting service delivery. Less popular mechanisms (established by fewer than half of the agencies) include patient and family education programs, legal counsel and consultants, ethics committees and ethicists, and the use of external resources such as an ombudsman program.

No significant differences in the variety of mechanisms used are found when considering the corporate status, auspice, community service area, or hospice provider status of agencies. It should be noted, however, that hospitals have established substantially more such mechanisms than other agency auspice types, although the difference fell just short of statistical significance. In particular, hospital-based programs are apt to use special-theme staff meetings and supervisory sessions more frequently. The use of increased numbers of special legal-ethical mechanisms (as measured by the LEMI) is positively associated with the increased occurrence of legal-ethical issues surfacing in agencies (as measured by the LEII), and, in particular, increases in the occurrence of patient rights issues and delegation of authority issues.

The Benefits and Drawbacks of High-Tech Care

Executive directors were given the opportunity to respond to a series of open-ended questions that inquired into the challenges associated with their agency providing high technology home health care services. These survey questions focused on the benefits and drawbacks of high-tech service provision, as well as assessments of those high-tech services delivered most and least effectively.

Three benefits to providing high-tech home health care dominate the responses of executive directors. Almost a third of those responding to the question believe that provision of high-tech care is resulting in greater opportunities for older persons to remain in the familiar environs of their own homes. Simply put, it has allowed them to age-in-place. This wish, of course, has traditionally dominated the thinking of older persons, regardless of their health status.

The following remarks are illustrative:

> Allows client to be at home in least restrictive environment.
>
> Improved quality of life for client and the family, development of a more normal lifestyle than institutionalization.
>
> Reduced alteration of client life style, ADLs and environment. People do better when they are able to retain as much of their usual surroundings and independence as possible.

Two additional, although somewhat less frequently mentioned benefits, can also be identified. First are the cost savings that can accrue from caring for older persons in their homes rather than institutional settings, regardless of the level of sophistication of the services and equipment needed. Approximately a quarter of the directors are of this opinion. An additional two in 10 directors maintain that recipients of high-tech care benefit in terms of increased levels of comfort and reduced stress while coping with a particular infirmity. Less frequently mentioned benefits of high-tech care provided in the patient's home include improvements in patient health status, the resultant availability of a more comprehensive package of services that agencies are consequently able to offer the consumer, and the increased involvement of patients themselves and their family in the care plan. One director went so far as to suggest that high-tech care's promotion of family involvement helps to prevent "family disintegration." Other benefits, much more seldomly mentioned, include the improved quality of services offered, a greater competitive edge for the agency, patients being exposed to less risk of infection and fewer side effects from immobility, and less visible care of the patient. One director, seemingly quite positive about the high-tech capacity of her agency, summed up the multiple benefits accruing from high-tech care in the home as follows: "Increased patient autonomy; allows patient to be care partner; keeps patient in home surroundings; involves family in patient care; decreases cost of medical care; increases patient comfort; easier access to care by patient; more personalized care."

Directors found it more difficult to identify drawbacks associated with the provision of high-tech care, testifying to what appears to be a relatively positive experience in service provision. The most common drawbacks are increased stress felt by family members and other personal caregivers, the absence of readily available third-party reimbursement for high-tech care, the unsuitability of some patient's homes for high-tech care provision, the scarcity of adequate numbers of staff trained in the provision of high-tech care, and difficulties associated with scheduling adequate coverage for those in need. Less frequently mentioned drawbacks to high-tech care include increased liability for agencies, increased risk to the patient, difficulties associated with accessing physician services when needed, and the inability to respond to patient-related high-tech needs during emergencies.

The Challenges of High-Tech Care

Asked to identify the major challenges associated with providing high-tech home health care, agency directors reaffirmed the difficulties associated with overcoming the kinds of drawbacks specified above. Several directors were able to communicate their concerns quite thoughtfully and compellingly. One director, who focuses on the more personal aspects of high-tech care provision, speaks of three particularly challenging features of this category of service:

1. To be able to help people in the environment they choose to live in.
2. To be able to cope and do the best you can when conditions are far from ideal.
3. To be able to accept and place life and death in perspective yet continue to choose life, if possible.

Many directors feel the major challenge revolves around the successful involvement of patients, family members, and other caregivers in the patient's plan of care. The following remarks by directors are illustrative of this kind of challenge:

Educating family to the needs of patient and ensuring family cooperation.

Family's knowledge base.

Teaching the patient/caregiver how to administer and care for IV.

Insuring that aseptic technique is followed by lay persons.

Educating patients so they can be independent in care.

Of course the teaching function represents a central challenge of home health care agencies not only for the patient and caregiver, but also for third-party payors, the general public, and all service staff, including physicians. The demands associated with on-going staff education and training permeate the responses of these directors, including especially the need to have competent, qualified staff who remain up-to-date on new technology (both procedures and equipment). Numerous directors emphasized that the equipment associated with high-tech home health care is undergoing rapid change in terms of its design and operation.

Other challenges for the agency that are cited include coordinating multiple patient services, including those offered by contracted agencies, pharmaceutical and infusion companies, private geriatric care managers, and the home health care team generally (comprised of the nurse, physician, aide, social work, physical therapist, and others). Still other directors speak of the challenge of convincing third-party payors to reimburse the patient or the agency for new and emerging high-tech modalities, scheduling adequate staff coverage, and responding in timely fashion to emergency situations. Finally, one director got right to the point specifying the ultimate challenge quite succinctly: "Getting 'it' [high-tech care] to succeed."

The Effectiveness of High-Tech Care

Each executive director was also offered the opportunity to identify the three most and the three least effectively delivered high-tech services offered by their agency. Because the full range of high-tech services and equipment are not equally likely to be offered by any given home health care agency, these data need to be interpreted with caution. The most prudent analytic strategy might well be to focus on comparisons of the frequency and percentage of time in which a particular high-tech intervention is mentioned as being most as compared to least effectively delivered. In those cases where the frequency of response is low for both categories of effectiveness (most and least) (e.g., personal emergency response systems, telecommunications/close circuit television, self-instruction computers, robotics, bone growth stimulation therapy, transcutaneous electric nerve stimulators) one might conclude that home health care agencies are simply less likely to be engaged in the delivery of such services and are thus unable to assess delivery effectiveness levels.

Given this approach to analyzing responses, it is clear that nutrition and hydration therapy is far more likely to be considered an effectively delivered service than an ineffectively delivered service. Similarly, antibiotic and pain control (palliative) therapies are, more likely than not, seen as being rather effectively delivered interventions. This holds true for tracheostomy, oxygen, pressure sore, and ostomy care as well. On the other hand, general infusion therapies emerge with mixed reviews in terms of effectiveness levels. Nearly equal proportions of respondents cite this high-tech intervention as their most and least effectively delivered service. Apparently, there is considerable variation in the ability to deliver different types of infusion therapy with equivalent levels of effectiveness. Furthermore, it is possible that one director could be referring to one type of IV therapy when speaking of general infusion therapy (e.g., antibiotics) and another director could be referring to another type of IV therapy (e.g., chemotherapy). Even more negative are assessments of the effectiveness of delivering ventilator care, blood component infusions, renal dialysis, and home chemotherapy. In each of these cases, greater numbers of directors identify the service as one of their agencies least rather than most effectively delivered intervention.

Several respondents insist that any high-tech service that is delivered least effectively should not be offered by the agency in the first place. Similarly, one director maintains that her agency does not accept clients that can't be served effectively. One respondent, apparently quite sincere, pointed out: "We do the best we can. . . . I trust our effectiveness. . . . The results we cannot control. . . . Some things help. . . . Some things don't. We try."

Final Thoughts

At the conclusion of the national survey, all directors were given the opportunity to add their personal thoughts about providing high-tech home care services. The majority of comments centered on shortcomings in the current system of care, including, in particular, the high costs associated with service provision. One director maintained it is prohibitive to anyone without an existing funding source. Another felt that third-party payors need to obtain a better understanding of high-tech home health care if they are going to make a genuine commitment to it. Still another spoke to the uneven availability of high-tech services, noting that high-tech services are not available anywhere on the island of Puerto Rico, and that the island's local medical plan does not have coverage for high-tech home care. The director of a rural-based home health care program further underscored the uneven nature of service availability. It was noted that there is little technical backup in his rural area. In fact, the home health care agency offers more specialized high-tech services than the local hospital, which is a regional medical center. The majority of referrals are directed to the home health care program because the hospital as recently as one year ago had extremely limited numbers of staff able to carry out necessary high-tech procedures. The director of one agency felt a strategy was needed to compensate physicians for managing high-tech home care patients.

Not all respondents, however, found fault with the system. One director, whose agency specializes in oncology services, focused on the positive consequences of service provision to vulnerable patients by pointing out: "I personally have found it to be very rewarding. We are providing a much needed and very appreciated service."

Special Practice Issues
and Applications

CHAPTER 8

Legal Aspects of High-Tech Home Health Care

By Raymond L. Albert

INTRODUCTION

The expansion in home care and its accompanying technological innovation, as this chapter discusses, is not without its problems. There is an
undeniable legal dimension to the convergence of technology and home
care, and home care agencies are correctly worried about the legal consequences associated with the use of high technology in the home. One
prominent scholar argues:

> [A]s home care becomes increasingly high-tech for many patients who
> previously would have needed institutionalization because of the severity of
> their illnesses or disabilities the chances for events to go disastrously wrong
> grow as well. [T]he permeation of home care services with sophisticated
> technologies, coupled with strong provider financial incentives to keep
> patients out of acute care hospitals altogether or at least to shorten their
> lengths of stay as much as possible, often results in a patient demographic
> picture characterized by a much higher sickness or acuity level than would
> have been found in the past. Sick home care patients demanding more com-
> plicated and time-consuming kinds of attention increase the potential risk of
> adverse outcomes, which are a central element of any negligence claim.

[T]he dissemination of home care services to patients through a complex web of sites and individuals presents challenging management information, monitoring, coordination, and supervision difficulties for home care agencies, which can make it more problematic to control legal risks (Kapp, 1995a, p. 32).

THE LANDSCAPE FOR LEGAL LIABILITY

The nature of home care is changing, a condition that also erodes the legal footing for home care administrators. A range of legal and ethical issues now confront agencies delivering technology-enhanced care in the home. Eighty-four percent of the home health agency respondents in the research reported in this volume indicated that the number of high-tech care requests had increased during the past 5 years, a condition that risks expanded liability (Kaye & Davitt, 1995a). Additionally, close to 81% of the respondents reported their risk of liability had increased since they began providing high-technology care. "The dominant factors contributing to this increased risk of liability were the resultant need for increased professional skill/expertise [and] the need to use complicated equipment and monitor/coordinate the activities of multiple service providers" (Kaye & Davitt, 1995a, pp. 41–48).

The home care field is governed by extensive regulations for both service delivery and the licensure of service providers.[1] At the core of this regulatory activity is a preoccupation with patient care standards (Johnson, 1991, pp. 126–127). The attendant legal duties are equally clear: home care providers must fulfill a standard of care, which is derived from the heavy overlay of legal regulations, accreditation standards, and the existent case law. All these sources, collectively, constitute the basis for legal liability (Johnson, 1991; Kapp, 1995a, pp. 33–37). The dearth of case law, particularly, on home health care is likely to change if lawsuits in this area mirror those in the nursing home field (Warner & Albert, 1997).

Perhaps the most distinguishing feature of the law in this area is its apparent unsettled nature. This is not to say that no law exists, or that existent law is idiosyncratic. Rather, current judicial decisions on home health care, whether derived from common law or based on regulations or accreditation standards, are practically nonexistent. One must, therefore, look to analogous areas, such as nursing homes and hospitals to draw conclusions about how the law will evolve. Notwithstanding, we know that negligence (injury caused by a failure to act under circumstances where there is a duty to act), vicarious liability (where a principal, such as an employer, is held liable for the negligent conduct of his agent, such as an employee), agency (where an agency acts for or represents a principal), and informed consent (a voluntary agreement based on knowledge of the nature and consequences of the agreement) comprise the conceptual framework. One might better appreciate this framework by conceptualizing it as akin to the thrust and parry involved in fencing, as the following table illustrates.[2]

TABLE 8.1 The Legal Framework of Health Care

Thrust	*Parry*
Hospitals have a duty to provide competent physicians and, for that purpose, to make proper investigation of complaints about physicians.	As a general rule, negligence is not absolute or to be measured in all cases in accordance with some precise standard.
One must act to avoid injury to foreseeable parties; all parties are required to use ordinary care to prevent others from being injured as a result of their conduct.	In the absence of statutory provision declaring an exception to that fundamental principle, no such exception should be made *unless* clearly supported by public policy.
No duty to protect against harm to self.	Except where defendant has control over the party, as in the case of a prison, or hospital.
A physician who treats a patient without consent commits a battery.	A patient's consent to medical treatment will be implied in some circumstances.
The doctrine of informed consent was developed to protect the right to self-determination in matters of treatment.	Where the patient is not competent to consent to medical treatment, an authorized person may consent on the patient's behalf.
Courts have upheld the right of a competent patient to refuse medical treatment, even if that decision will hasten his or her death.	The right to refuse life-sustaining medical treatment is not absolute.
A hospital may be held liable for acts of independent contractors, usually a doctor, if it can be shown that the contractor was an "ostensible agent" of the hospital.	A hospital could not be held liable for conduct of a physician under the theory of "ostensible agency" absent any evidence apart from the patient's complaint that hospital held physician out as its agent.

The challenge is to rationalize the pull and tug inherent in the controlling law and fashion rules that provide coherent guidance for those whose conduct must be regulated. Against this backdrop, then, the discussion below explores (a) the standard of care for high-tech home care, (b) several dimensions of liability for negligence of direct care providers, (c) informed consent and refusal of treatment, and (d) telemedicine/telehealth as the emerging model for high-technology home care.

THE STANDARD OF CARE

The applicable standard of care (the criteria used to evaluate whether certain conduct is negligent under particular circumstances) for home care providers is derived from the standard for delivery of health care in analogous settings, such as hospitals and nursing homes. *Darlington v. Charleston Community Memorial Hospital* (1966), a 1965 Illinois case, lays out the general rule: hospitals may be held liable for the administration or staff's failure to monitor and supervise health care delivery in the hospital. Underscoring the significance of both accreditation standards and state license regulations, the *Darlington* court found that both these legal bases were sufficient to impose liability on the hospital. The application of this standard to health care in nursing homes, however, is another matter. Johnson (1991), for example, discusses obstacles facing plaintiffs attempting to apply a *Darlington*-type standard to the nursing home setting; she is not sanguine, though not entirely pessimistic either, about its applicability to nonhospital situations.

In *Payton Health Care v. Estate of Campbell* (1986), the court found in favor of the deceased patient's estate, citing inadequate staffing at the defendant nursing home facility and other patterns of poor patient care. This result underscores the difference between the bases for liability for negligence within nursing homes versus home health care agencies. The locus of control is a critical feature that distinguishes hospital versus home care. From a clinical perspective, all care, tests, and daily activities are governed for the patient in the hospital. In contrast, when the patient goes home, the locus of control travels, so to speak, with the patient. Moreover, the patterns of poor patient care are certainly easier to isolate where an institution is in total control of such care, a circumstance in direct contrast to the home care situation, where care is typically provided by family members or paid caregivers who render personal service to the patient. Despite the potential obstacle embodied in the application of the control-of-care principle to the home care setting, there is a "heightened sensitivity to and demand for policing of the quality of home health care. Especially for high-tech home health care—where procedures are more invasive; more high-tech than 'high touch', and more likely to carry risk of severe complications—the potential for increased litigation and liability is great" (Johnson, 1991, p. 129).

One case directly addresses the convergence of government regulations and the home health standard of care: *Roach v. Kelly Health Care* (1987). In this case, the plaintiff's descendent, Edna Tuson, suffered personal injury in her home while under the care of Kelly Health Care, Inc. Having lost in the trial court, plaintiff Tuson appealed to the Oregon Court of Appeals, which reversed the trial court's verdict, holding that Tuson had sufficiently established the standard of care owed by the agency. Tuson won because she argued that the state regulations governing home health agencies constituted the standard of care, and negligence under these circumstances is tantamount to negligence, per se.

Mrs. Tuson, aged 87, lived alone in Portland. Her daughter, Mrs. Blaufus, having noticed evidence of her mother's forgetfulness, arranged for the Visiting Nurses Association to provide home visiting nurses several times a week. After several weeks under this arrangement, Mrs. Tuson suffered a stroke, and her daughter arranged with Kelly Health Care for 24-hour, live in care. Rather than provide the requisite home health aides, however, Kelly supplied Mrs. Tuson with certified nursing assistants. The difference between the two is their home-health training. Both receive 60 hours of training with emphasis on caring for patients in an institutional setting under direct supervision of a nurse, but home health aides receive an additional 60 hours of training, with special attention to home care, beyond the basic training. Mrs. Tuson's condition deteriorated gradually, with the result that she became less capable of caring for herself. She was eventually hospitalized for alleged negligence of Kelly's Certified Nursing Assistants (CNA) and subsequently transferred to a nursing home, where she died from other causes (*Roach v. Kelly,* 1987, p. 1192).

The court held that Oregon's licensure law required Kelly to provide home health aides to Mrs. Tuson, given that the range of services offered by the Kelly employees—the regular turning of the patient to prevent bedsores, the wound care treatment, the monitoring of medication, and so forth—pertained to the "curative, rehabilitative or preventive aspect of nursing" for which the Oregon statute requires a home health aide (*Roach v. Kelly,* 1987, p. 1193). Regarding the question of Kelly's liability for failing to properly supervise the CNAs placed in Mrs. Tuson's home, the appellate court remanded the matter, holding that the jury should have been allowed to consider the issue. Thus, while not finding Kelly negligent for failing to supervise the CNAs, the court nonetheless opened the door to such a finding upon reconsideration by the trial court.

The significance of *Roach v. Kelly,* then, is the court's clear willingness to look to state regulations, and certainly by implication accreditation standards, as a standard of care in negligence cases. Indeed, it may be reasonable to argue that, following *Roach v. Kelly,* an agency that violates existing administrative regulations pertaining to any aspect of home health care will be held liable, on a finding of negligence per se, for any resulting injury to the patient.

Another dimension of standard-of-care violations that has implications for home care, generally, and for high-tech home care, specifically, is chronicled in a *TIME* (Thompson, 1997) magazine investigative report depicting widespread neglect of nursing home residents. The report revealed residents dying for lack of food, water, or the most basic hygiene. It cited, among other things, the investigation of David Hoffman, Assistant U.S. Attorney, Eastern District of Pennsylvania, who sued a nursing home for failure to provide adequate care—as evidenced by the presence of festering bedsores on several residents. Hoffman (1997), in an unprecedented move, successfully used the federal False Claims Act (1997) to enforce quality care standards. He described three 1994 episodes in which the federal Nursing Home Reform Act was violated, resulting in a lawsuit against a Pennsylvania long-term care facility for inadequate care.[3] "The implications of this case," Hoffman argued, "are dramatic from a quality of care perspective: providing inadequate care now translates into a false claim to the government for payment [under Medicare or Medicaid]. The False Claims Act provides for treble damages and penalties of $5,000 to $10,000 per claim submitted for payment—enormous potential cost to any company that provides inadequate care" (p. 29).

In light of the above, the implications for potential liability in high-tech home care situations, such as inadequate or inappropriate staffing, is evident. The issues here would be the agency's failure to provide adequate numbers of properly trained staff. Failure to properly staff the agency in order to provide appropriate care is uncontroversial on its face, and liability can be grounded in negligence theory, at least, and other theories are possible.[4]

Failure to properly train staff is equally problematic and often arises in the high-tech home care setting in the form of paraprofessionals needing to be knowledgeable about, and capable of, identifying and responding to problems with patients or the equipment that they are using. Indeed, the federal Conditions of Participation (1997a) deal with the requirements for home health aide services, including provisions related to scope of practice, such as supervision. *Cahill v. HCA Management Co., Inc.* (1987) provides a related case in point. The court found that a hospital management corporation could be held liable under the doctrine of *respondeat superior* (where the master/employer/principal is deemed liable in certain cases for the wrongful acts of his servant/employee/agent) to a patient who allegedly suffered injuries from venipuncture negligently performed by a medical technician. The management corporation was responsible for supervising the technician. The situation, albeit based on the hospital setting, is easily transferable to the home care situation. Finally, an agency must also make certain to provide the adequate and appropriate supervision for all staff who supply care to home care patients. Agencies are well advised to keep copious notes in this regard, making certain to document how staff are oriented to agency policies and to the use of relevant equipment, afforded opportunities to participate in educational programs, and supervised.

Scope of practice issues also surface in this context. Two cases dealing with the matter for licensed nurses may prove illuminating: *Sermchief v. Gonzalez* (1983) and *Fein v. Permanente Medical Group* (1985). In both cases, the court was faced with determining the standard of care for nursing practitioners. Although nurses' independent actions are grounded in doctors' protocols and standing orders, there is still some room for independent judgment, a situation very likely to surface in high-tech home care. Nurse practitioners, therefore, may be subject to a heightened or enhanced standard of care, according to Johnson (1991), who states that "courts in malpractice actions against health care facilities have held nurses to the duty to 'second guess' and intervene in the negligent acts of physicians (p. 144). Moreover, as illustrated in *Capone v. Donovan* (1984), there is the related matter of joint tortfeasors, where two parties either act together to commit wrongdoing or, acting independently, unite in causing a single injury (American Law Report, 1997a). Although the case dealt specifically with a physician in a hospital setting, the nonseverability of the injury (i.e., it was impossible to uncover how each party contributed to the plaintiff's broken leg) and the court's finding of joint liability may have important implications for high-tech home care. "If the tortious conduct of two or more persons causes a single harm which can not be apportioned," the court stated, "the actors are joint tortfeasors even though they may have acted independently" (*Capone v. Donovan,* 1984, p. 1251).

LIABILITY FOR NEGLIGENCE OF DIRECT CARE PROVIDERS AND OTHER PLAUSIBLE AGENTS[5]

Vicarious Liability and Ostensible Agency

Put simply, home health agencies are responsible for those in their employ, and likewise responsible for any injury caused by an employee's negligence. The controlling legal theories are relatively straightforward: vicarious liability (where the employer is held liable for the employee's negligent conduct) and ostensible agency (an implied agency, where one induces another to believe that a third person is his agent, though the third person is not). There are exceptions, however, such as the relationship between the home health agency's attending physician and the agency itself. The usual employer-employee relationship does not hold in this last instance, at least not in the typical manner, and this dynamic has implications for the scope of duty for such physicians in relation to high-tech home care.

The theory of vicarious liability holds the employer liable for any harm caused by its employee. Hospitals, nursing homes, and home care agencies are subject to this general rule. There are limits on liability, such as when the employee acts beyond his or her authorized duties or without the express authority of the employer. But even these limits are not dispositive; and an employer may be found liable for conduct of the errant or irresponsible employee.

Ostensible agency, on the other hand, addresses instances where the employer-employee link is more tenuous, such as when the employer contracts with an independent contractor to perform certain services. Under this theory, the agency employer, such as a home health agency, would be liable for the negligence of its subcontractor authorized to act on the agency's behalf. In *Corrigan v. Methodist Hospital* (1994), the court held that under Pennsylvania law a hospital may be held liable for acts of an independent contractor, usually a doctor, if it can be demonstrated that the doctor was the hospital's agent. To assist in this finding, the court laid out several requirements, including "(1) whether the patient looks to the hospital, not to the contractor for care, and (2) whether the hospital 'holds out' the contractor as its agent" (p. 1213). That home health agencies delivering high-tech health care could easily meet these relatively broad requirements is all too apparent. Agencies, therefore, must take every step possible to ensure that home care patients are aware of who is and is not an agency employee.

Liability of Attending Physicians in Home Health Care

Physician responsibility for injuries to patient is poised to undergo a subtle shift from the aforementioned liability framework where home care is concerned. As a general rule, physicians may be held liable for injury or death resulting from an act of an individual under the physician's supervision. The duty here is to warn or to instruct the subordinate concerning a particular act. While this rule is easily applied in the hospital setting, its application to home health care is arguably not as clear cut. Complicating the matter is a court's willingness, on the one hand, to refrain from holding physicians liable where it determines that there is not duty to warn or instruct a subordinate if the act to be performed is a routine matter, that is, an act based on the subordinate's common knowledge pursuant to professional training. On the other hand, however, where the act to be performed by the subordinate is technical or otherwise beyond that person's apparent ken, then courts have been willing to find the physician liable for failing to warn or instruct an inexperienced or ignorant subordinate, such as a nurse or attendant (American Law Report, 1996).

The physician certainly retains responsibility for the patient's medical care, a responsibility that is implemented through the legally mandated approval of the patient's plan of care and treatment (Conditions of Participation, 1997b). An influential variable in the high-tech home care situation, however, is the fact that care is delivered not by the doctor but by the home health care agency and its employees and agents. The physician's conundrum is evident: care plan approval and monitoring is the physician's responsibility, yet the physician also depends on another party to actually implement that plan. High-tech home care introduces additional factors that are likely to further complicate this scenario.

Wickline v. State (1986) articulates the relevant principle, which is not drawn from home care, per se. Rather, *Wickline* stands for the proposition that physicians may be held liable for patient injuries resulting from negligent delivery of medical care, including home care, even when the physician has no control over the care that is ultimately delivered. Thus, after *Wickline,* the physician seems responsible for medical decision-making, however it unfolds. Although the *Wickline* case arose in connection with balancing cost containment activities with medical decisions, its relevance to high-tech home care is evident against the backdrop of increased cost-containment pressures, which have promoted home care—including high-tech equipment and sophisticated care and treatment plans—as a viable, cost-efficient health care option.

Plaintiff Wickline was diagnosed with Leriche's Syndrome, a vascular occlusion. Her doctor recommend surgery to replace part of an artery with a Teflon graft, which she received under the auspices of California's medical assistance program, Medi-Cal. Having obtained the requisite approval from Medi-Cal, Wickline had the surgery and went on to the allowed 10 days recuperative hospital care. One day before her discharge her surgeon and his assistant concluded that an 8-day extension was warranted given Wickline's difficult postoperation recovery, but the extension was denied. Following Medi-Cal's denial, Wickline's doctor discharged her from the hospital. His rationale for this decision converges on several points: (a) neither he nor his assistant felt her condition was deteriorating, (a) he assumed that Medi-Cal has the right and authority to discharge patients for whose care it had paid, and (a) he assumed Medi-Cal's decision in the matter was final and unlikely to be changed by his appeal to them. These assumptions would prove tragic for Ms. Wickline.

After returning home, Ms. Wickline developed problems with the graft in her leg, which showed signs of clotting and associated problems. She was re-admitted to the emergency room, but by this time her condition had deteriorated severely, with the result that her leg had to be amputated. She sued the party she believed directly responsible for her condition—Medi-Cal—alleging that their decision-making process was negligent, and such negligence caused her early discharge and its aftermath. At trial, Ms. Wickline was awarded $500,000.

The appellate court reversed the trial court verdict, holding that the facts did not support her contention that Medi-Cal was negligent. It reasoned that Medi-Cal's decision against extending care to Mrs. Wickline was one that was based on their usual practices, and her doctor could have appealed it had he believed that she really needed an extension. His acquiescence to Medi-Cal's guidelines, according to the court, was the real cause of Wickline's ultimate condition. The court concluded that Wickline's physician should not have abrogated his duty to ensure that his patient received care he deemed necessary and appropriate. Put simply, he should have spoken up and compelled Ms. Wickline to remain in the hospital, a move he could have made in conjunction with an appeal of Medi-Cal's decision. Medi-Cal had no opportunity to hear and evaluate such an appeal, according to the court, and therefore had no part in the medical decision that put Ms. Wickline on the path to an amputated limb. The court suggested that Wickline's physician precluded a challenge to Medi-Cal's decision and, consequently, foreshadowed the outcome.

The lesson from *Wickline,* then, in relation to home health care is that the physician retains responsibility for implementing treatment.[6] Home health care, presumably including instances where high-tech equipment is involved, is structured to simultaneously require physicians to develop a treatment plan and provide for its implementation via home health care agencies. Home health agencies and their attending physicians, therefore, must make every effort to coordinate care through a thoughtfully crafted treatment plan, and the agency must be prepared to supervise those responsible for implementing it. These expectations are voiced clearly by the Joint Commission on Accreditation of Healthcare Organizations.

Liability for Negligent Acceptance, Transfer or Discharge of Patients

Federal regulations explicitly set forth the expectation that a patient's care can be met adequately by the home health care agency in the patient's home. Implicit in this requirement, however, is the equally relevant expectation that an agency must exercise its independent judgment regarding admission of new patients. Thus, an agency may not simply rely on the attending physician's recommendation to admit a patient for care—both physician and agency have separate and distinct, albeit somewhat overlapping, responsibilities.

The agency must evaluate new referrals to ensure the patient's medical condition can be adequately managed in an appropriate and suitable home environment. This assessment must also include an evaluation that the agency itself can effectively meet the patient's needs (Erb, 1997). Attention must also be given to a coordinated discussion among patient (or surrogate), family, physician, and agency regarding the scope of agency services and any issues requiring informed consent (Brent, 1992; Davitt & Kaye, 1996; Indest, 1997). Certain Joint Commission on Accreditation of Healthcare Organizations standards provide the boundaries for high-technology dependent patients, as patient care in the home must be preceded by a careful determination of the home's readiness to handle high-technology equipment.

The transfer and discharge of patients in home care are bounded by considerations similar to those outlined above. The home health agency is the patient's case manager while the patient remains in the agency's care. Transfer and discharge of patients must be pursuant to written criteria established by the agency. Implicit in these requirements is the notion that patients must be not only informed about their status and any changes thereto but also given notice if it is determined that a change is warranted. The issue here is patient abandonment, a matter that can surface in the home care context if, for example, reimbursement for services is denied or the home setting becomes unsafe or otherwise deemed inappropriate (Johnson, 1991, p. 147; *Katsetos v. Nolan,* 1976; *Lee v. Dewbre,* 1962).

Liability for Injuries Associated with Medical Equipment in the Home

As noted earlier, home health agency employees and agents are assumed to act responsibly and competently, according to employer guidelines and applicable standards of care. If employees incorrectly or inadequately instruct patients in the use of high-tech equipment, or fail to properly install, operate, and maintain such equipment, they may be found personally liable for any resulting injury to the patient. The principal consideration here is whether employees properly discharge their duties in accordance with applicable standards of care. Employers, too, may be found negligent under some circumstances, owing to their failure to properly instruct or supervise their employees or agents who provide home care. Moreover, it should be noted that employee versus employer liability in this context is not mutually exclusive, and both may be found jointly liable, if warranted.

Home health agencies, therefore, must establish sound policies and procedures to guide employees and agents in relation to high-tech equipment. Staff training and monitoring must be emphasized, along with the proper hiring, training, and supervision of staff. A regular review of conditions of employment and service for all employees would be advisable under these circumstances, and this review should extend to all independent contractors with whom the agency has a business relationship. Joint Commission on Accreditation of Healthcare Organizations standards also specify the conditions of staff training and competence for suppliers of high-tech equipment, as well as duties for setting up and maintaining such equipment. Any professional nurse or home health aide who is uncertain about how to operate any medical equipment has a duty to inform someone in a position to supply the additional information. These obligations are underscored by the Safe Medical Devices Act (1990), which requires the health care provider to report information concerning a death, serious illness, or a serious injury related to the use of medical equipment to the Food and Drug Administration within a specified period of time. To back up these provisions, the Act provides for specific sanctions, such as reporting requirements and monetary penalties.

Tort liability (a private or civil wrong or injury, caused by a party's negligence) is yet another basis for remedying claims of injury caused by high-technology devices. Given the nature of the equipment, which may cause death if it malfunctions or is defectively made, the duty to warn associated with strict liability may arise. (Strict liability obtains when a manufacturer puts into the marketplace a product that is known to be dangerous if it is defectively made.)

(The inherently dangerous nature of the product or equipment is an essential component of this type of liability.) In a case involving a patient who was injured by the removal of a heart catheter by a nurse, the court in *Phelps v. Sherwood Medical Industries* (1987) laid out the contours of the strict liability principle. In *Phelps* (1987) the patient brought suit claiming that a defectively manufactured catheter broke while a nurse attempted its removal, which caused a portion of the device to remain inside his heart. The patient lost at the federal district court, appealed, and lost again. The Court of Appeals held that the manufacturer had no duty under Indiana law to warn users of the catheter other than the operating surgeon, nor any duty to warn the operating surgeon of danger of catheter breakage upon removal after suturing and routing to heart cavity. The court ruled that the manufacturer's duty to warn stopped with the operating surgeon—a so-called "learned intermediary" (the learned intermediary doctrine relieves drug and medical device manufacturers of the obligation to warn a patient when the manufacturer has provided an adequate warning to the patient's doctor)—and did not extend to either the nurse or to the patient. "The duty to warn of hazards," according to the court, "is part and parcel of the physician-patient relationship" (p. 303). The court argued that the learned intermediary concept, albeit borrowed from the prescription drugs context, had equal application to medical devices. Consequently, the court put the responsibility to warn squarely on the operating surgeon, who knew the risks associated with the catheter in question. The application of this concept to high-tech home health care may be problematic. The issues are likely to turn on a determination of whether the role of learned intermediary is fulfilled by the attending physician (comparable to the situation in *Phelps*) or by any of the many persons typically involved in caring for the patient in the home, such as the nurse, aide, or caregiver.

INFORMED CONSENT AND REFUSAL
OF TREATMENT IN HOME CARE

Informed Consent

It is well established that a patient has a right to refuse treatment, even if the decision is likely to lead to the patient's demise. The doctrine is applied equally in both the home and nonhome setting (*In the Matter of Farrell,* 1987) and thus has implications for high-tech home care (Indest, 1997). This ethic of self-determination has been codified in the Patient Self Determination Act of 1990 and reinforced in the United States Supreme Court's ruling in *Cruzan v. Director, Missouri Dept. Of Health* (1990), wherein it was determined that a competent person has a constitutionally protected liberty interest in refusing unwanted medical treatment. The subtext for this phenomenon is the concept of informed consent, which is inherent in a patient's claim to refuse treatment. Put simply, informed consent is the threshold issue, one that must be reached prior to refusal of treatment. Treatment may not be given absent of informed consent, and an attempt to perform treatment without the requisite consent can constitute a battery. For example, in *Corrigan v. Methodist Hospital* (1994), the court ruled that the "tort of failure of informed consent sounds in battery, not in negligence" (p. 1208). Interestingly, in this particular case, the court also found that material facts existed to show that the "hospital failed to oversee its doctors and failing to 'formulate, adopt and enforce adequate policies,' which may include policies governing obtaining informed consent" (p. 1212).

The doctrine of informed consent is based on the relatively straightforward notion, derived from the common law, that each of us has the right to our personal bodily integrity and to be free from assault (*Schloendorff v. Society of New York Hospital,* 1914). Informing the patient of the benefits and consequences of treatment, along with supporting reasons, is a threshold requirement for concluding that the patient actually participated in the decisional process. The aim is to be able to conclude that the patient had sufficient decision-making capacity, acted voluntarily, and received adequate information in a timely manner. As important as these elements seem, however, they may be difficult to discern in the home care setting where the patient's condition sometimes warrants an implied consent to treatment or where the patient's ability to think clearly is impaired. Blumenthal and Haynes (1995), for example, argue that the nurse, and presumably any caregiver, must be aware on a daily basis of the patient's condition and any changes thereto for the purpose of monitoring the extent to which the patient remains capable of giving consent to treatment.

Legal rules on the topic abound including federal regulations that explicitly impose on home health agencies the obligation to inform patients of their rights, and to act to protect and promote the exercise of these rights.[7] States have also enacted consent statutes, and the Joint Commission on the Accreditation of Healthcare Organizations has issued relevant accreditation standards. Finally, there is the aforementioned *Cruzan* (1990) decision, issued by the United States Supreme Court. Given this extensive legal framework, one might be properly puzzled by the array of cases on the topic. This outcome is not ironic, however, when one further appreciates the apparent exceptions to what seems like settled rules. *Estate of Leach v. Shapiro* (1984), for example, found that an incompetent patient's wishes may be expressed and achieved by an authorized person on the patient's behalf, or that, in some circumstances, a patient's consent to medical treatment will be implied. The task for a court, then, is to reconcile the discrepancies, to balance the individual's liberty interests on the one hand, and the state's interest in preserving and protecting life on the other. This potential clash of interests is most evident in cases dealing with refusal of treatment.

Refusal of Treatment[8]

As a corollary to the informed consent doctrine, the right to refusal extends the long-recognized right of a person to control one's own body. From this proposition, it is not a great leap to the assertion that a competent person may decide to refuse treatment, even if the decision is likely to hasten or result in death. As the court in *In The Matter of Farrell* (1987) stated, "a competent adult person generally has the right to decline to have any medical treatment initiated" (p. 410).

In November 1982, Kathleen Farrell began to experience symptoms of a degenerative disease known as amyotrophic lateral sclerosis (ALS, commonly known as Lou Gehrig's disease), a condition that left her incapable of movement but in possession of her mental faculties. The typical life expectancy for those suffering from the condition, as of 1982, was 3 years. She was admitted to a hospital, where she was eventually connected to a respirator, but subsequently released and allowed to go home as the hospital could provide no further relief for her condition. Thereafter she became paralyzed, requiring 24-hour nursing care. In November 1985, Mrs. Farrell informed her husband that she wanted to be disconnected from the respirator. She also informed her doctor, who arranged for a psychological review that concluded she was not in need of psychiatric treatment. In short, the psychologist concluded that Mrs. Farrell met the criteria for informed refusal of treatment: her decision was competent, voluntary, and based on reliable and timely information.

On June 13, 1986, Mr. Farrell sought appointment as Special Medical Guardian for his wife, with authority to disconnect her respirator. The trial court granted his petition on June 23, 1986, but stayed the order pending appellate review. Mrs. Farrell died, in her home, 6 days later, but the New Jersey Supreme Court agreed to hear the case and render a decision because of the case's importance and relevance to others in similar circumstances.

The court achieved two important goals in reaching its decision: First, it laid out a four-part test of the state's interest in this type of situation. Second, it set forth procedures applicable when a competent patient living at home requests the termination of life-sustaining medical treatment. Both aspects have implications for high-tech home care.

The four-part test recommended by the court is premised on the court's conviction that the right to refuse treatment, while fundamental, is not absolute. "The state has at least four potentially countervailing interests in sustaining a person's life: preserving life, preventing suicide, safeguarding the integrity of the medical profession, and protecting innocent third parties. When a party declines life-sustaining medical treatment, we balance the patient's common-law and constitutional rights against these four state interests" (*In the Matter of Farrell,* 1987, p. 411). In the *Farrell* case, the court concluded that none of these interests outweighed Mrs. Farrell's right to self-determination and privacy.

Because they had agreed to hear the case to give some guidance to families in circumstances similar to the Farrells, the court laid out the relevant procedures for these sorts of life and death decisions.

First, it must be determined that the patient is competent and properly informed about his or her prognosis, the alternatives available, and the risk involved in the withdrawal of the life sustaining treatment. [Second] it must be determined that the patient made his or her choice voluntarily and without coercion. After these assessments have been made, the patient's right to choose to disconnect life-sustaining apparatus must be balanced against the [aforementioned countervailing interests]. Generally, a competent informed patient's 'interest in freedom from nonconsensual invasion of her bodily integrity' would outweigh any state interest (*In the Matter of Farrell,* 1987, p. 413).

Interestingly, the *Farrell* court shied away from arrogating to itself or any court the primary responsibility for such decisions. It believed a court could play a role in instances where any of the parties were in conflict, but as a general rule, it wanted the courts to avoid entanglement with such matters. "In most cases," the court argued, "patients are presumed to be capable of making decisions about their own care" (p. 415). To allay fears of civil or criminal liability—fears that would normally force parties to turn to the courts—the court offered important protection: "In light of this, we specifically hold that no civil or criminal liability will be incurred by any person who, in good faith reliance on the procedures established in this opinion, withdraws life-sustaining treatment at the request of an informed and competent patient who has undergone the required independent medical examination described above" (pp. 415–416).

Despite the meaning and scope of *Farrell,* there have been instances where physicians or health care professionals have refused to honor a patient's refusal to consent to treatment. A leading case on the topic, *Estate of Leach v. Shapiro* (1984) articulated the relevant principle. Finding that a patient may recover for battery if the patient's refusal of treatment is ignored, the court in *Leach* held that a cause of action exists for ignoring the express requests of a patient or the family to terminate life-sustaining medical treatment. The court qualified its holding to some degree, arguing that "a patient has the right to refuse treatment, and this refusal may not be overcome by the doctrine of implied consent [unless the refusal fails to] satisfy the same standards of knowledge and understanding required for informed consent" (p. 1053). Notwithstanding, the decision nonetheless offers the prospect for recovery of damages in the event a health care professional disregards a patient's explicit intentions.

AN EMERGING MODEL
FOR HIGH-TECHNOLOGY HOME CARE:
TELEMEDICINE AND TELEHEALTH

Telemedicine/telehealth are an obvious marriage of high technology and home health care. Telemedicine, which Reid (1996) defines as the "use of advanced telecommunications technologies to exchange health information and provide health care services across geographic, time and social/cultural borders," is not new (McMenamin, 1997; Warner & Beller, 1997). Primarily focused on linking rural communities to physicians, it encompasses certain specialty areas along with its most common form, teleradiology (Warner & Beller, 1997). Telehealth might be characterized as a species of telemedicine, with special attention to not only patient access to health care but patient self-care management and education in the home. It is a "system of interactive telecommunications activities occurring directly between health care providers and their patients [that] supports the health care process by providing a means for more effective and more efficient information exchange" (Warner & Beller, 1997, p. 885).

While the relationship between the telecommunications technology and home care is in its embryonic stage, there is no doubt that telemedicine/ telehealth[9] will transform future health care (Sanders, 1996; Weissert & Silberman, 1996). Equally obvious, however, are the attendant legal dimensions of this technological evolution, which will raise issues that are distinct from, but not unrelated to, those for conventional home health care (Cepelewicz, 1997). Significant developments have occurred on the statutory and regulatory front, but these primarily focus on the legal context for infrastructure and reimbursement.[10] Case law on the topic is nonexistent.[11] Consequently, areas such as licensure, medical malpractice, and privacy and confidentiality are most relevant to high-tech home care, and each will be addressed briefly below (Rice, 1997).

Licensure

Licensure to practice medicine is a state-regulated activity, the authority for which is grounded in the state's so-called police power. The premise is straightforward: The state may regulate conduct that affects public health, safety, and welfare or otherwise advances important public policy (Young & Waters, 1995). Physicians typically obtain a license for each state in which they want to practice; conversely, absent a license, a physician may not practice within a state's borders.

The resulting "state-based licensure system in the United States discourages inter-state practice of telemedicine [and] runs counter to telemedicine's unique capability to transcend geographical barriers" (Sanders, 1996, p. 7). Reciprocity (where one state recognizes a professional license granted by another state) and "endorsement" (the acceptance by one state of a professional license granted by another state with similar licensure standards) are the logical remedies here, but the former is fading as a practice and endorsement varies among the states (Cepelewicz, 1997; Sanders, 1996). Under these circumstances, then, telemedicine and telehealth raise the specter of national licensure, that is, the requirement that every physician be licensed to practice medicine in every state—an unwieldy and possibly unwelcome prospect, at best. Ultimately, an individual who violates any of these licensure provisions runs the risk of being sanctioned or penalized, including the revocation or suspension of the license to practice medicine within a particular state. Suffice it to say that state medical practice licensure laws and regulations can effectively undermine telemedicine/telehealth's potential as a home health care strategy[12] (Center for Telemedicine Law, 1997b).

Medical Malpractice

Malpractice in the telemedicine/telehealth context may arise because of errors due to the lack of personal, physical contact with the patient. Telemedicine/telehealth presumes indirect (i.e., via telecommunications) patient contact and associated care—diagnosis, monitoring, treatment. The data obtained thereby, owing to technological defect or failure, may be corrupted or otherwise unreliable, with the result that the patient's care may fall below acceptable standards and thus give rise to possible liability. Sanders (1996) puts the matter succinctly, citing two categories of questions that are likely to shed light on the conditions under which malpractice will obtain in telemedicine/telehealth.

> The first set of questions relates to the safety and efficacy of the technology itself. Does telemedicine fail to serve patients according to prevailing professional norms and practices? If it does, what is the source of failure, and is the provider liable for it? Does telemedicine engender more error in clinical observation and reporting of signs and symptoms than is customary in the on-site practice of medicine? Is the patient's safety compromised, or the patient's right to privacy and dignity violated? Does data compression reduce significantly the quality of information transmitted? [And whose fault is it, if that occurs?] The second set of questions pertains to the litigation process, specifically. Does telemedicine expose providers to more litigation because of the impersonal nature of the service? Is the consultant [physician] at greater risk for litigation because he/she may be unable to establish rapport with the remote client? Who is better served by the availability of recorded information of clinical encounters, the client or the provider? Are the rules governing malfeasance and nonfeasance and the attendant liability for damages changed by virtue of having two providers attending to the same client? (pp. 12–13)

Clearly, the route out of potential liability lies with resolving these questions, some of which revolve around the sorts of issues discussed in the earlier section on standard of care. Others are unique to telemedicine/ telehealth but will nonetheless yield to careful guidelines regarding how health care professionals should conduct themselves when dealing with patients in a remote location.

Other bases for potential liability lie in telemedicine/telehealth's unique features. As one traces the link between health care provider and patient, the grounds for liability emerge. Patients may sue, for example, for assignment to inappropriate technology, improper software and hardware, or errors arising out of data transmission (Cepelewicz, 1997; McMenamin, 1997). The most apparent remedy here is at once obvious and difficult to achieve: appropriate systems design.[13] Vigilance in this regard will be rewarded, however, as all aspects of manufacturing must be made to serve patient needs.

Privacy and Confidentiality

Protecting patient privacy and confidentiality is a perennial concern in health care, generally, (Regan, 1995) and will be all the more important where telemedicine/telehealth are introduced. The presence of other actors, such as home health care agencies and third-party payers will further complicate matters. Encryption devices and other high-tech strategies can offer a significant measure of protection, and low tech solutions, such as passwords, appropriately-drawn release forms, and careful documentation, will also help maintain a patient's sphere of privacy (Rice, 1997; Warner & Beller, 1997). The real protection, however, will emerge from longstanding legal sources as well as long-established norms regarding the nature and confidentiality of the physician-patient relationship.

Essentially, the Federal Privacy Act of 1974 is the principal legislative framework for protecting patients from disclosure of confidential information. While the law is limited to federally operated health providers or nongovernmental providers and researchers who maintain or have access to federal government contracts, it does afford a comfortable measure of protection (U.S. Congress Office of Technology Assessment, 1993). Case law on the topic is available and will provide guidance as well (*Whalen v. Roe,* 1977). Finally, there is the array of state legislative rules, from legislation to protect privacy in the care of certain patients (e.g., HIV/AIDS), to requirements in professional practice acts (e.g., nurses, physicians), to state regulations for relevant agencies (e.g., licensure of home health agency), to accreditation standards and professional codes of ethics. Collectively, these sources comprise the basis for protecting patient privacy.

Telemedicine/telehealth's nascent development is an obstacle now, but only because we are uncertain how the convergence of technology and privacy considerations will actually shape rules and policy. Notwithstanding, the time devoted to attempting to lay out prospective rules will pay off in terms of forestalling potential abuses and providing concrete guidelines for an emerging area. Indeed, The American Nursing Association (1997), concerned that "existing laws, regulations, policies and protocols do not provide sufficient protection of health-related information," (p. 3) offers its recommendations to accompany the introduction of high technology in patient care:

> Previously established confidentiality and privacy protections for health information must be maintained as well as scrutinized to establish if they are sufficient for this new technology; patients who are the recipients of telehealth interventions should be informed of the potential risks (e.g., limitations to securing transmissions over the airwaves or by direct line) and benefits; patient access to information generated through telehealth is guaranteed; dissemination of patient data or identifiable patient images (e.g., voice) will be controlled by the explicit consent of the patient; patients are informed if other individuals outside the health team (e.g., technical staff, observers) are involved; and individuals who violate established privacy, confidentiality and security regulations and misuse information will be subject to enforceable penalties. (p. 4)

NOTES

1. For example, the Agency for Health Care Policy and Research (AHCPR), which was established in December 1989 under Public Law 101-239. AHCPR, a part of the U.S. Department of Health and Human Services, is the lead agency charged with supporting research designed to improve the quality of health care, reduce its cost, and broaden access to essential services. Its Office of the Forum for Quality and Effectiveness in Health Care has primary responsibility for facilitating the development and evaluation of clinical practice guidelines, which may themselves be framed to constitute a standard of care. The guidelines are designed to assist practitioners in the prevention, diagnosis, treatment, and management of clinical conditions and to provide consumers with information to increase their understanding and involvement in health care decisions. For a discussion of the legal implications of AHCPR Clinical Practice see Kurlander (1996). Other aspects of this framework include the Federal Conditions of Participation: Home

Health Agencies (1997a); the Standards for Accreditation of Home Care, Joint Commission on Accreditation of Healthcare Organizations (1997a); state professional licensure laws, including Nursing Practice Acts; the American Nursing Association Standards of Home Health Nursing Practice; the federal Omnibus Budget Reconciliation Act of 1987, and its amendments; and the various state statutes dealing with licensure of home health agencies.

2. The table incorporates principles from *Magrinat v. Trinity Hospital* (1987), *Wickline v. State* (1986), *Donaldson v. YMCA* (1995), *Estate of Leach v. Shapiro* (1984), *In the Matter of Farrell* (1987), *In the Matter of Conroy* (1985), and *Corrigan v. Methodist Hospital* (1994).

3. One of the government's three cases, for example, unfolded as follows: A nursing home patient was constantly restrained in her wheelchair, a situation that, according to the wound care expert retained by the government, may have caused the patients wounds and, more important, prevented them from healing. "Beginning in 1993, she developed multiple pressure ulcers. By late 1993, she had numerous Stage II and III ulcers, as well as multiple hospital admissions for dehydration and urinary tract infections. By January 1994, she was confined to bed with 16 pressure ulcers, including two Stage IV ulcers. Her serum albumin was 2.2 grams/dL at the time of percutaneous endoscopic gastrostomy (PEG) tube placement in February 1994. Tube feedings providing 1,500 kcal (29 kcal/kg) and 63 grams of protein (1.2 g/kg) per day were inadequate—she needed 2,060 kcal (40 kcal/kg) and 103 grams of protein (2 g/kg) daily. She died several months later. The LTC [long term care] facility's notes indicated excellent intakes, which clearly did not match with her clinical deterioration. Poor nursing care—the constant restraint in a wheelchair and poor, inconsistent documentation—and inadequate nutrition were both present in this case" (Hoffman, 1997, p. 27).

4. Kapp (1992) also suggests a possible contract-theory base for liability: "A home care agency may be held to have made express or implied promises to patients in the form of claims made about the quality or price of services contained in the agency's advertising or marketing materials. Promises placed in promotional brochures, for instance, may be introduced in evidence to establish that an agency undertook a specific duty. A home care agency may also be held liable for failure to fulfill promises made directly to clients (or their surrogates), either orally or in the form of written admission and service contracts. The guiding principle must be avoidance of any promise whose carrying out the agency cannot control or for whose violation the agency is not willing to be held answerable" (pp. 190–191).

5. This section will not address liability of health maintenance organizations (HMOs). To be sure, HMOs have created issues of liability in medical malpractice, and some of these may have implications for home health care.

The courts have typically analyzed HMO liability within the context of principles of agency or theories of respondeat superior or ostensible agency, or on the basis of corporate liability, breach of contract or warranty, and various tort theories. For a discussion of the topic, see, Frankel (1994), which fully discusses *Wickline* (1986) and related cases and American Law Report (1997b).

6. *Wickline* (1986) is also important in relation to liability for injuries due to utilization reviews. Health maintenance organizations (HMOs) utilization decisions may conflict with a physician's best medical judgment, and this could open the door for holding the physician liable for damages resulting from the HMO's decision to hold down costs. This clash of medical judgment and cost containment is present not only in *Wickline* but in two other cases described by Frankel (1994): *Wilson v. Blue Cross of California* (1990) and *Corcoran v. United HealthCare, Inc.* (1992, 1993). In this cost-containment situation, the physician is caught between giving care according to some cost-containment formula on the one hand and malpractice rules that may command that the physician ignore cost of services on the other. Indeed, under these circumstances, *Wickline* suggests the physician may even be held to a tougher standard of care. The implications for home health care, including high-tech care, are obvious, given the emergence of managed Medicare and its potential impact on payment for home care services.

7. The 1997 Conditions of Participation of Home Health Agencies (HHA) state: (a) Standard: Notice of rights. (1) The HHA must provide the patient with a written notice of the patient's rights in advance of furnishing care to the patient or during the initial evaluation visit before initiation of treatment. (2) The HHA must maintain documentation showing that it has complied with the requirements of this section. (b) Standard: Exercise of rights and respect for property and person. (1) The patient has the right to exercise his or her rights as a patient of the HHA. [c] Standard: Right to be informed and to participate in planning care and treatment. (1) The patient has the right to be informed, in advance, about the care to be furnished, and of any changes in the care to be furnished. (d) Standard: Confidentiality of records. The patient has the right to confidentiality of the clinical records maintained by the HHA. The HHA must advise the patient of the agency's policies and procedures regarding disclosure of clinical records.

8. This section will discuss the legal framework for instances in which patients refuse to consent to treatment. It's juxtaposition to the above section on informed consent is intentional. Attention will be focused on relevant principles and cases dealing with the right to refuse treatment phenomenon. I note two related topics that will not be addressed in this section. One concerns the matter of do not resuscitate (DNR) orders. A DNR order is an order placed on a patient's chart that directs health care providers to refrain

from administering certain emergency treatments in the event the patient suffers a specific emergency medical event while under the provider's care. For a discussion of the matter, see, American Law Report (1997c). The other topic deals with advance medical directives (AMD), which are written documents—usually living wills or durable power of attorney—completed in advance by an individual with express instructions for the conditions under which that person will or will not accept life-sustaining medical treatment, or the circumstances and the person to be designated to act as a surrogate decision maker on the individual's behalf. One might argue that the general principles associated with refusal of treatment constitute the framework for decision making with respect to these instruments (Davitt & Kaye, 1996; Weinberg & Brod, 1995).

9. I appreciate that telemedicine is built around connecting patients and images, usually at some remote location, to a physician's office or to a physician in a hospital; and that telehealth emphasizes home-based care to patients who are electronically linked to a home health care provider (usually a nurse). To be sure, these dynamics account for the fact that telemedicine and telehealth are defined differently, but their common focus on using electronic telecommunications to improve patient health care enables me, for the purposes of this article, to use the terms almost interchangeably. Thus, I will use the somewhat awkward construction telemedicine/telehealth.

10. The Center for Telemedicine Law, Regulatory Update (1997a), for example, describes major shifts in state law. The report indicates that over 200 bills were introduced in state legislatures regarding telemedicine, with 33 states enacting measures to influence financing, practice, or reimbursement for this technology. Most of the new state law (Arizona, Arkansas, Indiana, Minnesota, New Mexico, North Dakota, Texas, Virginia, Washington), according to the report, is designated to support telemedicine infrastructure, feasibility studies, and project development. The report goes on to cite four states (Alabama, Arkansas, Georgia, and Mississippi) that have enacted legislation addressing physician licensure and the practice of medicine via telemedicine. The thrust of the law in these states is to require a remote physician to obtain a special license or to obtain a full state medical license. Moreover, three states (Arizona, Oklahoma, Texas) passed statutes that mandated that patients be given the opportunity to give written consent to engage in telemedicine prior to engaging in such activities and that require confidentiality of all patient medical records generated via telemedicine and giving patients access to the resulting records. Finally, the report says four states (California, Minnesota, Oklahoma, Texas) now require reimbursement for some telemedicine activities. In addition, California's Telemedicine Development Act of 1996 relies on a registration program for out-of-state physicians seeking to practice telemedicine in California. The effect of this

law is to make telemedicine services reimbursable and equivalent for billing purposes to face-to-face consultations within California. Finally, at the federal level, there are the sections of the 1997 Budget Act (P.L. 105-33), which allow providers of telehealth services to counties designated as Health Professional Shortage Areas to be eligible for Part B Medicare payments beginning no later than January 1, 1999.

11. One California case, *Prince v. Urban* (1996), addresses the issue of personal jurisdiction within the context of the interstate practice of telemedicine. The basic question in the case is: How does a California court assume jurisdiction over the out-of-state physician who causes injury to a California resident? After some discussion of the requirements for assuming personal jurisdiction over the defendant Illinois physician, the California Court of Appeals affirmed the trial court's rejection of personal jurisdiction. In reaching this conclusion, the court stated, "[W]e must conclude that the present case is one where the assertion of personal jurisdiction is ultimately unreasonable and unfair. In sum, an out-of-state physician's follow-up care of a patient by telephone—even when the home state patient pays for it—is not a sufficient basis for personal jurisdiction" (p. 187). This case is important because it deals with the threshold issue of how to get jurisdiction over the out-of-state physician, a matter that must be reached prior to any consideration of negligence.

12. The discussion in this section has focused on physicians, but they are not the only actors whose licensure status matters in the telemedicine/ telehealth context. Nurses, too, are bound by state licensure requirements, and the American Nurses Association (ANA) is committed to telemedicine/ telehealth as a strategy to improve access to quality, affordable health care service. The American Nursing Association (1997) addresses the matter in its Policy Series Report. The report makes an important distinction between telemedicine and telehealth, not to define one as superior to the other; rather, to underscore the differences in the role of physician versus nurse and the scope of the services to be provided overall. "Because the use of telecommunications technologies in providing health care services is broader than the discipline or practice of medicine, ANA generally refers to 'telemedicine' as 'telehealth'—a much more inclusive and accurate term, and preferable to one predicated on solely a medical model" (p. 1). The report also makes an important point regarding the role of telemedicine/telehealth, one that also has implications for licensure. They state, " ANA strongly believes that the strength and promise of telehealth lie in providing increased access to health care services by augmenting existing services, not replacing them" (p. 2). Finally, it notes that there is confusion about the laws that apply to nurses providing telehealth across state boundaries, an issue that raises an important question: "Do the laws of one state requiring practice under a protocol or agreement with a physician

pertain if a nurse is providing consultation to a practitioner and patient in a state where no such requirements exist" (p. 2)?

13. Sanders (1996) suggests consensus exists regarding the use of so-called "open architecture" for telemedicine systems, which would enable the system to be comprised of modular parts that are upgradable. Modular elements would enable some degree of portability, adaptation, and component, as opposed to system, replacements, as needed. He also points out the importance of national and international standards to ensure system compatibility. The same concerns would hold for software development, and standards for important protocols would need to emerge to promote systems compatibility. There is also the obvious point that the system should be designed to be extremely user-friendly and have features that can allow the patient to contact a person in the event of an emergency.

CHAPTER 9

Ethical Issues in High-Tech Home Health Care

INTRODUCTION

Aside from the strenuous physical nature of many home care activities and the stressful conditions under which staff find themselves, home health care is a field rife with conflict and competing interests. The home care manager continually struggles with a variety of ethical dilemmas experienced by staff on a routine, if not daily, basis. These issues cover a wide range of concerns and are not limited to life-sustaining treatment decisions or high-tech care (Kaye & Davitt, 1995a). Rather, in the home health care arena, ethical dilemmas are more likely to arise around routine issues such as activities of daily living. In fact, the commonplace nature of home care can result in a tendency to overlook these mundane activities and the ethical issues intertwined within them.

This chapter is devoted to a review of the multitude of ethical dilemmas that staff may encounter. We begin with a review of several major ethical principles most applicable to this setting. These principles will surface throughout the chapter as we review specific ethical issues that can be expected to arise when delivering in-home services. Strategies to deal with such dilemmas will be discussed along with an analysis of how high-tech services may complicate certain ethical situations.

ETHICAL PRINCIPLES

Ethics is a branch of philosophy concerned with questions regarding morality and moral judgments. It is the study of the nature of morality and how particular values are established and justified in a society. It is a philosophy about what is right, good, or obligatory and how we come to know or establish this (Frankena, 1973). Morality is viewed as a social process or product; the practices defining right and wrong that are transmitted within a culture from generation to generation. Ethical analysis represents an attempt to make decisions, to resolve problems, or to discharge obligations in a formal, reasoned manner within this moral framework established by society.

The study of ethics offers a systematic approach to the ways in which we come to judge our world and the application of those judgments in specific situations. In this way, ethics can also be viewed in a more practical sense, that is, as applied within particular settings and professions. Ethics are rules of conduct for particular groups and in relation to a particular class of human interaction; they govern professional conduct toward patients and clients, other members of a profession, and society (Barton & Barton, 1984). Various professional codes of ethics are examples of such practical applications. In home health care several codes of ethics may be utilized simultaneously, including those of physicians, nurses, social workers, and therapists. Throughout this chapter we will be referring to both levels of ethical deliberation, the theoretical and practical.

Autonomy

The current liberal model of medical practice in this country places emphasis on patients as autonomous individuals who have ultimate control over their bodies. The competent patient is the responsible agent to whom all medical decisions are deferred. Liberalism emphasizes autonomy and neutrality—the state should tolerate differing views of the good life and should not impose a particular definition of what is worthy and good. According to Emanuel (1991) liberalism entails pluralism of conceptions of the meaning, purpose, and value of life. The idea of autonomy is vested in the liberal assumption, which places emphasis on respect of the individual. In other words, individuals should be free to choose their own version of the good life. As the term autonomy implies (from the Greek, autos which means self and nomos which means rule), the individual has a right to be self-determining (self-ruling). Individuals should be allowed to make decisions on their own behalf, which are voluntary. Implied then is the "the notion of self-determination, of freedom and liberty of choice concerning the various aspects of one's life" (Kapp, 1988, p. 2), including medical care.

Autonomy is a multifaceted concept. For example, the nature of informed consent to treatment assumes that the patient is an autonomous individual, capable of receiving information about the illness, processing this information in a reasoned manner, and making a decision about the course of medical treatment. It includes both a decisional element and an action element, and it assumes a specific functional level of the individual and a degree of independence within the decision-making process. Individuals should be free to choose among options but should also have the freedom to act on those options. Collopy (1988) has suggested a set of polarities, which could be used to map the concept of autonomy. They include decisional versus executional, authentic versus inauthentic, direct versus delegated, negative versus positive, and competent versus incapacitated autonomy.

Decisional versus Executional Autonomy

Decisional autonomy (autonomous choice) is the ability and freedom to make decisions on one's own behalf. Executional autonomy (autonomous action) refers to the ability and freedom to act out one's decisions. Therefore, autonomy may be constrained if choices are not meaningful or if individuals are restricted from enacting their wishes. According to Collopy, Dubler, and Zuckerman (1990), dependency on others can lead to an erosion of autonomy, especially in healthcare. Agency staff may begin to assume that patients who lack executional autonomy will likewise be unable to make their own decisions. "Because elderly clients cannot carry out certain choices or activities without assistance, caregivers may disregard their capacity to make choices or [to] have preferences about these activities" (Collopy, Dubler, & Zuckerman, 1990, p. 8).

Even though patients may be unable to independently enact their wishes, they do not forfeit their right to be self-determining. The agency's responsibility is to encourage and support decisional autonomy even in cases where the patients may need assistance in acting out their specific preferences. Agency staff have a positive obligation to support a patient's executional autonomy, for example, by developing a care plan that allows them to execute their individual wishes. For instance, Mrs. B, a home health care patient who receives daily tube feedings, has an opportunity to visit with her grandchildren on weekdays after school. She decides that having tube feedings in the afternoon interferes with these visits and she requests a change in schedule. This represents decisional autonomy. However, she cannot execute this decision without the support and cooperation of the agency. The staff's role in supporting her autonomy would be to develop a care plan that would allow her to execute that decision.

Authentic versus Inauthentic Autonomy

Autonomy can also be categorized as authentic or inauthentic. Individuals may make decisions in their lives that at first glance appear to reflect the function of an autonomous agent. However, a closer look may reveal that a particular decision runs counter to the patient's history and value structure. According to Collopy, "autonomy is authentic when it reflects the identity, decisional history, and moral norms of an individual" (1990, p. 10). Decisions that appear out of character for an individual, that is, "discontinuous with the individual's personal history and values" are inauthentic (Collopy, p. 10).

Authenticity is difficult to determine, especially if the patient is new to the home care agency. Collateral contacts may be necessary to determine the authenticity of a particular patient decision. This may be important for certain kinds of decisions that place the patient at imminent risk of harm or exploitation. For example, a patient may refuse a particular medical treatment that could potentially alleviate or reduce the medical condition. If this decision is based on a particular moral or value structure held by the patient for some time, then it may be indicative of an authentic decision and should be respected. However, if the decision not to comply with medical advice appears counter to the patient's values and or previous lifestyle, then some other factor may be constraining the patient's ability to act autonomously. Such factors could include depression, fear, ignorance, lack of confidence or emotional strength, concern for caregiver burden, possible cognitive decline (all internal constraints), or coercion or undue influence (external constraints) (Appelbaum, Lidz, & Meisel, 1987). Patients can also change their minds legitimately, and at times it may be difficult to distinguish such legitimate changes from altered patterns attributable to internal or external constraints. It is imperative that agency staff be aware of the potential for decisions to be inauthentic and to develop support systems to enable patients to make decisions based on their own values and preferences and to ensure that patients are not being pressured to change these patterns.

Direct versus Delegated Autonomy

Collopy also distinguishes between direct and delegated autonomy. Direct autonomy is simply direct control over decisions and actions, while delegated autonomy implies a granting of decision-making authority to another. Decision-making authority may be delegated on either an informal or formal basis. In the latter case, patients may choose to authorize, in writing, another individual who can make decisions on behalf of the patient, such as through a health care proxy or power of attorney. Patients may also choose to defer decision making to trusted family members on an informal basis, simply by asking the provider to "talk to my daughter, she handles all the medical decisions." Delegation may be comprehensive—the family member makes all decisions, or partial—only certain types of decisions are delegated.

Delegation of decision-making authority does not imply a complete loss of autonomy. First, for such delegation to be valid, it must be (or must have been) granted authentically. The main difficulty for providers is in determining when such delegation is authentic; it reflects the traditional value-base and preferences of the patient. Ensuring that such delegation is not occurring due to coercion or various internal constraints is a necessary but involved process. Second, as long as the patient is competent and capable of making decisions, such authority can be revoked at any time by the patient. This can be accomplished through formal written statements or verbally. Finally, patients continue to exercise individual autonomy in the choice to defer decisions to trusted family and friends.

The respect for the uniqueness and dignity of the individual refers to dignity as defined by the individual (not the macrosystem). Therefore, one person may obtain great dignity through mutual support and communal decision making while another may stress individual autonomy. Likewise, self-determination does not necessarily imply that a person must decide independently and isolated from others. Rather, self-determination can include the right to defer to others for support in decision making. Gostin (1995) notes that the boundaries of informed consent are shaped by the patient's right to self-determination, therefore patients have the ultimate authority over whether they wish to receive information or "whether disclosure should be made to the family." Some research has suggested that older people may have stronger preferences for family involvement in decision making than younger groups (Davitt, 1996). In addition, family participation may be more prevalent in certain ethnic or cultural belief systems (Michel, 1994) than in the current autonomy-based model of medical practice. "Many cultures place more emphasis on a communitarian approach to decision making with the family taking an active role in the process" (Davitt, 1996, p. 7). Agency staff will need to evaluate the process through which various patients make medical decisions to promote patient autonomy, including the right to defer decisions to others.

In the family-centered model of decision making, emphasis is placed on the individual within a family unit. The individual is not completely autonomous but a member of a community (family), and the rights of the family must be balanced against the rights of any individual member. The family becomes the unit of authority, and decision making is collective, balancing the shared interests of individual members. Individual members are never truly autonomous because they are imbedded in the family structure. This would replace the traditional view of informed consent that rests the decision-making authority exclusively in the patient. The family-centered model for medical decision making would place greater emphasis on participation of family members in the decision-making process.

Much research on shared decision making and collective autonomy has been conducted around long-term care and the delivery of services in the older person's home. "Decision making in home care should be an interactive process, involving negotiation, compromise and the recognition of reciprocal ties" (Collopy, Dubler, & Zuckerman, 1990). Long-term care needs can have a more direct impact on the needs and resources of the entire family unit because family members generally act as caregivers. Moody (1988) has suggested negotiated consent as a possible alternative in long-term care when the ideal cannot be achieved. According to Moody it is especially appropriate in situations where there may be "competing interests: there are multiple, legitimate views to consider (i.e., family, patient, agency). Kapp (1991a) suggests the importance of learning more about how "mentally competent older persons work together with their families . . . at shared healthcare decision making" (p. 619).

Another problem with delegation is to insure that the agent makes decisions based on what the patient would want, not necessarily based on what the agent thinks is best (unless this is what the patient wants). Other researchers are concerned with the potential for conflict of interest when family members become primary decision makers in relation to life-sustaining treatment decisions (Blustein, 1993). Problems with dysfunctional family systems and dysfunctional family members as decision makers have been noted in numerous studies of long-term care. Likewise the potential for misunderstandings between proxies and patients regarding what a particular patient would want in a given situation has been widely documented (Diamond, Jernigan, Mosely, Messina, & McKeown, 1989; Emanuel, 1991; Wetle, Levkoff, Cwikel, & Rosen, 1988). An important question, which must be considered by providers, is how would conflicting interests of family members and patients be balanced. Also providers must be concerned with supporting the preferences of patients who did not wish to have family involved in decision making.

Competent versus Incapacitated Autonomy

According to Collopy, professionals must also distinguish between competent autonomy and incapacitated autonomy. Competent autonomy is "informed, rationally defensible and judgmentally effective," while incapacitated autonomy "is substantially uninformed, unreasonable, or judgmentally unsound" (Collopy, 1988, p. 13). The determination of competency is pivotal in the process of justifying when others may intervene in the decisions of a patient. But this is a complicated endeavor. The President's Commission for the Study of Ethical Problems in Medicine and Biomedical and Behavioral Research (1982) has outlined the key elements of decisional capacity. "Decisional capacity requires, to a greater or lesser degree, (1) possession of a set of values and goals, (2) the ability to communicate and to understand information, and (3) the ability to reason and to deliberate about one's choices" (Smyer, 1993). The mere fact that a patient disagrees with the provider or with the recommended treatment plan is not sufficient evidence for incapacity. What appears rational to one person (refusing to comply with medical advice) may not appear rational to an outside observer. Rationality in this case must be viewed as a process, rather than as an end product. How the decision is made, rather than the outcome of that decision, must be evaluated. As long as the individual has a clear understanding of the potential ramifications of a decision (even if those ramifications are negative), then this is considered informed and reasoned. In other words, individuals retain the right to make bad choices as long as they understand the negative consequences (and as long as those consequences do not impact detrimentally on others) and as long as the choices are voluntary.

The ability to determine competency is more complicated in the home care setting because incapacity may be less pronounced. "Assessment of decision-making capacity is multifaceted and requires attention to a variety of factors" (Davitt & Kaye, 1996). The use of standardized tests alone may not be sufficient to determine whether the patient is capable of making decisions. Likewise, it is generally accepted that decisional capacity should not be assessed on a global basis but should be evaluated based on the individual decision confronting the patient. In other words, patients may have limited or fluctuating decisional capacity. For example, a particular patient may be able to communicate preferences regarding several aspects of treatment delivery, but may not have the capacity to execute an advance directive. "Since mental capacity is decision-specific and fluctuates along a continuum, some have proposed that it be evaluated according to a sliding scale, where less capacity is required for questions that are simpler or carry less serious consequences than for more complex or consequential decisions" (Kapp, 1990).

The method for informing patients must also be evaluated. Research has found that capacity may be undermined or enhanced based on the manner in which information is presented to the patient (Tymchuk, Ouslander, Rahbar, & Fitten, 1988). This study found that patients who received information in simplified and storybook formats understood the information better than when a standard format was used. Likewise the patient's medical condition, emotional well-being, and factors related to these (e.g., amount of pain experienced, medication contraindications) may influence the patient's ability to make decisions. These must be ruled out before a determination is made.

The timing of the assessment is also important. A patient's level of alertness generally will fluctuate throughout the day. This may vary from patient to patient; therefore it is important to base the time of the assessment on the individual patient's schedule. In fact, it has been suggested that these evaluations should be repeated because capacity may vary over time and with changing physical surroundings (Farnsworth, 1989).

Positive versus Negative Autonomy

In relation to autonomy, individuals have both negative and positive rights. These concepts relate to the idea of liberty and the distinction in modern Western thought that liberty consists of both negative and positive elements. Negative liberty implies that individuals are entitled to be free from interference or coercion in relation to choices and actions. For example, the right to privacy, or to choose to forgo certain medical procedures, are negative rights. Positive rights on the other hand relate to the concept of positive liberty, that is the freedom to act. Individuals have a positive right to the active support of their autonomy and their right to make decisions; it includes "positive entitlement, support and capacitation" (Collopy, 1988, p. 11). That is, they have a right to treatment.

Again this is a tricky issue for providers. It amounts to a balancing game between paternalism and autonomy. The libertarian view, which stresses the independence of each person and therefore the individual's right to be left alone, is juxtaposed with the competing ethical principle of beneficence (doing good). Choosing which principle to emphasize in a particular case depends on a variety of factors, including the patient's emotional and cognitive state, values, and informal supports. These issues are further addressed in the next section.

LIMITS ON AUTONOMY: COMPETING MORAL PRINCIPLES

Beneficence / Nonmaleficence

Autonomy may represent a prima facie duty but not always an actual duty in that it can at times be overridden. According to Faden and Beauchamp (1986), "a prima facie duty refers to a duty always to be acted upon unless it conflicts on a particular occasion with an equal or stronger duty". There are ethical principles that may compete directly with autonomy, such as, beneficence. Beneficence refers to the moral duty to do good. It encompasses both a positive and a negative obligation to prevent harm. The negative obligation refers to the concept that one ought not to inflict harm (nonmaleficence). Positive obligations refer to the active prevention or removal of harm or evil (Faden & Beauchamp, 1986).

Paternalism

The idea of promoting health or at least preventing harm leads to another competing principle—paternalism. This refers to the belief that interference by others is justified because beneficence should take precedence over autonomy. This idea has been translated into the legal doctrine of parens patriea or the view of the state as ultimate parent to its citizens (Kapp, 1988). Paternalism implies that some authority or external entity knows what is best for the individual and should therefore override the patient's decisions, such as, "the doctor knows best." This highlights a conflict or what might be referred to as an ethical dilemma between a positive duty and a negative duty. Paternalism implies a positive obligation on the part of healthcare providers to prevent harm and to therefore intervene in a patient's life in opposition to their wishes. "The autonomy of patients can be severely threatened by the paternalism of caregivers" (Collopy, Dubler, & Zuckerman, 1990, p. 7). A negative obligation, on the other hand, places greater emphasis on autonomy and therefore noninterference in the patient's life. Balancing these competing principles can be very complicated. However, in the United States paternalism in medicine has been justified only on a limited basis: (a) when the exercise of autonomy poses a threat of harm to self or others; or (b) when the person is not capable of autonomous choice.

The idea of intervening to prevent patients from harming themselves is complicated. Some argue that paternalism is always justified in such cases. However, others argue that it is justified only in very specific cases. The right to be free from interference can be complicated, especially in home care settings, by a variety of factors. The patient may be incapacitated or may not fully understand the ramifications of the decision. Also, the patient's decision may pose a risk to caregivers (both formal and informal). Finally, the patient may ask to be left alone due to emotional or psychological issues (e.g., depression, fear, anxiety), which warrant positive support rather than noninterference. However, providers must struggle to avoid the slippery slope of paternalism that can seriously disempower the patient. Reamer (1982) has suggested a possible framework (adapted from Gewirth's Principle of Generic Consistency) for making such decisions. "An individual's right to freedom takes precedence over his or her own right to basic well-being" (p. 77). Therefore, if the person is making an informed and voluntary decision and understands the consequences of the decision, then the person should be allowed to make this choice. This also assumes that any negative consequences will only affect the patient. Therefore, the right to choose can be interfered with if the provider has determined that the patient: is incompetent; is being coerced or unduly influenced (through internal or external constraints); or is uninformed about the nature of the treatment.

In addition, autonomy encompasses rights as well as obligations. In other words, my right to choose among options and to enact those choices is respected as long as it does not infringe on the rights of others. An individual's right to autonomy should not interfere with another individual's rights to safety, well being, and freedom. As in the classic works of John

Stuart Mill, individuals should be given maximum opportunity to pursue their own interests as long as this allows others to do the same. Reamer (1982, p. 77) has suggested the following guideline: "an individual's right to basic well-being takes precedence over another individual's right to freedom."

In home health care the question of balancing competing interests usually centers on the interests of caregivers versus the interests of patients. Balancing the rights of the caregiver to well being and freedom and the patient's right to complete autonomous choice can be difficult. Because both authority and responsibility are shared in home care settings among several parties, including the patient, family or caregiver, and agency staff, no one party may be completely autonomous. For example, the delivery of high-tech treatments at home may increase the burden on caregivers, which violates the principle of nonmaleficence in that it may increase both physical and psychological stress on the caregiver. "Thus the systematic exclusion of the interests of family and friends who provide care at home is untenable and unjust" (Arras & Dubler, 1994). Using Reamer's guideline, staff would need to evaluate the potential negative impacts of home care to the caregiver as well as the patient. In addition, the caregiver also has a right to autonomy and therefore the choice for home care may dramatically limit the caregiver's autonomy. Many theorists have suggested a model of autonomy, which reflects the mutuality, and interdependence of existence, especially for home care patients (Collopy, Dubler, & Zuckerman, 1990; Moody, 1988). "But a model that focuses on accommodating and reciprocating autonomies will be far more effective than one that focuses on the autonomy of the client alone and seeks chiefly to protect this autonomy from the paternalism of professional caregivers" (Collopy, Dubler, & Zuckerman, p. 9).

Justice

In addition, there is a justice factor that must be weighed in terms of caregiver burden and filial duty to care. How much should an individual be required to sacrifice of their own needs, interests, and aspirations to provide care for a dependent relative? Who in the family should provide this care, is another important question. Traditionally this has been a woman's duty. Although this has changed to some degree in recent years, the majority of caregivers are women. Therefore, women have historically been asked to sacrifice more of their own wishes and dreams to care for dependent relatives. Also, the burdens of caregiving in practice rarely prove equal. In many cases, one family member may carry a much heavier burden than others. "These observations about just caring suggest that accommodation and mediation of all legitimate interests, rather than the exclusionary pursuit of the patient's interests, are the most appropriate models for thinking about the justice of interpersonal relationships within high-tech home care" (Arras & Dubler, 1994, p. 25).

The idea of justice in caregiving is complicated by the virtue of filial responsibility, which is actually felt by family or caregivers. For many caregivers the notion of caring for a dependent relative is a given. "The caregiver's sense of moral obligation arises from a lifelong relationship where the duty is experienced as part of one's historical identity as a spouse, a son, or a daughter" (Moody, 1992, p. 34). However, this is not true for all families. Daughters and sons who were abandoned by a parent may feel less of an identification with the patient as a parent. Therefore the bonds of filial duty may be weak. Other dysfunctional family structures may likewise result in a reduced sense of moral obligation and reciprocity. Agency staff must be aware of the potential for such diverse family relationships and histories, rather than assuming that all families will volunteer to care (and do it adequately and sensitively) for a dependent relative.

Personal autonomy may also at times be limited due to concerns with distributive justice. For example, a particular patient may not be entitled to have as many home care visits as the patient wishes due to a scarcity of available resources to provide that level of care. "One significant implication of resource scarcity is the ethical imperative that, if we cannot provide every person with all the human services from which he or she could profit, at least we must devise a system for allocating our scarce resources in as fair and equitable a manner as possible." (Kapp, 1988, p. 2). Distribution of services can occur in several ways. First, we can choose to provide home care based on merit. That is, citizens will receive benefits based on their previous achievements or contribution to society. Of course, under this scheme the concept of merit would also need to be defined and could include such things as financial success, social contribution, occupational status, or educational achievement. Second, society could provide an equal share of services to each person, regardless of need or contribution. Third, services could be distributed based solely on ability to pay for them. Finally, services could be distributed so as to ensure that those with the greatest need receive the most service. This is Rawls' principle of distributive justice; public goods should be distributed to benefit the least advantaged in society.

Regardless of the basis for distribution, the fact that resources are limited requires curbs on individual autonomy. This is an important concern in home health care. Constraints on the amount and duration of services stem from reimbursement limits, agency constraints, and regulatory factors. Many patients will need much greater amounts of home care than can be provided. Therefore, the decision to admit a particular patient may require staff to address questions regarding distributive justice, that is, which patients are entitled to services, and how much service should they receive.

There are other potential limits to patient autonomy. The values and rules of the agency may contradict patients' preferences. Also, agencies may operate under specific regulations or guidelines that restrict their flexibility in handling certain patient requests. For example, the Patient Self-Determination Act (PSDA) allows providers to invoke a conscientious objection clause in relation to a patient's request to have treatment removed or stopped. Therefore, the professional is not required to act against their own value base. The law requires providers to transfer the patient to another provider that can honor the patient's wishes. In this example, the patient's autonomy becomes somewhat restricted due to the agency's values and government regulations. Just as patient autonomy can be restricted if a particular decision has the potential to negatively affect family or caregivers, it can also be restricted if it negatively affects formal caregivers. For example, the safety and well being of staff may take precedence over the patient's demand for particular services that staff are unable to provide. Likewise, the patient does not have the right to abuse staff emotionally or verbally. Limits in the pool of available workers may also restrict the patient's right to demand certain types of workers. This is a particularly difficult ethical concern. Many patients will express their own prejudices by indicating that they would not accept a home care worker of a particular race, gender, or religion. This request in most cases cannot be honored due to limitations on the agency and other overriding moral claims (such as fairness and equality).

PROCESSES OF ETHICAL DECISION MAKING

The Liberal (Patient-Centered) Bioethical Model

The traditional model of bioethics has developed over the years, mainly in the acute care setting, with a focus on crisis situations that warrant immediate action. This model has focused on the principles mentioned above, especially on autonomy, beneficence, and distributive justice (Moody, 1992). The method of decision making in this model focuses on the use of the case example to resolve ethical dilemmas. It is sometimes referred to as quandary ethics in reference to the ethical dilemmas that arise when competing principles conflict with each other (Moody, 1992). The focus is on rules and principles and an attempt to resolve conflicts between principles in a timely fashion. The analysis is action based, stressing the need for a decision that will lead to a course of action to resolve the fundamental conflict. "[I]t is always a specific, delimited act or choice that is the focus, not, for example, an ongoing human relationship or social institution or a still deeper question about character and virtue" (Moody, 1992, p. 33).

Critics of this model suggest that it lacks flexibility and interpersonal understanding so necessary in the home care arena. The model's basis in rights and duties (many of which we discussed above) establishes a disjuncture between theory and practice. For example, the complicated nature of autonomy and the multiplicity and mutuality of the caregiving relationship in home care results in a complex weave of autonomy demands. In these situations there is no simple answer that one person's right to autonomy takes precedence over another person's right to autonomy. As in a game of chess, if one player is allowed to move, it affects the potential movement of all other players and therefore cannot be thought of as an independent, time-limited act. According to Moody (1992, p. 33) "what is missing in the dominant model is an appreciation for the more intuitive and interpersonal ingredients of ethical deliberation: the role of individual character, the texture of lived experience, and the importance of interpretation and communication."

It is clear that the current health care delivery system in the United States affords great weight to the view that the individual patient is an isolated individual. The law is meant to protect that individual from external interference. However, in reality, human beings are embedded in relationships and an environmental context that cannot be ignored (Michel, 1994). Current models for decision making in healthcare emphasize the individual while downplaying the environment. This focus, however, also fails to consider the degree of cultural diversity in this country. Many patients espouse value systems that stress family-centered or collective decision making. Therefore, the dominant model of ethical deliberation fails to respond to the value systems of various cultures.

The Ecological Model

The function of an individual's values and belief systems can have a great impact on people's perceptions about control, dignity, autonomy, death, and many other personal issues. Our value systems generally stem from the culture to which we belong. Simply put, culture is a set of shared meanings, values, ideologies, language, norms, and beliefs. It provides a set of symbols that establish the standards for human behavior within that culture. According to Kottak (1978) culture includes, "that which is transmitted through learning—behavior patterns and modes of thought acquired by humans as members of [a] society". The culture defines values of the good life as perceived by its members. Certain values may be viewed as important (highly cherished) in one culture while deemphasized in another culture. These values create structure and consistency and define appropriate interactions (role expectations) between members of that culture as well as those external to the culture (i.e., health care provider). "In other words, the cultural environment in which the system finds itself will set different norms and expectations for role occupants" (Compton & Galaway, 1979, p. 86). Culture is a set of collected adaptations that maintain a community and provide a shared sense of expectations related to behavior and ways of thinking.

Social roles are very important elements of any culture because they define our interactions with others and how we perceive ourselves. A role is defined as the "set of behavioral expectations that constitute a particular status" (Passuth & Bengston, 1988). Therefore, social roles are defined by the culture but also help to define the individual. "The individual is born into an a priori set of societal values and expectations . . . [which] are passed on through socialization . . . and provide the context for a social definition of personal meaning" (Reker & Wong, 1988, p. 227). Therefore personal meaning cannot be understood apart from the cultural context (Reker & Wong, 1988). For example, research shows that different cultures have their own definitions of such constructs as health, illness, ethnicity, family, and self (Sankar, 1984).

The value system and role expectations of a particular culture can impact how its members view medical decision making as well. Such values as autonomy, truth-telling, and self-determination that predominate in the United States may run counter to the prevailing values of a particular culture that emphasizes communal authority and positive interaction in medical decision making. For example, specific cultures may emphasize the benefits to advance medical care planning while others will view planning as negative or harmful. Therefore, certain patient groups may be interested in planning for incapacity while others may avoid the subject completely.

Likewise, cultural beliefs regarding role expectations can impact on how patients interact with various healthcare providers. For example, in some cultures patients expect a paternalistic approach from the physician (especially in relation to truth-telling practices with terminal patients). Other cultures may expect the physician to include the family in all patient care conferences due to their emphasis on cooperation and communal decision-making. Therefore, practitioners should have an increased sensitivity to the potential for diverse views among their patients.

Members of ethnic groups who ascribe to different norms and values based on their ethnic culture may not condone the approaches used to elicit medical decisions in the current liberal model. A recent wave of research has demonstrated the varying belief systems and preferred methods of decision making employed by certain cultural groups (Blackhall et al., 1995; Carrese & Rhodes, 1995; Gostin, 1995; Michel, 1994). The concept that all patients should expect and welcome informed consent disregards the cultural impact on the patient who does not hold strong convictions of autonomy and self-determination. In this way the concept of autonomy becomes almost deontological, that is, ethical obligations must be satisfied even if the consequences of fulfilling them are unfortunate. Here duty becomes independent of its practical outcomes. To some extent the state defines the meaning of the good life as equivalent to autonomy, rather than in the pluralist commitment underlying liberalism.

Assumptions regarding what is meaningful to one person may not hold true for the next both within and across cultural groups. The greater the amount of acculturation to the majority culture, the more likely one is to place emphasis on the traditional patient-centered liberal model of medical decision making (Blackhall et al., 1995). The individual's context is influenced by culture, education, socioeconomic factors, and degree of acculturation to the majority culture as well as personality factors (Michel, 1994). Therefore, agencies will need to support multiple decision-making models and avoid the pitfalls of generalization and stereotyping, that is, assuming that one knows how a patient will behave because the patient belongs to a particular cultural group. The use of virtue ethics, ethics of care, or an ecological approach have been suggested as alternatives to a current patient-centered liberal model that relies heavily on rules and principles to make ethical decisions. These new approaches rely more on a view that ethical decisions are unique and that sensitivity to the specific situation is more important than specific rules or principles.

PRACTICE-BASED ISSUES

Admitting the High-Tech Patient

In determining whether a particular patient should be discharged (from an institutional setting) with high-tech home care, providers must both assess the patient's medical needs as well as the potential benefits and burdens of treatment at home. In this way the decision has an ethical component. As mentioned earlier, this relates to the concept of nonmaleficence. If the burden to the patient overrides the benefits, then home care may not be the best solution because it may in some cases actually generate negative consequences for the patient. Ivan Illich (1976) first spoke of the iatrogenic nature of health care and the medicalization of every day life. Implied here is the idea that turning the home into a satellite hospital may not always be the best option for the patient, the patient's family, and caregivers. First, this can generate stress for the patient and for caregivers. Such stress can be overwhelming, especially if the patient's care needs are complex or the technology is complicated and intimidating. Families and patients may live in constant fear that something terrible will happen. In addition, the amount of care the patient needs may also generate stress for family and caregivers not to mention physical exhaustion. Therefore, a balance must be struck between benefit and burden. Patients and caregivers should be informed of the benefits and burdens of home care prior to discharge from an acute or subacute setting as well as the alternatives to home care.

Use of Restraints

At first glance the debate around restraint use in home health care appears to be a legal concern. However, this issue reflects a fundamental change in the ethics of care. In the past restraint use was much more widely accepted in a variety of health care settings. "This regulatory approach reflected a model of care long unquestioned in both acute and long-term care, a model that tended to be paternalistic and highly interventionist, with heavy decision-making power vested in professional caregivers" (Collopy, 1992, p. 6). The new focus is on the least restrictive care alternative, with an emphasis on patients' quality of life and their rights to be self-determining.

Much research has established the clinical risks related to restraint use in institutional settings, including physical and chemical restraints (Marks, 1992; Miles & Irvine, 1992; Powell, Mitchell-Pederson, Fingerote, & Edmund, 1989; Robinson, Sucholeike, & Schocken, 1993). In this case the use of restraints violates several ethical principles, including benefi- cence (doing good) and nonmaleficence (not doing harm). "The imposi- tion of restraints without the person's valid informed consent also runs afoul of the precept of autonomy or self-determination, and arguably shows disrespect for the individual's dignity as a person" (Kapp, 1995b). Home health care staff must be very careful in assessing the need for restraints in the home situation. Restraints should not be used to substitute for quality care, for communication with the patient or caregivers, or for individualized care plans (Collopy, 1992).

Prior to initiating restraint use for a particular patient, staff should re- view several factors including: any potential underlying and treatable causes to the patient's disruptive behavior; alternative responses on the part of caregivers (both formal and informal) to such behavior; alterna- tive treatment modalities that might minimize the disruptive behavior; and the adequacy of the level of care currently provided to the patient. Agencies should have explicit written policies on the use of restraints that can guide staff decisions in this area. If restraints are indicated, then the least restrictive alternative should be employed and usage should be continually monitored. Above all the dignity and autonomy of each patient should be respected.

Life-Sustaining Treatment Decisions

The ethical issues related to life-sustaining treatment decisions in home health care are similar to those covered earlier in this chapter in relation to medical decision making in general. The U.S. Supreme Court decision in *Cruzan v. Director of Missouri Department of Health*, 110 S.Ct. 2841, 2855-56 (1990) set the stage for greater emphasis on written advance directives to guide treatment decisions for incapacitated patients. Advance directives are written documents (including but not limited to living wills and durable health care powers of attorney) completed by an individual in advance of an incapacitating illness or injury, which: (a) describe what types of treatment the patient would or would not want should they be- come incapacitated (living will); (b) designate a surrogate decision-maker to act on behalf of the incapacitated individual (durable power of attorney for health care or health care proxy); or (c) provide general guidelines regarding the patient's value-system and preferences pertaining to a quality life. The Patient Self-Determination Act (PSDA) of the Omnibus Budget Reconciliation Act of 1990, (P.L. 101-508), was therefore enacted to promote education and understanding related to the benefits of advance directives to clearly document a patient's preference in advance of incapacity (LaPuma, Orentlicher, & Moss, 1991).

Through the PSDA health care providers have been given very specific criteria that they must follow to promote patient self-determination. The PSDA requires Medicare- and Medicaid-certified health care providers to: (a) maintain written policies and procedures regarding state law on advance directives; (b) inform patients upon admission of their rights under state law to direct their medical treatment and to execute an advance directive; (c) inform patients of agency policy on advance directives; (d) document the existence of an advance directive in the medical chart; (e) not discriminate in admissions or service based on advance directive status; and (f) educate agency staff and the community about advance directives.

There are several underlying assumptions in *Cruzan* and the PSDA. First, advance directives are assumed to be the best and most accurate method to determine patients' wishes should they become incapacitated. Emphasis on the use of formal advance directives has raised serious questions as to whether such documents accurately and comprehensively communicate patients' wishes. Second, education in the form of written materials provided at the point of admission to a health care system is assumed to be the best method to educate the general public about advance directives and to encourage their use. This method may have been chosen more for its ease of implementation rather than its ability to enhance public knowledge. Related to this is the third assumption that providers will establish and implement appropriate policies and procedures to protect and promote patient wishes regarding life-sustaining treatment decisions. However, researchers have continually noted their concern that agencies are merely satisfying the minimum requirements of the PSDA (Davitt, 1992; Davitt & Kaye, 1996; Sabatino, 1993). Fourth, it is assumed that patients will understand and voluntarily choose to execute a directive once they have been educated. Planning for the future has traditionally not been a primary focus of the majority of citizens in the United States, including planning for future financial, residential, and medical needs. Likewise, with the multicultural nature of the United States, one cannot assume that all health care consumers will be equally open to such planning. Certain cultural groups view such planning for death as a negative process, and other cultures view discussions with a patient regarding a poor prognosis as taboo. Therefore, the assumption that all people should welcome the opportunity to think about incapacity and death and express their wishes in a directive may (at best) run counter to prevailing sentiment regarding such planning and may (at worst) be culturally insensitive.

One of the main problems in the legal interpretation of the *Cruzan* decision is the assumption that the only way to determine accurately someone's preferences in relation to life-sustaining medical treatment is for them to provide detailed written instructions. This assumes that those individuals who do not have an advance directive have intentionally chosen not to execute one because they would want everything medically possible done should they become incapacitated. It also emphasizes the liberal model of bioethics previously described, which focuses on the patient as an autonomous, isolated decision-maker. However, many people do not execute a written directive simply due to ignorance or procrastination, and it should not be assumed that the absence of written instructions implies a desire to always be treated. In this situation, the state becomes the decision maker by default, rather than the people who know the patient best— close family members. (Throughout this chapter we use the terms family or family members in a broad sense to include biological, legal, and nontraditional members of a client's immediate support network.) With this system many clients will not have their wishes followed simply because they did not sign a piece of paper.

Many states have attempted to circumvent this problem by recognizing in statutory law the authority of family members to make life-sustaining treatment decisions in the absence of formal written instructions. Commonly referred to as family consent statutes, these laws explicitly grant family members, usually in a specific order of preference based on degree of kinship (i.e., spouse, adult child, etc.), the right to make health care decisions for other family members in nonemergency situations (Sabatino, 1993). However, many state statutes do not recognize nontraditional family configurations, and nonkinship based significant others such as close friends or lifetime partners.

A second problem in relation to this false assumption stems from the emphasis on instruction directives, rather than surrogate decision making, since the *Cruzan* decision. It has yet to be determined whether such directives are helpful in communicating clearly the patient's actual preferences. In many cases directives can be too vague or broad to help providers understand patient preferences in specific situations. Many advance directive forms currently being distributed simply provide a checklist of treatments for consumers to accept or refuse. These forms offer little guidance as to the type of situation in which the patient would or would not want treatment to be withheld. Therefore, instruction directives do not always provide a clear picture of the patient's expressed wishes and can therefore erode patient autonomy.

The expressed intent model that places emphasis on instruction directives, rather than surrogate decision making, may also ignore certain cultural value systems. Patient's who would prefer to have their families make or participate in medical decisions will be less likely to have their wishes honored if a proxy directive has not been executed. Many patients, due to their cultural background and ignorance of the law, will assume that family members will make these difficult decisions if the time comes and therefore will not execute a durable power of attorney for health care or a health care proxy. In states without family consent statutes, such patients may not have their true wishes (for family-centered decision making) honored.

In cases in which clients are open to discussion, home care agency staff can begin by educating clients about their rights: to informed consent; to determine the course of their medical treatment; to refuse treatment; and to execute an advance directive. If clients have specific preferences about life-sustaining treatment decisions, then they should consider: (a) discussing preferences with their physician and family; (b) discussing preferences with the agency staff (who should document these discussions); or (c) executing an advance directive. The staff can assist the client to clarify some important issues by discussing varying scenarios of prognosis and functional status with the client to determine in what situations the client would want or not want treatment. In addition, detailed information regarding treatment options and the drawbacks and benefits to certain treatments should be explained to clients to assure that they fully understand what they are requesting (or not requesting as the case may be) in their advance directive. Again, these discussions should be documented because they might provide necessary clarification later.

If a client decides to put it in writing there are theoretically three choices. (Actual legal authority for these options varies from state to state. Some states allow all three while other state laws limit the means for advance planning.) First, individuals can provide written instructions pertaining to the types of treatment they would or would not want (commonly referred to as a living will or instruction directive). Second, they can designate a surrogate decision-maker either through a durable power of attorney for health care or a health care proxy. (Surrogates at times may be referred to as agents, proxies, or attorneys-in-fact.) Finally, clients can combine an instruction directive with a health care proxy. This last option allows the client to provide specific instructions to the surrogate to ensure that the surrogate understands the client's wishes.

Agency staff can support clients throughout the execution process by: providing sample forms for clients to review (along with a verbal explanation of the forms); assisting clients to complete the forms; and encouraging clients to discuss their wishes and plans with their physicians and families. If the client wishes to appoint a surrogate decision-maker, the staffperson's role in this situation would be to assist the client in identifying the best person to act as a surrogate (keeping in mind that it is the client's choice). Likewise, the staff can assist in educating surrogates about their new role, when and how it becomes effective, and what their responsibilities would be. Finally, the staff can ensure that surrogates understand that their role is to make decisions as the client would have, not as the surrogate would and not necessarily in the client's best interests. Staff should promote and facilitate ongoing discussions between clients and their designated surrogates. (See Table 9.1 for a list of tips for choosing a surrogate.)

TABLE 9.1   Tips for Choosing a Surrogate Decision-Maker

1. Be sure the surrogate is someone the client trusts.
2. Attempt to find someone with similar values and belief systems as the client.
3. If the proposed surrogate has dissimilar values, be sure that they respect the client's values and belief system.
4. Be sure the surrogate is reasonably accessible (i.e., someone in the same geographic location as the client, someone who can get to the hospital in a crisis situation, etc.).
5. Be sure the surrogate has the ability to "question authority" and is willing to act as an advocate on behalf of the client's wishes.
6. Make sure the surrogate understands the role and responsibilities prior to accepting the appointment. (They should understand that they may have to advocate to have treatment removed and/or not provided, rather than advocating what is in the client's best interests.)
7. Be sure that they understand when they become responsible, only if the client is decisionally incapacitated.
8. Promote regular discussions between clients and surrogates to ensure understanding in light of the potential for clients to change their minds.

From J. K. Davitt. (1996). Promoting cultural pluralism in advance care planning. *Geriatric Care Management Journal, 6* (4), 2–10.

Once clients have documented their wishes, either through an instruction directive or through a durable power of attorney for health care, the staff can assist clients with dissemination and maintenance of their documents. The first step is to distribute copies of the directive to physicians, surrogates, family members, and health care agencies involved with the client. Likewise, the home care agency should receive a copy for its records. (This will ensure a safe place for the document in the event that a crisis occurs and a copy of the document cannot be located.) An accessible place should be located in the patient's home to maintain the document. Remember a safe deposit box at the bank or a locked safe in the client's home are not accessible should the client become incapacitated. A note (indicating where the directive is) can be placed on the refrigerator or above the telephone to direct emergency personnel to the document. Also, many states have wallet-size versions of the directives or cards to alert medical personnel to the existence of a directive.

Patient education is a key focus of the PSDA. However, the law only requires providers to ask if the client has an advance directive and to distribute written material on advance directives and patient rights under state law. Providers who adhere to the letter of the law and only distribute written materials to clients, without discussion or verbal explanation, may not be promoting true patient understanding and autonomy. In most cases, information is being distributed during the admissions process (as required by the PSDA). This only exacerbates the problem. The admissions interview may not be the best time to ask a patient to complete an advance directive (Davitt, 1992). Clients may sign a directive (along with the many other forms they are handed) without true understanding. In addition, facile execution of an advance directive is more likely to occur with individuals who have less education, poor language skills, or atypical value systems. Also, lack of understanding regarding specific medical treatments on the part of health care consumers raises questions regarding their understanding of the advance directive that they have executed.

Finally, a client's cultural background may influence openness to such discussions. The requirement (in the PSDA) that providers must ask every patient if they have a directive may violate certain cultural beliefs simply by asking the question (Michel, 1994). This is especially true for those cultures that do not believe in discussing negative concepts or who expect the doctor or family to automatically make these decisions should they become incapacitated (Carrese & Rhodes, 1995; Michel, 1994).

Studies of various ethnic cultures in the United States have demonstrated variation from the traditional patient-centered model, which stresses informed consent. The Navajo culture, for example, believes in positive thought and discussion. Carrese and Rhodes (1995) found that an advance care planning discussion would be viewed as harmful to the patient in the Navajo culture. Blackhall and colleagues (1995) found that Korean Americans and Mexican Americans were less likely to support telling a patient the truth about a terminal diagnosis than African Americans or European Americans. Therefore, a blanket requirement to discuss these issues with every client may be culturally insensitive.

TABLE 9.2   Planning for Incapacity

Step 1	Assess client's cultural background, level of family support, and knowledge of their medical rights.
Step 2	Begin client education. Re: medical treatment rights
	a. Right to determine the course of one's medical treatment
	b. Right to informed consent
	c. Right to accept or refuse medical treatment
	d. Right to execute an advance directive
	Remember, if clients are not interested in such discussions or such planning that is their choice. It should never be forced on them.
Step 3	Begin planning discussions: Support and encourage clients to discuss their preferences with family, significant others, physician, clergy, and so forth.
Step 4	Assist interested clients in obtaining and completing necessary forms (if they wish to execute a directive).
Step 5	Assist client to schedule and coordinate discussions with family or assist by mediating such discussions, especially in families with conflict.
Step 6	Document patient preferences (especially for those clients who are willing to discuss their feelings and preferences but not willing to actually execute a directive).
Step 7	Assist client with distributing copies of advance directives to all necessary third parties (i.e., agents, family, physician) and storing originals in an accessible place.
Step 8	Follow-up to ensure that client has not changed his or her wishes, (at least annually).
Step 9	Educate other providers about client's wishes.
Step 10	Advocate if the time comes.

From J. K. Davitt. (1996). Promoting cultural pluralism in advance care planning. *Geriatric Care Management Journal, 6* (4), 2–10.

Agency staff first and foremost must understand patient rights to assist the client in planning for possible incapacity. Although, many patients will never need an advance directive in that they will never become decisionally incapacitated, the need for planning is important for all individuals because in most cases one cannot predict who may become incapacitated. Of course, those clients who may be in the early stages of dementia or other progressive diseases would be primary targets for such planning.

Planning does not always have to mean executing an advance directive. Rather, creative strategies may be utilized to assist clients from various cultural backgrounds to begin the planning process in a way that is comfortable for them. For example, with cultural groups that emphasize collective responsibility for medical decision making, agency staff can facilitate family meetings to support discussions in advance of a crisis. These discussions do not have to solely revolve around the client either. This is a great opportunity to have other family members begin to think about and discuss these issues for themselves because planning is important for people of all ages. Discussions can happen prior to executing a formal directive to understand how one truly feels about these issues. Or, they can occur after completion of the directive, using the directive to guide discussion. Agency staff can help patients prepare for these discussions by thinking about how they feel, anticipating the potential reactions of family, and role playing possible responses to these reactions. Staff can also document such discussions to ensure that conflict may be avoided if ambivalence among family members arises, especially for those patients who are not willing to execute formal directives. (See Table 9.2 for steps in the planning process.)

CONCLUSION: PROMOTING CULTURAL PLURALISM IN HOME HEALTH CARE

It is clear that the current health care delivery system in the United States affords great weight to the view that the patient is an isolated individual. The law is meant to protect that individual from external interference. However, in reality human beings are embedded in relationships and an environmental context that cannot be ignored (Michel, 1994). Current models for decision making in health care emphasize the individual while downplaying the environment. In relation to home health care, any system for decision-making must be able to accommodate multiple perspectives.

One person may obtain great dignity through mutual support and communal decision making while another may stress individual autonomy. Self-determination does not necessarily imply that a person must decide independently and isolated from others. Rather, self-determination can include the right to defer to others for support in decision making. An ecological perspective would support multiple decision-making models. This pluralistic approach would allow each patient to define and delineate the decision-making process of preference (including those who would choose not to define such a process). It would stress sensitivity to diversity in meaning for such concepts as quality of life, death, health, self-determination, truth, and dignity.

Ethical decision making in home care situations cannot be subject to rigid criteria and guidelines. Although it is always helpful for agencies to have written policies and procedures that can guide staff, many ethical conflicts will warrant review and discussion among multiple parties with competing interests. Such cases may require greater emphasis on virtues, such as compassion, empathy, and understanding, than on principles such as autonomy, justice, and beneficence. Moody (1992, p. 34) suggests that, in fact, the "ethics of rules and the ethics of virtue need not be understood as mutually exclusive." At the vary least, ethical conflicts in home care require an eye toward the complexity of relationships, the interdependence of existence, and the mutuality of interests.

CHAPTER 10

The Challenge of Providing High-Tech Care: Reimbursement Issues

INTRODUCTION

Few patients have the resources to pay privately for unlimited home health services. This fact is even more crucial for high-tech patients, who tend to need more expensive services and additional units of service than the traditional home care patient. Therefore, many patients (and agencies) rely on third-party reimbursement, either public or private. Whether the patient's care is covered under private or public insurance, the amount, type, and duration of benefits may be limited. Therefore, it is essential for administrators to be well versed in the eligibility and coverage criteria for each insurer. In addition to private insurance and private pay, several federal programs exist that cover home health care expenses for older adults. These include Medicare, Medicaid, and Veterans Administration programs. This chapter describes particular details of the three main public insurance programs that offer home health care as a benefit. A summary of the recent changes in Medicare and Medicaid reimbursement policies for home health care brought about under the Balanced Budget Act of 1997 (BBA) is also provided. These changes have dramatically altered the reimbursement policies and procedures associated with the home health care benefit.

MEDICARE

Medicare was enacted in 1965 as an amendment to the Social Security Act (Title XVIII). The goal was to increase access to medical care for older adults by providing a publicly sponsored health insurance system. Medicare, is a national health insurance program administered by the Social Security Administration for individuals 65 and over. Prior to Medicare, private insurers denied many older adults coverage due to old age or health status. Most older adults receive Medicare Part A (hospital insurance) and some choose to purchase Medicare Part B for an additional monthly premium. Home health care benefits have historically been paid out of the hospital trust fund (Part A) (Rosenzweig, 1995). However, after enactment of the BBA, some home health care costs will be shifted to Part B. In particular, those visits not related to a previous hospital stay or that extend beyond the 100 visits will be shifted out of Part A (Moon, Gage, & Evans, 1997).

Eligibility Criteria and Covered Services

Patients must meet certain eligibility criteria before Medicare will approve reimbursement. First, the patient must be considered homebound. Although the patient is allowed to leave the home, they must be able to do so only with the help of an assistant or with the use of a device (cane, walker, wheelchair) or with considerable difficulty. These absences from the home must be infrequent and of limited duration or specifically for the receipt of medical care. Thus, a patient who needs temporary assistance with intramuscular injections of interferon (for hepatitis C) but is otherwise able bodied may not be eligible for home health care benefits. Second, the patient's need for home care must be certified by a physician. The physician must order the services, establish a care plan, and must periodically review the treatment plan. Third, the patient must need intermittent skilled nursing care, physical therapy, or speech therapy. Intermittent care is defined very broadly and can include anything from service needs that occur every 60 days to patients who need more intensive care (such as every day) but for a short period of time. Finally, the agency providing services must be Medicare certified. (Recent changes in eligibility criteria are described in the next section of this chapter.)

In the arena of home health care, Medicare covers mainly skilled medical services, such as skilled nursing, medical social work, physical therapy,

TABLE 10.1   Eligibility for Medicare Reimbursement for Home Care

The patient must be homebound.

The patient must need intermittent skilled nursing care, physical therapy, or speech therapy.

The services must be ordered by a physician.

The agency must be Medicare certified.

speech therapy, occupational therapy (usually in conjunction with physical therapy or speech therapy), and home health aide services (always in conjunction with one of the above listed skilled services). There is no set limit on the number of visits one can receive, and the patient does not have to have a hospital stay prior to receiving benefits. Services provided by a skilled professional are fully covered (i.e., no deductible or copayment), and durable medical equipment ordered by the physician and necessary due to the patient's medical condition are covered up to 80%. Medicare does not cover services for clients who only need custodial care (personal care services such as bathing, dressing, or shopping). Medicare does not pay for full-time nursing care at home, prescription drugs, blood transfusions, or home-delivered meals. Medicare coverage must be authorized as both necessary and medically reasonable before Medicare will actually pay for such services.

Medicare also covers hospice care. Hospice agencies provide comfort care to patients who are terminally ill. Care must be provided by a Medicare-certified hospice agency and includes: physician services, nursing services, medical appliances and supplies, home health aide and homemaker services, physical therapy, speech therapy, occupational therapy, medical social services, counseling, and short-term inpatient respite care. To use the hospice benefit under Medicare, a physician must certify that the patient is terminally ill with only about 6 months to live. However, hospice care is limited to two periods of 90 days each with an additional 30-day extension. Individuals who use up the 210 days of hospice coverage may be able to get a permanent extension by having a physician clarify the nature of the patient's terminal illness.

Expansion of the Medicare In-home Benefit

Interestingly, the original focus of Medicare was on acute care benefits. However, various factors eventually converged to lead to an expansion of the home health benefit. According to Rosenzweig (1995), these included elimination of the 3-day prior hospitalization clause and the limit on visits (previously 100) in 1980 and development of the prospective payment system (PPS) in 1983. The PPS resulted in a reduction in hospital stays due to the creation of diagnostic related groups that determined maximum hospital-based payments for a particular diagnosis. The new reimbursement system created an incentive for hospitals to discharge patients sooner to reduce financial losses. This resulted in a shift in care settings from hospital to home, greatly expanding demand for home health care.

Also, in 1989 the home health care benefit was further liberalized as a result of a national class-action law suit, *Duggan v. Bowen,* which increased both the number of beneficiaries and the amount of service received by each patient (Komisar & Feder, 1998; Rosenzweig, 1995). Patients could now receive services if they had either a part-time or intermittent need (rather than part-time and intermittent). According to Komisar and Feder (1998, p. 6),

> [t]he revised regulations specified that beneficiaries could get, on a weekly basis, up to 28 hours of skilled nursing and home health aide services combined (and up to 35 hours subject to review on a case by case basis). The revisions also permitted beneficiaries to receive full-time care (that is, 8 hours per day) for up to 21 consecutive days, or longer in exceptional cases where the need for care was finite and predictable.

Changes in regulatory practices around this time also made it more difficult for intermediaries to deny home health claims (Komisar & Feder, 1998). The review switched from a focus on general patient characteristics (i.e., for patients with similar diagnoses) to a review of the patient's actual medical condition. In this respect, denials were more difficult to achieve in addition to making the process more costly for intermediaries. All of these changes positioned home health care to respond to changing medical practices, including shorter hospital stays and advances in medical technology.

The shift in focus from acute care benefits to in-home care resulted in a dramatic expansion in home health care. Growth in Medicare expenditures for home health care have increased by an average annual rate of 29% from 1990 to 1996, while total spending for Medicare only grew by 11% annually (Komisar & Feder, 1998). "The majority of the growth in expenditures resulted from increases in the number of visits per home health user and the number of home health users per 1,000 Medicare beneficiaries" (Lewin Group, 1998, p. 7). Although much of this expansion can be attributed to policy changes in health care in general, such growth aroused concerns about whether services were being provided in the most efficient manner.

Since the initial focus of the postacute benefit under Medicare was on skilled services, concern naturally centered on the question of whether long-term care support was being provided to patients. Questions began to surface related to the increase in the number of visits on the lower end of the reimbursement scale (i.e., for personal care services) and the inability of agencies to develop efficient methods to control costs. It seemed that the focus was shifting from skilled care to custodial care. For example, agencies had little incentive to reduce the number of visits because reimbursement was based on an average cost limit per visit. Therefore, agencies could offer additional visits (especially in lower cost services) and still remain within the payment limit (Komisar & Feder, 1998).

> [E]ach agency's payment limit was calculated as the sum across visit types of the per visit limit for each of six visit types multiplied by the number of visits of that type provided by the agency. The limit was set at 112% of average labor and non-labor costs for each of the six disciplines (nursing, physical therapy, occupational therapy, speech therapy, social services, and home health aide). However, since an agency's payment limit increased with the number of visits it delivered, it had no reason to curb volume as long as the average cost per visit did not exceed the average limit. (p. 7)

Another important trend that has been reported in the literature is related to the growth in the number of proprietary, Medicare-certified home care agencies (Benjamin, 1993; Komisar & Feder, 1998). Such growth was considered a clear indicator that Medicare reimbursement policies based on cost were too lucrative. These concerns were addressed in the Balanced Budget Act of 1997, which included major revisions to the Medicare home care benefit (in addition to other Medicare programs).

The Balanced Budget Act of 1997 and Changes to the Medicare Home Health Benefit

Prior to the BBA, agencies were reimbursed via a formula that allowed agencies to sum allowable costs for all visits. In other words, if an agency was under the limit in speech therapy, they could then be over the limit in another service. According to Komisar and Feder (1998, p. 8) the goal of the BBA is "not simply to control the price of home health services but to constrain volume per person served." This is accomplished through several changes in the way agencies will be reimbursed. These changes include: creation of the interim payment system (IPS) after October 1997; implementation of the prospective payment system (PPS) after October 1999; basing payment limits on the location of service rather than the location of the agency's billing office; and changes in eligibility criteria. Each of these changes will be described and potential drawbacks will be highlighted.

The interim payment system constrains expenditures by limiting the overall average per patient costs. After October 1, 1997, agencies were paid based on the lowest of three limits: (a) the actual allowable costs; (b) 105% of the median national costs for free-standing agencies (a change from 112% of the average national costs); or (c) per beneficiary limits (Komisar & Feder, 1998; Lewin Group, 1998). The per beneficiary limits are based on a blended average utilizing 75% of an agency's costs per beneficiary and 25% regional average costs from 98% of fiscal year 1994 (base year) costs (Moon, Gage, & Evans, 1997). This is based on an aggregate figure that means that any given patient's costs could be greater than the limit as long as the average is below the limit.

There are several important areas for concern under the IPS that are particularly related to the delivery of high-tech services. First, high volume users are most likely to be adversely affected under both the IPS and PPS, since the focus is to curb the number of visits provided per beneficiary. The per beneficiary limit under the IPS establishes an incentive for providers to limit the number of visits a client receives as well as the cost per visit (Komisar & Feder, 1998; Lewin Group, 1998). Therefore, high-end patients (either in use rates or in cost of service used) may be least able to access home health care services. This is due to the fact that "the per beneficiary limits do not incorporate changes in the number or mix of visits per person served" (Komisar & Feder, 1998, p. 14). The lack of a case-mix adjustment in this interim process may negatively impact on patients needing high-tech services because these patients generally warrant highly skilled professional care or additional units of service more than traditional home care patients. This could also impact patients without informal caregivers. According to Williams (1994) these patients tend to receive more units of service than patients with a caregiver. Therefore, those patients most in need of home care, because they lack other resources for care at home, will be the most adversely affected by these changes.

Agencies may choose among several strategies to avert financial hardships. First, they may severely restrict the types of patients admitted to their home care service. Second, they may restrict the number of visits that a given patient will receive. Third, they may attempt to substitute lower cost services, potentially compromising quality of patient care. For example, agencies may choose not to serve high-tech patients because of the potential for overexpenditures. Finally, they may discharge patients that appear to be too costly or refuse to readmit patients that have already received home health care that year (Komisar & Feder, 1998). In this case many patients will be left with few options because current regulations do not provide patients with an opportunity to appeal decisions denying them access to the home care benefit. In addition, beneficiaries in regions with limited community-based alternatives may end up in a nursing home if their benefits are restricted or they are denied access to home health care (Schor, 1994). These options could have serious repercussions for patients in terms of quality of care and safety issues and would be especially problematic in high-tech care situations.

Patients may be asked to pay out-of-pocket for additional services. This will, of course, most dramatically affect those with the least ability to pay, those with lower incomes and insignificant savings or other assets. In addition, it may affect those patients with the greatest care needs or the most expensive care. In some cases this may prove to be a double-edged sword because many low-income patients will have poorer health and therefore will be more likely to need additional care or more costly interventions.

Agencies that have chosen to care for patients with more intensive care needs (such as those receiving high-tech services) will be more restricted by the new limits. Agencies that do not maintain a low-cost mix of patients may need to slash per patient visits even more dramatically to stay within the cost limits. This will be especially problematic for agencies whose care mixes have shifted to the higher end after the base year. In other words, those agencies that expanded into the high-tech arena after 1994 will most likely have a higher cost mix than their base year, leading to a gap in reimbursement. The idea behind this change was to curb inefficient practices, however, many agencies that have switched to high-tech patients are not less efficient, but rather altering their care to meet patient needs and market trends. This cap may make it difficult for such agencies to continue to provide adequate care to high-tech patients. In addition, the failure of the IPS to take into account regional variations in agency costs (due to demographic and market trends) may also negatively affect agencies that provide services to patients with more intense needs, simply because there are few alternatives for care elsewhere in that region.

Concerns abound regarding the quality of care issues raised by these changes. Research has demonstrated that cutting back on services may in fact lead to poorer health outcomes for home health care patients

(Schlenker, Shaughnessy, & Hittle, 1995). Rather than supporting patients and their ability to improve, the new reimbursement limits may negatively affect patient care outcomes, leading to a greater overall need for assistance.

These changes may also impact the agencies directly, thereby having an indirect affect on patient care. For example, many agencies may not be able to maintain their current labor costs due to ceilings on reimbursements. This may mean that agencies will be less able to attract and maintain qualified personnel, which may affect the quality of care that patients receive (Lewin Group, 1998). Such changes could result in agency closures due to financial losses especially for those agencies that are unable to simultaneously reduce overall number of visits and the unit cost per visit. An increase in agency mergers between home health agencies may also become commonplace. This is due to the fact that agencies can increase the overall volume in order to reduce average number of visits and per person costs (Lewin Group). However, due to the limited size of the potential Medicare home health beneficiary pool, many agencies will not be able to take advantage of this option and a merger may be the only way to increase overall volume and therefore avoid closure. Also agencies may have less ability to invest in new technology (Lewin Group). At a time when they will need computerized patient tracking systems most, agencies will be least able to purchase such technology due to increased fiscal constraints.

These changes, according to the Lewin Group (1998), will especially impact small agencies, rural providers, agencies that expanded services after 1994, and new providers. In particular, high-tech agencies may be hard-pressed to reduce unit cost per visit because many high-tech interventions cannot be provided by lesser skilled and therefore lesser compensated staff.

The second change requires the Secretary of Health and Human Services to develop and implement a Prospective Payment System (PPS) for home health care on or after October 1999. The theory is that such a system will encourage agencies to be more efficient and effective in the care they provide by eliminating unnecessary services. Many of the specifics related to the PPS (e.g., definition of the unit of service, standard rates, and necessary cost adjustments) have yet to be developed (Komisar & Feder, 1998; Lewin Group, 1998; Moon, Gage, & Evans, 1997). "[T]he Secretary shall consider an appropriate unit of service and the number, type and duration of visits provided within that unit" (Balanced Budget

Act of 1997, P.L. 105–33). The adjustments will most likely include case mix and regional variation factors.

The PPS will be based on an episode system, that is, a "fixed, predetermined payment for all services provided during an episode" (Komisar & Feder, 1998, p. 15). The important issue will be in deciding whether to limit the episode based on length or to base it on a period preceded by specified time periods in which the patient receives no care. It could also be limited by number of visits. Finally, an outliers exemption policy could be utilized to deal with visits that occur outside of the episode limit.

The BBA also requires that the PPS incorporate some type of case-mix adjustment. Case mix has been used in other healthcare settings (acute and long-term care) as a method to account for the potential for differing care needs of an agency's patient mix. This is hoped to counteract the disincentive created by a PPS for agencies to admit higher-needs patients, promoting equal access across all patient types for home health care. However, research has demonstrated that the Medicare home health prospective payment demonstration has not accounted for much of the variance in home health use (Goldberg & Schmitz, 1994). Other systems such as the hospital-based diagnostic related groupings (DRGs) system and the resource utilization groups (RUGs) demonstration in nursing homes in New York State have been better predictors of resource utilization. Therefore, the case-mix system in home health care will need to be dramatically improved if it is to reflect actual resource use across patient types.

Adjustments for regional variations in costs to providers due to forces or market trends beyond individual providers' control are also recommended. For example, researchers have demonstrated that a number of factors may impact costs to providers, including: availability of nursing home beds, the demographic and health characteristics of patients, and state Medicaid policies. These factors vary from region to region and from state to state and therefore may need to be adjusted for to protect agency fiscal stability (Cohen & Tumlinson, 1997).

The main concern with the PPS is the potential for a profit incentive to develop as it did in the acute care setting. The case mix adjustment (if adequate and appropriate) should reduce problems regarding reimbursement limits for agencies that serve patients who are sicker or have more complex care needs. This will depend on how well the adjuster accounts for actual difference in care needs. Also, the PPS may require increased reviews to assure that patients are being served appropriately and to curtail patient dumping (Lewin Group, 1998). In addition, there is very little time to collect the necessary data to develop an effective case-mix adjuster prior to the established implementation date. This may result in the use of a poor case-mix adjuster, which could potentially aid less efficient agencies while hurting those that are efficient (Komisar & Feder, 1998). The need to develop an adequate method to handle rare cases that legitimately fall outside of the limits established under the PPS is also crucial for agency stability as is the need to create an incentive for agencies to take on difficult (i.e., more costly) cases. One important issue included in the BBA is that rates must be initially set 15% lower than what they would have been, regardless of whether the PPS has been developed (Lewin Group). This will increase pressure on agencies to reduce costs.

The third major area of change relates to alterations in eligibility criteria and coverage. The Act eliminates venipuncture as a covered service for those patients who only need venipuncture. In addition, the act alters the definition of intermittent skilled nursing care. This is now defined as "skilled nursing care needed on fewer than 7 days each week or less than 8 hours each day for periods of up to 21 days (or longer in exceptional circumstances when the need for additional care is finite and predictable)" (Komisar & Feder, 1998, p.9). This represents an expansion in eligibility criteria. The BBA also redefines part-time and intermittent skilled nursing and home health aid. This is now "care provided for less than 8 hours each day and 28 or fewer hours each week (or less than 8 hours each day and 35 or fewer hours each week subject to review on a case-by-case basis)" (Komisar & Feder, p. 9). This represents a contraction in eligibility criteria. Patients who may need more than 8 hours per day of care but do not need this on a daily basis will not be able to get the full care that they need. Likewise, patients who need intensive care (8 hours per day) for a limited period of time, for example for postacute recovery, will not be able to receive the level of care they require. Many of these patients will have to use a subacute facility or nursing home for such recovery, especially if they lack informal supports or the resources to pay privately.

The final important change relates to the surety bond as a condition of participation under both Medicare and Medicaid. The bond amount is the greater of $50,000 or 15% of the agency's Medicare revenues with no maximum limit (National Association for Home Care, 1998). This may prove to be an exorbitant expense for agencies with large Medicare budgets. This is exacerbated by the fact that home care agencies are required to hold separate bonds for both Medicare and Medicaid. These requirements will be especially problematic for voluntary, not-for-profit home health agencies because collateral and guarantees are required from board members. However, volunteer board members may not be able to personally guarantee the value of the bond, which, in some cases, could exceed $1 million (National Association for Home Care, 1998a).

Initial determinations of eligibility for Medicare are made by the home health care agency. This can be problematic, especially if agency staff are not well versed in Medicare procedures and regulations. Reimbursement under Medicare can be inconsistent. Medicare denial of claims is usually due to inconsistent interpretation (on the part of agency staff) of the Medicare criteria concerning intermittent care, homebound or skilled care. Because the agency has already provided the service in anticipation of later reimbursement, denials can be critical to the fiscal stability of the agency. These issues become more problematic given the recent and dramatic changes in eligibility and coverage. Training for agency staff will be crucial to avoid denials. Likewise, the increase in medical reviews since the BBA may result in an increased denial rate (National Association for Home Care, 1998b).

MEDICAID

Medicaid, or Title XIX of the Social Security Act enacted in 1965, also focused on acute care. As Medicare offered a restricted home health care benefit available only for skilled care needs and for postacute situations, Medicaid placed greater emphasis on institutional alternatives to a postacute stay. Medicaid provided incentives for states to subsidize institutional care (Stevens & Stevens, 1974). States were not forced to fund in-home services even at minimal levels. Simply mentioning such services in legislation or regulations was deemed sufficient to meet the legislative mandate. It was not until 1967 that amendments to Social Security made home health care mandatory rather than optional under Medicaid.

Eventually, as with Medicare, concerns mounted over the increase in medical costs, and home care was considered as an alternative solution that would reduce overall health care expenditures. Also, Medicaid expansion into home care provided an alternative to premature institutionalization. Recent figures demonstrate the expansion in the Medicaid home health care program. Next to Medicare, Medicaid is the second most significant funder of in-home services. According to Applebaum (1997, p. 3) "in 1982 1.2% of the long-term care Medicaid expenditures were allocated to home care." By 1987, 9.8% were spent on home care, and by 1996 20.7% of Medicaid expenditures were allocated to home care.

Medicaid is a joint program pooling federal and state resources to aid low income individuals. Benefits and specific eligibility criteria (categoric and financial) vary from state to state. However, patients must generally meet an income requirement, must require nursing supervision, must have physician authorization of need, and must have a periodic review of care provision. States have a great deal of flexibility in relation to the types of services that will be covered (Rosenzweig, 1995). Generally speaking, states are required to provide services uniformly throughout the state. Medicaid can pay for such services as: home nursing care, home health aides, personal care services, medical supplies and equipment, physical therapy, occupational therapy, and speech therapy. Medicaid benefits are extremely limited, usually only covering part-time care. Also, Medicaid usually reimburses at a lower rate than Medicare. However, Medicaid does not require a skilled need to provide home care services, such as nurse aids, attendant care, and so forth.

States provide Medicaid home health benefits under three options: (a) home health services; (b) personal care optional service; and (c) home and community-based waiver programs (Burwell, 1997). Under the home health services plan states must provide mandatory services on a part-time or intermittent basis, including nursing, home health aides, and durable medical equipment and supplies (Rosenzweig, 1995). Many states also cover optional services including physical, speech, and occupational therapy (Folkemer, 1994). However, states can severely limit the amount of service provided because the federal government sets no minimum.

States can also choose to provide optional home care services. These include: personal care, private duty nursing, respiratory therapy for ventilator-dependent patients, hospice, and optional home and community care for functionally impaired older people (Rosenzweig, 1995). Although many of these services would focus on the traditional home care patient, they could also be used to expand available services to the high-tech patient in some cases. This will depend on whether patients are dually eligible for Medicare and Medicaid and at what levels of eligibility they fall. Those with lower incomes may be eligible for Medicaid to cover additional services. Whereas those with higher incomes may only be eligible for coverage of the Medicare premium and copays through Medicaid.

Medicaid waiver programs were initially authorized in 1981 "to allow states to apply for a federal waiver to use Medicaid funds for nonmedical long-term care services" (Applebaum, 1997, p. 3). Generally speaking eligibility for waiver programs is the same as eligibility for Medicaid subsidized nursing home care in each state. In other words, states apply for a waiver to provide in-home services for patients who would otherwise be institutionalized. The plan allows for service to chronically ill and disabled persons or persons over age 65. In addition to service criteria, Medicaid has program criteria, including financial and categoric criteria (O'Keefe, 1996).

Although these programs have traditionally focused on serving patients with chronic care needs, such as providing personal attendant services, home health aid services, case management, adult day care, rehabilitation, and respite, there may still be potential benefits under waiver programs for high-tech patients. First, these programs might be used to provide additional support to the patient for the less technical care needs, such as bathing, laundry, and housekeeping. This might allow patients with limited or no informal support mechanisms to remain at home with high-tech care. In addition, waiver programs more recently have expanded the types of care and services they will reimburse, including more technical types of services. For example, support from the waiver program might be utilized to assist the patient in purchasing or renting the necessary equipment that may not be covered by their insurance or Medicare, for example a new refrigerator to store medicine. Also, waiver programs can expend resources for home adaptations that might allow a patient on a ventilator to come home once the electrical support has been upgraded. It might also be used to supplement additional hours of nursing or therapeutic services.

VETERANS BENEFITS

Veterans may be eligible for a limited amount of home health care under the Veteran's Administration (VA) medical system. The main home care program under the VA is referred to as aid and attendant care. This is available to any veteran with an honorable discharge who also has a permanent and total disability either nonservice connected or service connected. These veterans receive an additional pension or compensation that can then be used to cover the costs of in-home care. Veterans who have a

service connected disability may also be eligible for grants for prosthetic devices and home modifications.

PRIVATE INSURANCE

Some patients will have private insurance that they pay for independently or that they receive through employment or retirement benefits (i.e., through a union plan). Many private insurance plans, including both indemnity type plans and managed care plans, offer some amount of home health care coverage. The home health care benefit, however, is likely to vary from plan to plan. This will be true for both traditional home health care services and high-tech treatments. These plans usually limit the number of visits allowed and may also set limits on the types of services covered or may charge various copayments or deductibles for specific services. It is essential to check with the patient's insurance company to determine what services are covered if feasible in advance of patient admission. If possible, an actual copy of the policy or contract that details available benefits and restrictions on those benefits should be obtained. Getting it in writing is a beneficial yet frequently overlooked strategy for protecting patient rights and agency financial stability.

Home health care administrators should be well acquainted with state and federal law establishing standards of practice both in relation to third-party reimbursement and basic medical care. In the latter situation, the law may restrict insurance limitations or special conditions for eligibility. For example, if certain treatments are required under the state licensing board or practice act to be provided by professional staff, then the insurance company cannot demand the substitution of paraprofessional staff. Likewise, they would have to reimburse at a rate consistent with the degree of professional involvement. In addition, insurance providers are generally restricted in relation to changes in benefit packages during the benefit cycle.

In many cases agency staff may become patient advocates to protect patient rights and insure that patients receive the benefits to which they are entitled. This may include assisting the patient or patient's family in filing an appeal of denial of benefits with the insurer or with the state insurance commission. If the home health agency is a member of the insurance company's provider network, there may be a conflict of interest. In such cases the home care agency may choose to refer the patient to a community-based advocacy group, such as the ombudsman, or community legal services.

PAYING FOR HIGH-TECH SERVICES

Not all high-tech services are approved for provision in the home. It is important to check the specific insurance (Medicare, Medicaid, private insurance) to determine whether the particular treatment prescribed can be covered. Also, there may be limits on the types of medical equipment that the insurer will cover. For example, Medicare covers durable medical equipment only if prescribed by a doctor and required for the patient to remain at home. Medicare covers 80% of the cost of purchase or rental, whichever is cheaper. Patients can consider whether to purchase or to rent equipment, depending on the amount of time the equipment will be needed and the cost for either.

SUMMARY

Although much research has demonstrated the cost effective nature of many high-tech home care services, reimbursement for those services will not always be available. Regardless of the insurance coverage, providers must be fully aware of the review practices of third-party payers (either public or proprietary) toward high-tech services. The amount and duration of coverage are essential factors to weigh in deciding to admit a specific high-tech patient or to provide a range of high-tech services. For example, if a particular treatment is viewed as experimental, especially by the Health Care Financing Administration (HCFA), then many proprietary third-party systems will not offer that service as an approved benefit. If the patient is admitted to the high-tech service prior to receiving approval and the patient cannot afford to pay privately, the agency may incur the financial burden of serving the patient until an adequate discharge plan can be implemented.

A thorough understanding of the patient's insurance coverage is essential to protect the health and safety of the patient as well as the fiscal stability of the agency. Such issues as duration of benefits, amount and type of benefits covered, limits or restrictions on coverage, and the nature of eligibility criteria should be obtained in writing from the insurer if the patient has private coverage. In addition, agency staff should be familiar with reimbursement policies under Medicare and Medicaid. This is especially important given the recent changes under the BBA. Staff will need training to remain up-to-date on policy changes. Likewise, given the new

limits on reimbursement, decisions surrounding the admittance of patients and the amount of service that can be provided will become even more complicated.

Staff may need to be creative in their efforts to identify other funding sources for patients. In this light, medical social work may become an even more important service in home health care. Social work staff may be asked to assist in identifying additional sources of funding for patients, including community-based agencies, religious groups, and so forth as well as coordinating informal support systems. The mandate to maintain patients safely in their own homes justifies such advocacy efforts in home health care.

CHAPTER 11

Taking the Plunge into High-Tech Care: Guidelines for Providers

INTRODUCTION

As demand for high-tech services increases, and all projections indicate this trend will persist, more and more agency administrators will choose to plunge their agencies into the high-tech world. In choosing to provide high-tech services (or for that matter to expand existing high-tech services), agency administrators enter a realm of transition and challenge. The decision warrants detailed consideration and evaluation of agency resources, market forces, and potential pitfalls. This chapter will consider the major areas for concern and will raise important questions, which should be considered by those agency directors pondering the decision to provide high-tech care. This information will also benefit those agencies that have already entered the high-tech pool; providing helpful strategies and methods for evaluating the existing structure and organization of such services. The chapter will review organizational and management issues, patient-centered concerns, quality assurance and improvement techniques, and matters related to fiscal management. The purpose is to provide practical and straightforward recommendations for responding to the demands of delivering high-tech services safely and effectively.

TESTING THE WATERS: INITIAL STEPS
IN DEVELOPING A HIGH-TECH UNIT

There are a variety of ways that an agency can begin providing high-tech services. The most expedient strategy might well be to contract with another health care agency already experienced in providing a particular service (e.g., IV antibiotics) or group of services (e.g., all infusion therapies) (dipping a toe in the high-tech pool, if you will). An agency with adequate resources that is less interested in complex contracting arrangements might choose to provide services directly. This can be pursued as a gradual process (perhaps getting one's feet wet, to stick with our analogy) of selecting one high-tech treatment and providing it directly. Another approach would be to offer a range of services that are specific and limited, such as infusion therapies. Finally, the agency can choose to establish itself as a provider of any high-tech service that is determined to be needed in a particular community. Whether you merely dip a toe (i.e., subcontract) or you take the plunge (provide an exhaustive list of high-tech services) depends on a variety of factors.

Several factors, which include market forces and trends, agency resources, and market saturation, warrant thorough assessment prior to program implementation. A feasibility study is an important first step in determining whether to develop a high-tech service unit, even if that unit only provides one technologically enhanced therapy. This planning process may focus on "a whole system, one or more subsystems, or specific program areas or target groups" (Witkin & Altschuld, 1995). For example, the agency may wish to provide a particular type of high-tech treatment to a particular target group (e.g., IV antibiotics to older adults) or offer a full range of services (e.g., all infusion therapies to adults and children). Although the market may be larger in the latter case, the degree of complexity of providing such a menu of services is important to consider as well. We will come back to this in a moment.

Assessing Need

Whether providing a range of services or one service, a determination of need must first be made. What is the potential market for high-tech services? What is the actual need or demand for these types of services? To what extent will your agency be able to satisfy the existing need or demand in the community? The assessment should illuminate both the prevalence of need as well as the specific services needed. The latter issue relates to specific target groups and the kinds of services that particular patients may need. Prevalence, on the other hand, will provide information on general need as well as the degree or severity of need within particular target groups.

Accessing Data Sources

A variety of data sources may be used to gain an understanding of the scope and prevalence of need. In many cases administrators may be able to utilize existing data for this analysis. For example, census data can give information on the number and proportion of older adults in a particular geographic area. Agency (e.g., hospitals, adult day care programs, senior centers, and other health and social services organizations) data bases can also provide useful information about potential target groups, such as persons with disabilities, or the prevalence of particular diagnoses that may be more likely to warrant high-tech intervention. In particular, hospital admissions and discharge records may indicate prevalence of need for certain types of follow-up care as well as the types and amount of high-tech services currently being used in a particular community or region. For example, increased use of subacute facilities may indicate the need for high-tech home care (Kaye & Davitt, 1995c).

On the other hand, existing data may be inaccurate or may lack the comprehensive qualities desired. In this case the assessment may require original data collection. New data may be generated through key person or expert interviews, surveys, creating agency data bases, or focus groups. Whether using existing data or collecting new data, the data should provide a thorough understanding of the need for high-tech care. It should afford an opportunity to estimate overall prevalence of need as well as to identify need within particular target groups.

Determining Service Groups

Once the scope of the need is determined, the next factor concerns whether existing providers are adequately meeting the need. The range of high-tech providers already operating in the service area must be determined. The important issue is whether the market can bear another high-tech provider. By entering the market the new provider may duplicate existing services, fragment the service delivery network, or orchestrate its own drowning and ultimate demise in an overcrowded pool of providers.

Through the assessment it may be discovered that the entire market is saturated or that a particular service is saturated leaving room for another agency to offer those less available services. If the entire market is saturated, the choice to enter the market may be unwise. Costs to the agency in establishing any new service (for administrative overhead, staff training, recruitment, and marketing) are substantial, and the agency may not be able to recoup these in a highly competitive market (Kaye & Davitt, 1995c).

Agency Capacity

The agency's capacity for providing specific high-tech services must also be evaluated. This is the final component in the feasibility study and is similar to a resource study in that it examines issues related to personnel, training, fiscal stability and available capital, and expertise. The agency must either have the capacity, given existing resources or the ability to expand the existing agency resource base through creative use of capital to develop a high-tech service unit. Such expansion issues may include: providing staff with additional training; hiring new, specially trained staff; purchasing special equipment; and developing new systems for 24-hour coverage and crisis intervention.

Internal agency issues such as maintaining congruence with the mission statement, insuring future fiscal stability, and committing the organization to on-going self-evaluation also must be assessed. The agency's mission statement may clearly limit the types of treatments that can be offered, as, for example in the case of hospice providers. A hospice might provide infusion-based palliative care, such as morphine drips, but might not provide in-home chemotherapy because the latter is more often viewed as an active form of treatment. However, an agency with a more broad-based mission may provide all types of high-tech services. Expanding services can also create fiscal instability in that the initial investments in the expansion may be exceedingly high. Therefore, agencies with existing cash-flow problems may need to stabilize prior to expansion. These issues warrant consideration regardless of whether the agency decides to provide only one high-tech service or a comprehensive set of services.

Market Trends and Forces

The range and type of services provided ultimately become a function of market trends and agency resources. An agency administrator may in a competitive market choose to provide services gradually, beginning with a particular service(s) that is (are) not currently available. In a less competitive market, a broader range of services may be initiated simultaneously but only if the agency has the resources for such extensive augmentation. By looking at both market forces and agency resources, the feasibility study may also help to determine which approach to service delivery is most appropriate, direct service delivery or subcontracting. In an intensely competitive environment, agencies may opt to subcontract. Other agencies that specialize in a particular intervention may be better equipped to continue providing these treatments. The agency may also choose to subcontract due to resource constraints such as size, staffing shortages, or limits on staff expertise.

THE PARTIAL PLUNGE: SUBCONTRACTING HIGH-TECH SERVICES

Subcontracting of high-tech services generates different but related concerns from direct provision of services. The most important concern in this case is assuring that the subcontracting agency has the requisite resources, experience, and technical expertise to provide the services. Although the contracting agency may not have to provide initial staff training and ongoing in-services, direct staff supervision, emergency or trouble-shooting interventions, nor patient education related to the high-tech services, it still needs to have policies and procedures in place to ensure that quality services are being delivered. It is essential that the contracting agency thoroughly assess and evaluate the capabilities of the potential subcontractor. Several questions must be answered prior to establishing such a relationship. These questions, which are listed in Table 11.1, will help the contracting agency to assure that quality services are being provided and that patients are being supported safely in their homes.

Interagency Cooperation and Quality Assurance

The need for open communication and cooperation between agencies is pivotal to the successful delivery of high-tech care. Although the subcontractor is responsible for direct delivery of the high-tech service, contracting agency staff will (in most cases) be interacting with the client and therefore may need to have some understanding of the high-tech treatment or at least should be familiar with that aspect of the treatment plan. Concerns

TABLE 11.1   Essential Questions in Subcontracting Relationships

* How long has the subcontractor been providing the services in question?
* Do they have a strong track record or have they violated any regulatory requirements in relation to this service?
* Do they have a comprehensive quality assurance plan, including staff training, supervision, coverage issues, and agency evaluation?
* How does the agency handle 24-hour coverage and emergency intervention?
* What training does the agency offer staff? (frequency, duration, and content)?

pertaining to interagency communication and cooperation arise both in everyday care delivery as well as in emergency situations. For example, if a patient receiving IV antibiotics begins to show signs of anaphylactic shock, which agency would the caregiver call and which agency would be expected to respond in this situation (the contractor or subcontractor)? The manner in which these types of concerns will be handled must be mutually resolved prior to the crisis and therefore warrant much discussion between the two agencies prior to admitting any patients under a subcontract arrangement. They also require procedures to assure continual communication between agencies.

Questions may also arise regarding who is responsible for direct supervision of high-tech staff. This must be decided in advance of admitting patients and must be agreed to by both agencies. It is logical that the subcontracting agency would supervise those staff responsible for high-tech treatments, however, this does not necessarily mean that the contracting agency has no responsibility in providing quality care. Again, it is essential for the contractor to determine that the subcontracting agency has adequate policies and procedures for supervising such staff in addition to quality education and training. The contracting agency may still by held legally responsible for negligence on the part of the subcontractor. (Please refer to chapter 8 for a more detailed discussion of legal liability.)

Other issues must be considered prior to entering a subcontracting agreement. Most notably client confidentiality procedures must be reviewed for both agencies. Procedures for sharing information must be established that promote the cooperative effort essential to these cases while protecting the patient's privacy. Such procedures must also be explained in detail to the patient. Informed consent to share information between agencies should be obtained directly from the patient whenever possible or from the patient's

TABLE 11.2   Interagency Cooperation and Quality Assurance

Establish open channels of communication.

Determine each agency's responsibilities in advance (e.g., who is responsible for staff supervision?; how will emergencies be handled?).

Establish procedures for sharing information to protect client confidentiality.

Insure that the subcontractor has established procedures for client appeal of decisions.

Develop procedures concerning the handling of reimbursement arrangements (through primary agency or directly to the subcontractor?).

---

attorney-in-fact, healthcare proxy, or guardian or conservator if the patient is unable to give informed consent.

Reimbursement Issues

Reimbursement questions can also be more complicated in a subcontracting arrangement. It is important first to determine whether a particular third-party reimbursement source will accept such an arrangement. It would be irresponsible to admit a patient for high-tech care only to discover that the agency cannot provide such care through a subcontractor because the patient's insurance does not approve the provision of such service. In this case the patient would either have to be transferred to another agency or the agency would have to provide the service without reimbursement. Given the expensive nature of high-tech services, an agency could quickly approach a fiscal crisis under these circumstances. Likewise, it would be essential to determine whether subcontracting is cost effective, either for a particular service or for a particular patient. It is possible that the level of reimbursement will not be adequate to support the administrative expenses of two agencies.

If it is determined that reimbursement is adequate and acceptable, then the logistics of payment must be arranged between the two agencies. For example, will the lead agency accept the third-party reimbursement and then pay the subcontractor; or will the payment go directly to the subcontractor? At times these questions may be decided at the source. For example, the insurer may reimburse the subcontractor for high-tech services while reimbursing the lead agency for all other services. Or the insurer may choose to pay a capitated rate to the main agency out of which the agency then reimburses the subcontractor.

Although subcontracting high-tech services may appear less burdensome and may be an appropriate strategy, this is not always the case. As mentioned earlier, several factors warrant assessment to make an appropriate decision whether to engage in the provision of high-tech care and the modality or modalities of that provision.

TAKING THE PLUNGE: PROVIDING HIGH-TECH SERVICES DIRECTLY

Providing high-tech services directly (or expanding existing high-tech services) requires careful consideration and planning. Agencies may decide to phase-in services gradually; or, they may decide to begin by providing a full range of high-tech services. This decision may be affected by market competition; the greater the competition, the smaller the range of services initiated. In either case, there are several issues that warrant consideration prior to actually admitting patients to the high-tech service.

Personnel Management: Ensuring the Pool Has Enough Lifeguards

Education and Training

Once the agency has determined (through the feasibility study) the level and types of expertise staff will need to provide the specific high-tech services selected, the next step is to ensure that there is ample access to staff with this expertise. Lack of adequate numbers of trained staff is one of the top mentioned challenges in providing high-tech care. Certain strategies may be utilized to ensure that the agency has access to properly trained staff. This may include expanded staff training, recruitment and hiring of new specially trained staff, as well as generally expanding the number of staff because patient census should rise due to the new services.

Agencies may choose to hire new staff with special skills related to the specific treatments to be offered. However, these staff will benefit from ongoing education and training. Although the professional staff will come to their positions within the agency with some very essential training and knowledge acquired in previous settings, continuing education is crucial to provide the training that was not received prior to employment and is essential to the position to be filled. Changes in regulations, treatment modalities, and technologies are just some of the challenges for which staff will need ongoing training. Training and education is even more important when utilizing existing staff for high-tech service delivery. Expansion into new service delivery modalities requires that staff skills and education be continually updated. Equipment and treatment modalities change rapidly in the high-tech arena. New innovations are surfacing every day. Staff are expected to master these new modalities to remain competitive with other home health providers. Therefore it becomes the agency's responsibility to ensure that their personnel are trained in contemporary high-tech methods and techniques. Direct care staff are the pivotal element of home health care delivery. They provide the regular hands-on care to patients as well as conducting ongoing assessments of the patient's health status. Therefore, it is important to ensure that these staff are trained to provide the services the agency has committed to provide to the patient.

Training and education are essential to quality practice for a variety of reasons. First and foremost, education and training can enhance staff skill and knowledge related to the provision of service. This can be important in terms of alleviating problems related in transition from one staff member to another. Perhaps more importantly it reduces staff burnout, improves staff morale, and provides incentives to deliver quality care because it provides opportunities to grow and advance in the field. Because nurses take an active role in teaching patients and families how to use equipment or monitor treatments, they will also benefit from training in teaching methods. It should not be automatically assumed that all staff will make good teachers. But teaching methods can be taught.

Agencies can employ both internal and external resources to fulfill training requirements. Specifically, experienced staff may be utilized as trainers for existing staff. On the other hand, external training programs may offer comprehensive educational packages that are more expedient. In either case, it is essential with new services that supervisory staff attend the same or very similar training as the direct care staff to insure that services can be monitored effectively. Content of training programs will vary according to the individual treatment. However, at a minimum training should cover specific treatment-related procedures; identifying signs and symptoms of problems; proper use of equipment; training patients or family on treatment; and troubleshooting in emergencies.

Training a Full Range of Staff

Agencies may use paraprofessionals to provide services or support the professional staff. These staff need ongoing training as much as the professional staff. Unfortunately, not all home health care agencies are committed to training all staff in relation to high-tech services. The focus of most high-tech training seems to be on nurses, with other professional (therapists, and social workers) and paraprofessional groups (home health aids, homemakers, home attendants) not receiving training as frequently. However, many home health aides and other paraprofessionals are in the home more frequently than skilled nurses and may at times be called on to troubleshoot in relation to equipment or complicated treatment routines. For example, if the caregiver wishes to leave the home when the aide is present for respite or other responsibilities, it may be expected that the aide would then monitor the patient's care needs and treatment. In fact, our research confirms that many home health aides are assisting regularly in the delivery or monitoring of high-tech services, as are professionals other than nurses, such as social workers and physical therapists. Unfortunately, only one in every two home health aides and professional staff other than nurses are participating in specialized agency training as compared to nine of every 10 nurses.

This inevitable and perhaps unanticipated spread of responsibility by staff other than nurses into the area of high-tech service provision is worrisome if it occurs without the benefits of continual upgrades in their practice knowledge base. If these staff are not receiving training in the

TABLE 11.3   Staff Training Tips

Target your staff population—Interdisciplinary vs. discipline-specific training, professional vs. paraprofessional, nursing vs. all staff, etc. In many cases the topic or subject matter will help you to decide.

Keep abreast of new developments—Service innovations, new equipment, policy changes, research, etc. Plan regular inservice programs using input from all staff.

Encourage staff participation—Allow staff to be directly involved in planning and presenting education programs both for staff and patients. Mutual responsibility enhances learning, motivation, and loyalty.

Use adult learning principles—People learn differently. Alternate training methods. People learn most by doing, rather than simply reading or listening. Remember to provide handouts in all training that provide staff with a summary and quick reference tool to use in their daily work.

Don't overwhelm or bore staff—Make sure material is meaningful to staff.

---

*For additional tips on training see Kaye, L. W. (1992). *Home health care*, Newbury Park, CA: Sage.

particular treatments to which they are exposed, the patient may be left in a precarious situation. It is important for agencies to be aware of this problem and to provide essential training to all staff who may be called on to provide high-tech care directly as well as provide ancillary assistance including monitoring such services. All staff should be provided with training on dealing with emergencies and crisis intervention. The variation in training protocols for different staff will be reflected in the focus and intensity of training. At a minimum the training for all staff should consist of teaching similar to that provided to families.

Coverage Issues

Providing adequate patient care coverage is another challenge to home health care, especially for high-tech patients. Because staff may specialize in particular categories of treatment, there may be problems with coverage if there are not adequate numbers of trained staff who can handle a particular patient's care needs. Providing 24-hour coverage is especially tricky for high-tech providers, because many patients may need to be seen in the middle of the night or on weekends rather than during the traditional business day. For example, home dialysis patients or patients receiving infusion-based nutrition may prefer to initiate treatment during the night hours to avoid interruptions in work schedules. Unless or until the patient is trained and able to administer the treatment independently, agency staff will be required to visit at night. Even after the patient has been adequately trained, emergencies may still arise that will warrant in-person staff assessment.

When considering patient services, full-time employment status may serve to reduce the amount of turnover that clients sometimes experience when receiving home health care. If more staff work full time, there will be less variation in the staff who see each patient. Likewise, lesser use of part-time staff can reduce the amount of logistical planning and coordination necessary to schedule adequate coverage. However, dependence on full-time staff can also reduce the number of available replacement staff, leading to potential difficulties in ensuring that coverage is readily available when staff are sick, on vacation, or otherwise unavailable to work.

When providing high-tech services it is essential to develop back-up and emergency intervention plans should regular staff be unavailable when a crisis arises. Such procedures may include site visits to assess the patient, to deal with faulty equipment or power outages, or to provide crisis-based treatment interventions. Emergency interventions can also be problematic

TABLE 11.4   Policies and Procedures of High-Tech Providers

- Admissions criteria and procedures
- Staffing requirements
- Discharge criteria and procedures
- Quality assurance procedures
- Informed consent
- Ethical decisions
- Dealing with conflict
- Monitoring staff performance
- Monitoring service delivery
- Ongoing evaluation
- Advance directives

if in fact there are not adequate staff to cover such emergencies. While part-time staff will seem to have certain drawbacks in relation to issues of turnover, increased use of part-time staff may actually be one solution to the problem of emergency coverage. By having more staff who work fewer hours the agency can spread coverage demands across staff, thereby reducing the potential for staff burnout due to coverage issues or emergency interventions. For example, a larger staff may reduce the number of nights and weekends per month that any individual staff member is required to be on call. In addition, the agency may be able to offer patients greater flexibility regarding the scheduling of appointments, offering more evening and weekend visits.

Quality Assurance

We have already discussed the need for policies and procedures on training and education and staffing requirements. Quality assurance is another policy that should be established and enforced throughout the agency. Quality assurance should be used to improve quality, not just to monitor quality. This can help improve patient outcomes by enhancing staff performance and providing best practice methods for service delivery. The most important aspect of quality assurance is to establish consistent policies and procedures. This promotes consistency in service delivery, enhances staff morale, and provides a source of guidance for staff in difficult situations.

In addition to training and education, staff need adequate supervision. This is important both from a quality assurance perspective and from a staff support perspective. In the latter case, staff need to feel that they have an accessible resource for troubleshooting difficult cases and for understanding new treatment modalities. The National HomeCaring Council defines supervision as "the means by which an agency assures itself, the community and the policy body that its programs and services are provided in the most effective and efficient manner. As a process, supervision is the means by which workers are helped to perform the jobs for which they will be held accountable" (Gilroy, Trager, & Kinney, 1982 p. xvii). Home health care supervisors are responsible for staff accountability, evaluation of staff performance, coordination of staff service schedules, and ongoing education and training of staff. Some of the tasks that a home care supervisor may be involved in include: staff recruitment and selection; new staff orientation and continuing education; worker assignments and scheduling; ongoing monitoring of staff performance and worker-patient relations; administrative responsibilities; and providing staff support in difficult cases.

Supervisory staff need knowledge and skills in direct service delivery. They must understand the difficult nature of providing care in the home to very frail and disabled populations. Without this knowledge it is very difficult to support and assist staff in the field. Likewise, they must have a complete understanding of agency policies and procedures as well as regulations and standards of practice. Finally, they need advanced skills in communication, training, organizational process, and problem solving.

The increase in demand for high-tech in-home care has been documented in the research reported here as well as elsewhere (Estes et al., 1993; Mehlman & Younger, 1991). Even so, the assignment of high-tech patients is not always consistent across staff. Some staff will have no high-tech patients while others will have all high-tech patients. The fact that some staff may be handling all high-tech patients could lead to burnout, if in fact these are very complicated cases. Given the intense nature of service delivery to such patients the issue of burnout may well be even more important for agencies serving high-tech patients.

One method for alleviating burnout is to involve staff in the planning of high-tech services at the agency. Maximizing the involvement of personnel in agency planning has its advantages and should be seriously considered by agency directors. Staff are able to more readily appreciate the connections between overall agency systems and procedures and individual patient needs. This may be an important strategy for building allegiance and commitment among both professionals and paraprofessionals in a field of service that has traditionally been beset with high turnover and burnout rates. Engaging more field staff in the planning function will also better use their direct and often intimate knowledge of the status and needs of the consumer population, and it is an appropriate strategy for promoting total quality improvement.

There are a variety of options available to administrators who wish to seek staff feedback on agency procedures and service delivery. The most expedient method may be to incorporate staff feedback into existing supervisory activities, such as supervisory meetings, staff meetings, and case reviews. These methods can be used in an ongoing fashion to promote the agency's ability to respond quickly and effectively to changes in market forces and to client demands. Other, more formal approaches may be used as well. These will generally be conducted less frequently and may be more focused on overall agency issues and concerns, such as whether to include a new treatment in the service package and how to establish the new service. Such formal methods may include: focus groups, staff surveys, and staff participation in long-range planning meetings.

Admissions Criteria

Each agency should have very specific admissions criteria that staff can use as a guide in making high-tech home care admissions decisions. These criteria will help to avoid potential problems, such as insufficient service to meet patient needs, lack of monitoring and emergency intervention, or inadequate agency reimbursement. Use of a screening tool, such as an intake form, will promote consistency in making such decisions. This information can be gathered from several sources. However, one should always begin with the patient. If necessary, collateral contacts can be made later to clarify or obtain additional information. Intake and screening are essential components of a well-run high-tech program. Several factors related to the specific patient must be reviewed prior to admitting a patient for high-tech service. These issues are summarized in Table 11.5.

The ability of the patient to learn to handle his or her own care is frequently cited as an admissions criterion by agencies. High-tech patients in particular tend to have heavier care needs of greater duration and intensity. Rarely are enough resources available to maintain 24-hour staff presence in the home. Unfortunately, many high-tech patients receive treatment around the clock (e.g., tube feedings and infusion therapy). Limitations on the amount of service that can be provided to the patient

TABLE 11.5   Intake and Screening Questions

- Does the patient have sufficient informal support (is there an available caregiver)?
- Can the patient/caregiver do self-care tasks? What potential does the patient/caregiver have to learn treatment-related tasks?
- Is the patient/caregiver intimidated by complex equipment?
- Is the home environment adequate and safe for the provision of high-tech care (e.g., sanitary, electrical access and supply, space for equipment)?
- Do you have staff available who have the expertise and experience to handle the patient's specific treatment?
- Has the patient ever received this treatment before (e.g., in hospital)? Does the physician approve home care?
- What is the patient's prognosis? Will this affect the ability to be cared for at home?
- How will the patient pay for services (insurance, private pay, Medicare)?
- How much service can the patient receive (i.e., afford or get under insurance)?
- Is the patient in a reasonably accessible location?

increase the need for the patient to become an active participant in the provision of treatment.

Clearly, providers should be concerned about the complex nature of high-tech patient care. Given the potential frailty of the patient population served, agencies legitimately should be concerned that patients may not be able to handle their own care needs and therefore will need caregivers who can be available when staff are not there. However, it is important in terms of this issue for agencies to recognize the potential for bias in patient admission. As indicated in previous chapters, high-tech beneficiaries are substantially different from the traditional home care patient demographically. Certain types of patients may be eliminated from the high-tech service pool simply because they lack a caregiver. These include older women, African Americans and other people of color, and those living alone. However, patients without a caregiver should not be automatically rejected from high-tech care. Rather, a complete assessment should be conducted to determine if these patients can manage their own care and or to identify other informal supports on which they may be able to rely. Creativity in relation to the care plan may be the key to ensuring that all patients have equal access to such services in their homes.

Among the most pivotal issues considered during screening is the safety of the home environment. Many home environments may not be suitable to support the complex equipment or procedures needed by the patient. For example, patients' homes may not have adequate power supplies to handle sophisticated electrical equipment, or patients' homes may be unsanitary, or lacking adequate space or other utilities.

When reviewing a case for admission, keep in mind that one must determine eligibility for service as well as the appropriateness of service provision. In other words, a patient may have a clear need for medical services, but service provision by a home health agency in the patient's home may be inappropriate given the level of need and inability of the patient to complete even minimal self-care tasks or the adequacy of the home environment.

Also, the administrator must address the problem that arises related to reimbursement denials. Providing additional unreimbursed services to high-tech patients may exhaust financial reserves much more quickly than it would with traditional home care patients. Careful assessment of the reimbursement environment for a particular patient is essential to the overall fiscal health of the agency. (See chapter 10 for a more detailed discussion of reimbursement factors.)

Agencies that lack admissions criteria may end up providing service to all types of patients regardless of diagnoses or treatment modality. This triggers questions regarding quality of service, training needs of staff, and the capacity of agencies to respond to all care needs and to provide all types of treatments. It also raises questions pertaining to agency liability. At what point is the agency responsible for ensuring that a particular patient's care needs can be adequately met? Likewise, if an agency does not have set criteria for staff to follow, how then are admissions decisions made?

The need for admissions criteria may not be applicable for certain types of agencies with very specific missions. For example, hospice providers are less likely to have such criteria (Kaye & Davitt, 1998). This may be due to the nature of the service provided by such agencies. Although the patient may be receiving high-tech services, the emphasis is on palliative care, maintaining the patient in a comfortable setting until the patient dies. The fact that hospice providers only serve terminal patients in the end stage of their illness may be a sufficient criterion in and of itself.

Patient Education and Training

Patients and their relatives more often than not can be expected to participate in various aspects of their own high-tech care. To do so safely they need to be well versed in proper procedures. Education and training of patients and caregivers is therefore essential and must be innovative, thorough, and geared to the specific patient. Some families' learning may be enhanced by reading written descriptions of tasks to be performed. Others will prefer demonstrations or videotaped reviews. In addition, staff should be aware of the learning abilities of each patient or family. For example, research has shown that older adults retain more information when there are less distracting background noises to contend with.

The following tips may be useful when teaching older adult clients. Consider the patient's learning potential and use different training styles and media for different patients and family members based on their learning styles and abilities. Physical ability can be affected by declines in sensory abilities including vision, hearing, and tactile sensitivity as well as mobility and dexterity. These can impact the patient's ability to absorb information provided in a teaching session, as well as the ability to implement newly taught skills or tasks. The trainer should be aware of specific deficits for each patient to design the most appropriate educational program for that patient. For example, if a patient has severe visual impairment, written descriptions of self-care tasks will not be helpful. It is important to observe the patient in action to ensure that the procedure has been learned and, more importantly, that the task can be accomplished independently.

In addition, the patient's illness may in some cases impact the ability to learn or perform required tasks. The illness itself or the treatment may negatively affect sensory organs, cognitive abilities, and physical strength. For example, if a patient is receiving pain killers, this may have a dulling effect on the patient's senses. Also, if the patient is receiving chemotherapy, the side effects may so weaken the patient that they will not be physically able to perform requisite tasks. This again highlights the need for a caregiver for certain patients. However, patients will respond differently to treatments and therefore will have differing capabilities for self-care. The need for a caregiver must be assessed on a case-by-case basis.

Likewise, the aging process can impact cognitive processes. Research has shown that processing time for older adults is longer, while response time is slower. Therefore the speed at which information is presented is crucial when working with an older population. (It is even more essential when working with patients who have pathological cognitive deficits.) Older adults need longer exposure to material with more time between exposures for processing. Because background noise can be very disruptive to older adults, the trainer should be aware of the environment in which training will occur. Depending on the patient's physical and cognitive abilities, the trainer may want to use some of the strategies highlighted in Table 11.6.

Ethical and Legal Issues

Choosing to provide high-tech services can also increase the risk of liability. The most common contributors to this heightened liability risk are the need for increased professional skill, the use of complicated equipment, the need for more frequent communication with the physician, the increased frailty of the patient, the need for continual monitoring of treatment, and the responsibilities of monitoring multiple service providers.

The increased provision of high-tech services in the home is accompanied by the likelihood that home health care agency staff will increasingly need to face a variety of patient's rights, right to die, and delegation of authority issues. Agency participation in patient and family decisions around foregoing life-sustaining treatment, preparing living wills, using durable powers of attorney and guardians is not uncommon. Agencies may also find themselves involved in decisions determining patient competence and addressing conflicts between family and patient wishes.

TABLE 11.6   Patient Training Tips

- Use self-paced training materials.
- Check understanding frequently and before moving to the next topic.
- Use several training approaches combining written, verbal, and hands-on cues.
- Repeat key points.
- Use pictures, large print, magnifying aides, appropriate contrasting colors.
- Employ audio aides (remember to eliminate background noise).
- Have patient/family repeat their understanding and perform task.
- Provide adaptive equipment or adapt environment for those with mobility or dexterity deficits.
- Start where the patient is, determine what is already known, correct any misconceptions.
- Assess the psychosocial situation. What fears exist? Beliefs about healing. and medical care? Support from family and friends? Motivation to learn?

Home health care agencies would be advised to consider establishing, if they have not already done so, policies regarding how staff should handle decisions about life-sustaining treatment as well as policies for dealing with patients who have questionable decision-making capacity. For a more detailed discussion of the legal setting see chapter 8 and chapter 9 for ethical considerations.

MARKETING SERVICES

Given the public's lack of familiarity with many high-tech procedures, sensitive marketing of this component of a home health care program is particularly important. Marketing services can be especially important in a highly competitive market of novel in-home treatments. The most common approaches for advertising and publicizing home health agency services include printed brochures and flyers, directory listings, personal presentations and speeches delivered in community programs, and in-person outreach. While personalized forms of marketing such as in-person presentations, community outreach, and operating focus groups with potential service users may require considerable time and energy, past experience confirms that these are considered to be most effective by agency executives. Other appropriate marketing techniques include: placing newspaper or magazine ads, planning special promotions, running public service messages, carrying out consumer surveys, and airing television and radio commercials.

Actually, a variety of direct service home care staff can play an important role in the marketing process. Remember that the home care practitioner has the most direct access to patients, is most likely to receive consumer feedback, is out in the community on a regular basis performing in effect a public relations function during the course of service delivery, and can be counted among those best able to recognize the appropriate targets for marketing, as well as for program expansion and innovation. Agencies should use their own in-house knowledge and expertise to its fullest potential in any marketing or program development plan.

National survey data underscore the advanced age of home health care recipients as well as the predominance of unmarried women receiving in-home services of all types. A large proportion of service beneficiaries is over the age of 75. Home health care has an undeniable gender-specific, gerontologic focus. And, home health care patients are an increasingly aged cohort (Institute for Health and Aging, 1986). These facts highlight the importance of agencies recruiting staff who are sensitive to the special needs of working with an older, female, functionally impaired population. In similar fashion, marketing efforts need to be responsive to changes in the demographic profile of service consumers as well.

SUMMARY

As this chapter clearly indicates, choosing to plunge an agency into the high-tech pool is no simple matter. Prior to expanding agency services a number of factors must be assessed. First and foremost, there must be adequate need for the service to warrant expansion into new treatment modalities. Second, market forces and trends should be thoroughly evaluated to ensure that service expansion is a prudent option both for the agency and the community. This includes determining which specific types of patients the agency may potentially serve. Finally, agency capacity to augment service is a pivotal component in the successful expansion of services.

The agency has several choices when considering expanding the service base. First, managers can choose to provide a full range of services within a specific service area or they can specialize in one type of high-tech service. They can also choose to provide services through a subcontracting arrangement or can develop their own high-tech service package (again this can be a full or limited package). Both market patterns and agency capability will determine the decision to subcontract as well as the decision to provide a full array of high-tech services. If markets are highly saturated and competition is intense, then subcontracting may be the only option. Likewise, in this type of scenario agency administrators may decide to offer a limited number of new services, perhaps those that are not currently being offered elsewhere. If the market is less saturated and competition is low, then a more broad range of services may be provided directly by the agency. The agency must also be both functionally and fiscally capable of taking on new treatments. Agencies with cash flow problems will need to stabilize prior to expanding the service base. In addition, agencies may need to hire new staff or train existing staff to ensure their capacity to serve high-tech patients.

In choosing to provide high-tech services directly or to expand an existing high-tech unit, agency managers need to consider a variety of issues.

First, the agency must have adequate staff with the necessary skills to provide quality treatment to patients in their homes. Expansion into the high-tech care arena may result in additional staff training as well as increased difficulty related to patient care coverage. Plans for emergency interventions and 24-hour back-up may need to be revised to handle the complex treatment plans of high-tech patients. Policies and procedures need to be revised to ensure that quality care is being provided to all patients. This will include a review of patient education programs, patient assessment and admissions criteria, reimbursement issues, and ethical concerns. Finally, to ensure that the new services do not become a financial drain on the agency, a proper plan for outreach, marketing, and patient recruitment is essential. Once these issues have been thoroughly evaluated and proper policies and procedures have been developed, the agency will then be prepared to plunge into the high-tech home health care pool.

CHAPTER 12

Guidelines for
Serving Consumers

INTRODUCTION

Advances in medical technology (miniaturization and portability of equipment, remote electronic patient monitoring, etc.) have dramatically altered the nature of health care delivery in the United States. Greater emphasis on cost effectiveness and on serving the patient in the least restrictive setting have lead to an increased willingness on the part of patients to receive and providers to deliver exceedingly complicated treatments in the home. Patients are discharged sooner and frequently with more complex aftercare needs than ever before (Estes et al., 1993; General Accounting Office, 1996; Kaye and Davitt, 1995). Many patients return home with complex treatments and complicated care needs that are collectively referred to as high-tech care. As defined earlier, high-tech home care service refers to a variety of monitoring devices, sophisticated procedures, and medical equipment that enable treatment in the home that was, until recently, available only in hospitals and other intensive health care facilities. The increased demand for high-tech home health care services has spurned a related increase in the number and types of agencies offering such services (Applebaum, 1997; National Association for Home Care, 1997). With such a rapid influx of providers into the field, concerns abound regarding the quality of care provided (Kaye & Davitt, 1995).

This chapter highlights the advances in high-tech home health care services and reviews the information necessary to insure that patients receive quality services in their home. The focus is on assisting professionals in the home care or health care field counsel clients on the selection of high-tech care in the home. This chapter will provide strategies for assessing the relative benefits and drawbacks to high-tech in-home care for specific patients, as well as important information on how to choose a home health care agency.

THE BENEFITS AND DRAWBACKS
TO HIGH-TECH CARE

There are clear benefits and drawbacks to receiving high-tech services at home. When discussing the positives of high-tech in-home care, providers tend to focus on the great benefit to being home while recuperating from an illness or surgery. Being at home is, for most patients, a more pleasant experience, which, in turn, reduces their stress and increases their comfort. Greater familiarity with surroundings can enhance the patient's comfort. In addition, being at home means that the patient may have enhanced autonomy and flexibility in relation to everyday life activities (Davitt & Kaye, 1995). For example, having family and friends in for a visit (especially children) may promote patient emotional well being. Such arrangements will naturally be more flexible in a home setting than in an institution due to the need in institutional settings to protect the rights of multiple patients. Likewise, patient autonomy in regard to everyday decisions can be enhanced in the home. For example, the patient can have greater flexibility and control over such routines as deciding when to eat meals or whether to watch television or listen to the radio. Although these may seem like trivial matters, they can be very important features of a quality care environment.

However, the potential for enhancing patient comfort is also not foolproof. The influx of staff into the patient's home actually can reduce patient autonomy and flexibility in daily routines. Agency staff need to fit patients into a global schedule for each day, where the routine consists of multiple patient visits. In many cases arranging staff visits around the patient's schedule may prove impossible. This can be somewhat disruptive for patients, especially if the visit involves some form of invasive treatment that may be upsetting to family or friends present during the process or it may simply be embarrassing to patients to have certain family or friends present.

Although cost savings are frequently alluded to as an important benefit of home health care interventions, the actual cost savings that are realized during the delivery of high-tech services at home has been questioned (Dombi, 1992; Haddad, 1992). Cost-effective service delivery in the home care setting depends on a variety of factors, not the least of which is the complexity of the service itself. In some cases the cost to provide a particular service at multiple remote sites may actually increase overall expenditures. For example, patients using durable medical equipment need to have this equipment in their home. In an institutional setting, equipment may be shared among patients, resulting in a lower overall expenditure on equipment. Other factors can impact on the overall expenditure for high-tech services, including: duration and intensity of service need; the type of service and delivery modality; and the novelty of the treatment to the in-home setting. The potential for out-of-pocket expenditure is much greater for high-tech care than for traditional home care. Some patients will not have the resources to cover these costs, and the agency may end-up delivering services without adequate reimbursement.

The uncertainty around new treatments being provided in the home creates anxiety as to whether services will be reimbursed by Medicare or private third-party insurers. These concerns must be addressed by agency administration to ensure that the agency remains fiscally solvent, while still providing quality care. It has been clearly documented in the literature that denials by Medicare are a well known part of the home health game and are likely to increase given recent Medicare reform initiatives. It is sometimes very difficult for agencies to be certain that patients' care needs will be covered under Medicare. This is especially problematic when the service is new to the home health arena. In fact, research conducted by the authors demonstrated that patients are, on the average, receiving services for less than 1 year and less than three visits per week. This attests to the limits of third-party reimbursement in assuring that patients receive adequate services for a sufficient period of time. This problem is exacerbated in the case of high-tech treatments. It is the agency's responsibility to determine prior to admission whether the patient can be served safely in their home and for how long.

One of the biggest challenges in delivering high-tech care is matching the patient's expectations with the agency's obligations. Many patients do not understand why they cannot have additional units of care, either for professional or paraprofessional services, and may express their dissatisfaction with the agency. In many cases what patients demand and what insurers will cover varies tremendously. For example, the limits of Medicare appear to be impacting the type, amount, and duration of services provided. Patient satisfaction with services is a complicated construct to measure. Although many patients are satisfied with the quality of services they are receiving, they may be dissatisfied with the quantity. Any assessment of patient satisfaction should be careful to address these two issues separately. Perhaps it is accurate to translate patient satisfaction into a sense of personal relief for patients that they are receiving additional increments of support in their home, albeit limited, which enable them to more easily forestall decisions around considering institutional forms of care.

The nature of high-tech home health care encourages considerable sharing in the responsibility of care among formal and informal caregivers. This partnership in the responsibility of care may be emphasized more during the course of providing home health care services than any other health or social service intervention. On the one hand, such an emphasis may be seen as helping to prevent the disintegration of family ties during an impaired relative's time of need. On the other hand, such responsibility placed on friends and relatives can serve to seriously test the integrity of the bond that exists between the patient and his or her loved ones. The heavy care needs of the high-tech patient coupled with the limited availability of reimbursement for such care places much of the burden for daily care on family and other caregivers. Because staff are generally not on-site 24 hours each day, much of the burden of responsibility rests with informal supports to monitor and provide patient care. Providers are well aware of this and appear to be concerned that the consequence of this responsibility is more likely to breakdown than bolster patient-caregiver bonds of affection.

Informal support is usually provided by daughters and then by spouses (Brody, 1990; Kaye & Applegate, 1990; Kaye & Davitt, 1995). Most of the informal support provided is personal care. Again, this comes as no surprise given the limits on reimbursement for custodial care. However, some caregivers are clearly providing or assisting with complicated medical care, especially for high-tech patients. Teaching family members to care for high-tech patients can be more difficult and time consuming than teaching the self-care tasks of traditional home care patients. Monitoring artificial nutrition and hydration can be very complicated and intimidating to the layperson. It requires not only clear instructions on equipment and modality, but also reassurance and sensitivity to the anxiety and concerns of caregivers. This may translate into additional staff time to teach patient

TABLE 12.1   Potential Benefits of High-Tech Care

Increased patient comfort and reduced stress

Patient is in familiar surroundings

Patient and family are more involved in care

Enhanced patient autonomy and increased flexibility

Cost savings

care or additional staff hours in the home to actually monitor patient care while the family becomes comfortable with the routine.

Patient anxiety regarding the treatment is another potential drawback to in-home, high-tech care. Patients will be naturally concerned with safety and security pertaining to the receipt of services in the absence of institutional supports. In many cases this anxiety can be minimized through comprehensive and sensitive patient training. However, some patients may be overly anxious, and this may interfere with their ability to learn the appropriate procedures for monitoring their care or administering aspects of the treatment. Staff may need to first address the concerns of the patient before training can even begin.

Another important challenge to receiving home health care in general, and high-tech care in particular, is the loss of privacy that accompanies service receipt. Although this may be less intrusive to the patient's lifestyle than institutionalization, it is still an important area for concern in the home setting. With multiple caregivers (formal and informal) interacting with patients, the latter can begin to lose their sense of self-control and self-determination. Staff and families need to be alerted to this issue, so

TABLE 12.2   Potential Drawbacks of High-Tech Care

Increased stress placed on caregivers

Problems with gaps in insurance coverage

Increased risk to patient, especially during off-hours and in
   emergencies

Loss of privacy

Decreased patient autonomy and flexibility

Unsafe conditions in the patient's home

Not enough hours of service

that the loss of privacy and self-determination can be minimized. (For a more detailed discussion of self-determination refer to chapter 9.)

CHOOSING HIGH-TECH CARE

The process of determining whether a particular patient should be served at home is multifaceted. An appropriate hospital discharge plan must be developed for each patient and must be based on a comprehensive assessment, which reviews their diagnosis and treatment plan, patient status and resources, and the home environment. It is important to determine if a particular patient can be safely and adequately served at home. For a variety of reasons, which will be discussed shortly, some patients may not benefit from home care. Rather, they may need continued hospitalization or discharge to a subacute facility or other institutional setting.

Type of Treatment Needed

The first factor to be assessed is the type of treatment the patient will need when discharged. Although a wide variety of high-tech treatments are now available for in-home delivery, and even more new treatments are being continually tested, there are limits as to the types of treatments that can be provided in the home. (For a current list of high-tech services refer to appendix C.) The foremost question is can the treatment needed in this case be delivered safely in a home setting? In other words, certain treatments may not be available for in-home delivery simply due to the treatment modality or complexity. This is especially important if specialized equipment is needed. It must be determined whether the equipment is available and covered under the patient's insurance as well. Equipment may also warrant the use of subcontracts with durable medical equipment suppliers that can further complicate the home care service scenario.

Another factor related to the treatment itself is its longevity as an in-home modality. If a treatment has been offered on an in-home basis for some time (and for which most of the kinks have been worked out), then it is much more likely to be successful. Services with a longer history of in-home delivery will benefit from an enhanced predictability factor. Home care staff have a better understanding of the risks and potential problems related to the treatment due to experience and can, therefore, establish a care plan that anticipates such contingencies. Treatments that have a less extensive track record in the home setting may be more volatile and unpredictable. If this is a novel treatment that has rarely been offered in the home, then additional caution must be followed in assessing the patient's status (both clinical and psychosocial status). The potential risk to the patient must be determined, and this can be very difficult for treatments that have a limited track record of in-home use.

Patients who have been difficult to stabilize in the hospital may not be acceptable candidates for in-home high-tech care. Home care agencies generally require that the patient receive at least one course of treatment prior to discharge from the hospital to stabilize the patient and to resolve any problems with the treatment. For example, a patient needing IV antibiotics for osteomyelitis may experience an anaphylactic reaction to the medication. This can be determined in the hospital with much less risk to the patient and a new medication prescribed and tested. This issue may also be related to the novelty of the treatment itself, with newer treatments being potentially more unstable due to inadequate field testing.

Patient Status

The second factor relates to patient status. Patients must have either the capacity to monitor and, in some cases, administer their treatments or they will need a responsible and accessible caregiver. For example, patients with dementia will, in most cases, not be able to understand treatment directions nor monitor or troubleshoot problems. However, it should not be assumed (either due to diagnosis or age) that a patient cannot complete all or some self-care tasks. A comprehensive functional assessment must be conducted to determine each patient's ability for self-care. This assessment should consider factors related to the pathology that can affect a patient's self-care capacity, but should not rest solely on one factor (e.g., age or diagnosis). Included in this assessment should be an evaluation of the patient's psychological or emotional status as well. Are they motivated to complete self-care tasks? Is the patient depressed and will this depression affect the ability for self-care? At a minimum, the patient should be able to identify signs and symptoms of trouble, know whom to contact in an emergency, and be able to understand any specific administration tasks. We deal with these issues in greater depth when we discuss patient education.

For those patients who are assessed as incapable of managing their own care, an appropriate caregiver needs to be identified. Appropriate is a twofold concept. First, the caregiver must be available, in some cases on a 24-hour basis, to the patient. Second, the caregiver must be able to perform the self-care tasks as the patient would. In many cases it may be necessary that the caregiver live with the patient (or vice versa). However, the fact that they reside with the patient does not solely determine their capability to act as a caregiver. They must be assessed in the same way as the patient. They must be able to understand the treatment; monitor and identify problems; and administer, where necessary, certain aspects of the treatment. (This final capability, of course, depends on the treatment.) The caregiver must also enter this agreement voluntarily and with open eyes. They should be informed in detail about this commitment and the responsibilities related to it.

Patient resources also include financial resources. Patients' insurance coverage should be reviewed prior to admission, with the goal of determining the amount and duration of services that will be approved. Likewise, the patient's ability to pay privately must be determined. (For more information on reimbursement issues see chapter 10.)

Assessing the Home Environment

The final factor that must be assessed is the setting itself. Patients may not understand that certain high-tech treatments require specific (and sometimes specialized) conditions and equipment. Therefore, the patient's home needs to be evaluated for such requirements as proper electrical support, storage for medications (which may need to be refrigerated), sanitary conditions, accessibility, and so forth. For example, older homes may not be wired properly to support electrical equipment, such as telemetry monitors or dialysis machines. In addition, patients may need to mix medications in sterile environments. Inadequate utilities, unsanitary conditions, or the lack of running water may make it impossible to serve patients safely in their own home. (They may, however, be able to be served in a family member's home.)

The use of highly technical services in a patient's home can be very complex. Many factors need to be considered before deciding to go home with high-tech care. Careful consideration and assessment and discussions with various health care professionals can aid in making such determinations. Table 12.3 lists the kinds of questions that a patient, patient's family, or advocate should ask when deciding whether to use high-tech services in the home.

TABLE 12.3   Questions to Ask When Choosing High-Tech Care

- Can the care I need be effectively provided in my home? (Is the electricity sufficient to support equipment? Is there enough space for the equipment? Where will I store supplies?)

- What is my doctor recommending? Home care? Rehabilitation hospital? Personal care? Subacute care? Nursing home?

- Will I need someone besides agency staff to help with my care? Is someone available?

- Will I need any equipment? Who will provide the equipment? Who will service the equipment if it breaks down? How quickly will equipment be replaced?

- What happens in the event of a power failure? Is there a back-up power supply for equipment? Does the agency notify local fire and police that the patient is using high-tech equipment or life support?

- Will these high-tech services be covered by my insurance (Medicare, Medicaid)? If no, can I afford to pay privately for such services?

- What potential emergencies might arise? Who will help me handle these emergencies?

- Will I be expected to monitor or complete aspects of my own care? Do I feel comfortable with my (or my family's) ability to do self-care?

- What type of service do I need to go home? Nursing care? Physical therapy? Other therapies? Home health aide services?

- How many hours of service will I need?

- How long will I need the service for?

CHOOSING THE PROVIDER

Once home care has been determined to be an appropriate and safe option for a given patient, the next step is to choose the right provider. When deciding whether to choose home health care, it is essential to review carefully the agency that will be providing the care. Selecting a home health care provider is an important and difficult decision. Agency experience in home health care and with high-tech services (especially the service needed) is very important. The agency must be able to demonstrate that they have adequate numbers of properly trained and supervised staff to care for the patient. Likewise, they should have adequate experience in providing the particular service requested. Talking to trusted family, friends, and professionals (such as a doctor) about the agency is a worthwhile strategy for patients.

As we discussed previously, not all high-tech services will be available as in-home services. (A list of current high-tech services is provided in appendix C.) Likewise, not all services will be offered by all agencies. It is essential to determine (through the physician, hospital discharge planner, etc.) whether there are home health care programs in the community that provide the specific services needed. Certain high-tech services are more commonly available in the home and include nutrition and hydration therapies, pain management, antibiotic therapies, bedsore care, and chemotherapy. Others are just beginning to be used and will be more commonly available in the future. These include self-instruction computers, telehealth technology, closed circuit television, and even robots that can help patients manage better in their home.

Subcontracting Services

It is important to know whether the agency provides a given service directly through their own staff or whether they use other agencies on a contract basis to provide the service needed (referred to here as subcontracting). One example of this practice is with intravenous therapy. Many general home health care agencies do not provide infusion therapy services. Instead they arrange for another agency (a subcontractor), which specializes in providing intravenous services, to deliver that specific part of the patient's care. Although the primary agency will continue to monitor care delivery, the subcontractor will be more directly responsible for nursing care needs. Therefore, it is wise to also investigate the subcontractor because staff of this agency will also be coming into the patient's home and will be responsible for direct care needs.

In many cases the patient's treatment may require specialized equipment. Many home care agencies do not provide equipment directly. Rather, they arrange for a durable medical equipment supplier to install and service necessary equipment. It is important also to evaluate the supplier. For example, the patient would need to know which agency would be responsible for problems with the equipment. How is equipment serviced? Will staff of the supplier need to check on the equipment regularly and if so how often? Are these employees bonded? Such questions should be asked prior to approving a particular supplier.

Table 12.4 provides a list of questions that can be used as a guide in determining whether a particular agency can meet specific patient needs. These questions are appropriate from both the patient's perspective and from the primary provider's perspective and are particularly important in a subcontracting arrangement. (They are presented here from the patient's perspective.) The primary agency must be alert to these issues due to its obligation to provide the best services to each patient as well as from a liability standpoint. (These issues are addressed in greater depth in chapter 8.)

As is the case for the primary agency, the subcontractor should be certified or licensed to provide the specific services in question. Likewise

TABLE 12.4   Questions Regarding Agency Capability

- Does the agency provide the services and equipment your doctor says you need?

- Does the agency offer a full range of services? Can you get all the services you need from this one agency? Do they also have all types of staff needed?

- Does the agency provide these services directly or do they contract with another agency to provide them?

- How soon can the agency begin providing these services?

- How long has the agency been providing home health care?, High-tech services?

- Is the agency a licensed home health care provider? Medicare certified? Medicaid certified? VA certified/approved?

- Does the agency provide itemized bills/receipts?

- How are staff licensed or certified? What type of training do staff receive (and how often)? Are they certified for the treatment you will need?

- How are staff recruited and selected? Are references checked for all staff?

- Are staff bonded or insured?

- How will the agency monitor your care to ensure that you are receiving quality care?

- Does a supervisor make periodic visits to observe staff performance?

- Does the agency check with clients to see if they are satisfied with their care?

- Can the agency respond to an emergency, 7 days per week and 24 hours per day?

- Does the agency inform you of the risks and benefits of this treatment and of receiving this treatment at home?

- Does the agency have a written description of your rights as a patient?

their staff should have required certificates or adequate training for each service provided.

Procedures should be outlined in advance for handling emergency situations and providing back-up coverage. Specific concerns regarding emergency coverage are addressed in greater detail in chapter 11. From the patient's perspective, however, there are several important issues. First, the patient needs to be reassured that help will be forthcoming and in an expedient fashion if an emergency arises. This may help to ease some of the anxiety experienced when receiving high-tech services at home. Second, clients need to understand who to contact in an emergency, as well as how to identify potential problems that could result in a medical crisis if not attended to immediately. Therefore, patient education should include a review of emergency contact procedures.

TEACHING PATIENT AND FAMILY

Another important issue related to high-tech home health care is how much of the care will need to be provided by someone other than agency staff. Do patients or their family and friends feel comfortable with their ability to monitor, manage, and even provide some of the care? For example, patients who are receiving food and water through a feeding tube may be expected to: change the feeding bag as needed; cap the tube when not receiving fluids; and monitor the wound site for infection or the tube for back-ups. All of these tasks are continuous responsibilities. However, staff will not be in the home at all times. Therefore, patients and their families may be expected to complete these tasks when staff are not in the home.

Agency staff are responsible for teaching patients and their caregivers self-care tasks as well as how to monitor the treatment and identify problems. This training is very important, not only to ensure safety, but to increase peace of mind. Open communication between staff and patients is key to successful patient education. Patients should be encouraged to ask questions or voice concerns. In addition, staff trainers should determine whether patients feel comfortable with the self-care requirements and that they are able to complete the tasks independently.

If the patient is in a hospital or other facility prior to receiving home health care, teaching should begin before discharge. Hospital staff should begin working with the patient and family on these self-care tasks. It is

TABLE 12.5   Questions Regarding Patient Education

- Who will teach me the required self-care tasks?
- What will I be expected to learn?
- Will a family member be taught also?
- When will teaching begin, now or after I get home?
- How much service will I get while teaching is being completed?

These questions are provided as a general guide. Other questions may need to be posed depending on specific patient situations.

also a good idea to have more than one family member learn how to provide the treatment in case the primary caregiver is unavailable. Teaching may continue after discharge with the goal of gradually transitioning the responsibility for direct care to the patient and family. Therefore, the agency may provide more intensive services at the outset with a gradual decrease in the number of visits as the patient becomes more comfortable with self-care tasks. It is important for patients to understand this scenario from the beginning; otherwise they may feel abandoned as the agency reduces the number of visits. The goal—patient independence—needs to be clearly communicated (whenever that is the case). Table 12.5 offers a list of questions that should be asked in relation to patient education.

PAYING FOR HOME HEALTH CARE

Another important factor in deciding to receive home health care services is related to how a patient will pay for such care. There are some important issues that must be considered in relation to payment by Medicare, private insurance, and other sources before choosing to receive care at home. Insurance generally limits the amount, type, and duration of care for which coverage is provided. Therefore, it is essential to check with specific insurance carriers to learn what type of coverage can be expected. Issues around reimbursement are covered in more detail in chapter 10.

Paying for High-Tech Services

Not all high-tech services are approved for provision in the home. It is important to check the specific insurance (Medicare, Medicaid, private insurance) to determine whether the particular treatment prescribed can be covered. Also, there may be limits on the types of medical equipment that the insurer will cover. For example, Medicare covers durable medical equipment only if prescribed by a doctor and required for the patient to remain at home. Medicare covers 80% of the cost of purchase or rental, whichever is cheaper. Patients can consider whether to purchase or to rent equipment, depending on the amount of time the equipment will be needed and the cost for either.

PATIENT RIGHTS

Consideration of the legal and ethical dimensions of providing high-technology care to older adults, the disabled, and other vulnerable populations in their own homes is destined to be an issue of central importance in the years ahead. Patients receiving home health care services have certain rights. It is important for the patient to be aware of these rights to ensure

TABLE 12.6   Patients Have the Right to

- Be informed about the risks and benefits of treatment
- Be informed about alternatives to the recommended treatment
- Make decisions about their treatment
- Refuse, discontinue, or withdraw treatment
- Be informed about their rights under state law to create an advance directive
- Create an advance directive that gives health care providers guidelines for making life-sustaining treatment decisions for a patient, if the patient becomes incapacitated
- Appeal decisions made by the agency or insurance company regarding the types of services they will provide or cover
- Maintain confidentiality of their medical records
- Participate in developing the plan of care and to be notified about changes in the plan
- Be informed about liability for payment
- Be given adequate notice of termination of services or transfer to another agency
- Have access to bills for services received
- Be treated with dignity and respect

the receipt of quality care. Many of the areas covered under patient rights can also be considered in legal or ethical contexts. Therefore, these issues are more thoroughly addressed in chapters 8 and 9.

HOW TO FIND A HIGH-TECH PROVIDER

Finding an appropriate high-tech care provider may be a very difficult and time-consuming task for consumers who have little experience in this area. This is especially true if the needed intervention is fairly novel to home care. There are several places to turn to learn about high-tech home care services. One is the hospital social worker or discharge planner. Another is the local office on aging or area agency on aging. These agencies, which are found in all states and generally in each county within a state, provide information about home health care services in specific areas. Home health care agencies also publicize their services in various places including the local telephone yellow pages and the local directory of community services for older adults. Patients' physicians are also likely to know about home health care agencies able to meet their needs. Neighborhood senior center staff may also have such information. Finally, the National Association for Home Care in Washington, DC and state associations for home care can identify agencies that provide high-tech home care services in particular communities.

One of the best methods for determining the quality of care and therefore selecting an agency is through word of mouth. Patients may have family or friends who have recently received home health care services

---

**TABLE 12.7   Contacts to Help Clients
Find a High-Tech Home Care Provider**

Hospital social worker or discharge planner

County office on aging

Phone book

Physician

Senior center staff

National Association for Home Care

State associations for home care

Friends and family

---

and have had a positive experience. These personal referrals, in some cases, are the best source from which to determine whether an agency can meet patient needs adequately and safely. Checking the complaint record of home health care agencies under consideration by calling the Better Business Bureau is also recommended.

SUMMARY

There are both benefits and drawbacks to delivering high-tech care in the home. It should not be automatically assumed that home care is the best option for every patient. Rather, a thorough assessment of each patient, his or her diagnosis and treatment plan, resources, and home environment must be conducted prior to admission to a home care service. The agency should determine that the patient's needs can be adequately and safely met in the home environment. This is especially important for patients receiving high-tech care because they will generally have more complex care needs. When possible, treatments should be initiated in an institutional setting to stabilize the patient and test for possible adverse reactions to the treatment. The type of treatment, complexity, duration, and amount of care required must be determined prior to admission. The longevity of a particular intervention in the home care field is an important factor to consider as well. Finally, patients must be able to monitor their own care or must have appropriate caregivers willing to act in this respect.

In choosing to accept high-tech home care, patients should be made aware of several factors. First, they should understand the benefits and drawbacks to the particular treatment and its delivery in a home setting. Second, the role of the provider and agency staff should be thoroughly explained to prevent later misunderstandings. If other providers are used to assist with the service, patients should be informed of their role and responsibilities and which agency to call in the event of an emergency. Finally, patients should understand their (or their caregivers') roles in monitoring and administering the treatment. Patient education should be provided to ensure adequate understanding as well as to reduce patient anxiety regarding possible emergencies or negative side effects of the treatment.

CHAPTER 13

Conclusions and Recommendations: Gazing into the Future of High-Tech Care[1]

INTRODUCTION

This chapter draws conclusions and offers interpretation based on findings arising from both stages of the research, the national and local surveys, reported on in section II. Recommendations are also presented for home health agency operation and future home health research, which are enunciated in the form of best practice guidelines. The latter part of this chapter considers several emergent trends and developments in the field of high-tech home care including some of the most promising technologies that we predict are going to be applied more and more commonly in the context of the patient's home. We close by identifying a series of issues that are now positioning themselves on the health care horizon and that are likely to impact home care's evolutionary path in significant ways in the years to come.

INTERPRETING THE OBSERVATIONS
FROM THE FIELD

A Note on Those Agencies Choosing Not to Participate
in the Research Reported on in Section II

For-profit, proprietary home health care agencies, serving primarily urban neighborhoods are underrepresented in the national sample of responding executive directors reported in section II. The unwillingness of a large proportion of these agency directors to share their experiences in providing high-tech home health care services is disappointing. One can speculate as to the reasons behind their lack of response. It is possible that urban-based programs (many of which are proprietary) have comparatively higher ratios of patients to staff and find it difficult to find the time to respond to what are likely to be all too frequent requests for information from curious academic researchers. On the other hand, the highly competitive nature of home health care service provision in metropolitan regions may also dissuade such agencies from willingly sharing their experiences with other agencies like themselves. This tendency to protect experiential information may be especially strong when it comes to the provision of emergent and novel services in the field such as technologically enhanced in-home care. If the former explanation is the accurate one, then the poor response is understandable and excusable. On the other hand, if the latter explanation holds merit, then one can only express a degree of concern that the critical process of information dissemination in the field of high-tech care is being stifled by a closed-door, dog-eat-dog provider attitude. Novel service interventions must benefit, in particular, from open lines of communication and experience sharing in order that delivery strategies are perfected at the earliest possible point in time. The survival of neophyte home care agencies and the well being of their patients may lie in the balance.

Issues of Gender, Age, Education, and Work Schedules

It should not be surprising that women dominate the home health care field. This is the case both in terms of service providers and those persons receiving services. Gender imbalances in the health and human services, both in terms of those who comprise the ranks of direct service staff and those who are beneficiaries of their services, have always been commonplace (Davitt & Kaye, 1995). Women have traditionally dominated the ranks of the nursing, social work, home health aide, and therapy (occupational, physical, and speech) professions. Furthermore, those accessing and ultimately utilizing social and health services are more likely to be women than men (Miller, 1987). These gender imbalances are highlighted in the research reported here, particularly by the large numbers of female nursing assistants and home health aides participating as subjects in the Philadelphia survey.

Also consistent with the data presented here is the level of education attained by a majority of home health care staff. The fact that a majority of staff have received posthigh school education is not surprising given the large numbers of professional staff in the survey (e.g., nurses, therapists, and social workers). What is surprising is that one quarter of the staff have completed more than four years of college. This is especially interesting given the low number of management and supervisory staff participating in the local survey. One might anticipate that supervisory staff would be more likely to have acquired advanced degrees. If, however, the local staff interviewed in this research are reflective of the home health care field generally, it would appear that direct care personnel have completed advanced education as often as their administrative counterparts.

The national data confirm that agencies employ more part-time staff than full-time staff. This is not the case for the four local agencies that were studied; there a majority of staff work full time. This difference in employment status may be attributable to size variation among agencies. Also, it may be based on the geographic location of the local agencies and employment trends associated with those locales.

When considering patient services, full-time employment status may serve to reduce the amount of turnover that clients sometimes experience when receiving home health service. If more staff work full time, there will be less variation in the staff who see each patient. Likewise, lower use of part-time staff can reduce the amount of logistical planning and coordination necessary to schedule adequate coverage. However, dependence on full-time staff can also reduce the number of available replacement staff, leading to potential difficulties in ensuring that coverage is readily available when staff are sick, on vacation, or otherwise unavailable to work. This may be why staff interviewed at the local level indicate that scheduling adequate coverage and lack of adequate numbers of trained staff are high on their list of challenges to providing high-tech home care. This, of course, may also explain why staff are used on a full-time basis—because it is so difficult to find additional adequately trained staff.

National survey data underscore the advanced age of home health care recipients as well as the predominance of unmarried women receiving in-home services of all types. Large proportions of service beneficiaries are over the age of 75. Home health care has an undeniable gender-specific, gerontological focus. And, home health care patients are an increasingly aged cohort. These data highlight the importance of agencies recruiting staff that are sensitive to the special needs of working with an exceedingly old, female, functionally impaired population.

The recipient of high-tech service is different in substantial ways from the traditional home care patient. High-tech beneficiaries are much more likely to be younger, male, married, and living with others. They are also slightly more likely to be White than African American or Hispanic. These data may simply reflect a different profile that characterizes those persons in need of technology-enhanced services or they may signal particular biases reflected in the consumer population served by high-tech agencies (Kaye & Davitt, 1995b). If the latter explanation is the accurate one, then these findings are worrisome. It raises questions concerning whether women, those who are not married and living alone, persons of color, and older adults have experienced impeded access to needed high-tech services. Certainly, the importance of having an available informal caregiver has been clearly identified as a critical criterion for determining high-tech service eligibility. Such a factor will undoubtedly provide married men with a special advantage when it comes to high-tech service eligibility. Whether those who are classified as old-old (those over 75 years of age), living alone, and people of color are being discriminated against in similar fashion can only remain conjecture at this point in time. Further study is warranted.

The Meaning of High-Tech Care
and Its Implications for Training

Staff surveyed locally were not provided with a definition of high-tech home health care until after they answered certain questions. The goal was to have staff define high-tech care from their own perspective, prior to our offering a formal definition. Although much research on this subject equates high-tech care to specialized equipment (e.g., ventilators and apnea monitors), it became clear during both phases of this research that providers do not necessarily define high-tech care in that way.

As is demonstrated in this research, various factors interplay to make a service technologically enhanced, according to staff (Davitt & Kaye, 1995). Although most staff think highly specialized equipment could make a service high tech, many also feel that other factors play an influential role as well. For example, if the service or treatment provided by the nurse requires very specialized knowledge and a high degree of intensity, that would be enough for many staff to view a service as high-tech. Intravenous chemotherapy seems to be one example of a high-tech service meeting these definitional criteria. The potential for adverse reactions and the toxicity of the medication makes this treatment high tech when provided in the home regardless of how it is administered.

Many staff also feel that the novelty of a particular treatment provided in the home for the first time may make it high tech. The extent to which a particular service has been provided on a frequent basis over an extended period of time appears to impact on perceptions of its complexity. This may be the case for such services as ostomy care, pressure sore and wound care, and incontinence care, which are now interventions commonly available through many home health care agencies. At one point in the evolution of health care provision, providing nutrition and hydration infusion in the home was likely to be viewed as extremely risky. Now, based on the responses of subjects in this research, many home health staff would apparently describe this as a fairly simple service to provide. More importantly, many more family members and informal supports are providing the assistance home care patients need with feeding tubes. The important lesson here, from the point of view of staff, is that there is not a simple unidimensional definition that can delineate automatically high tech from traditional home health care services.

Some staff apparently do not know how to define or describe the phrase high-tech home health care. Based on the local analysis, a majority of staff having this difficulty are home health aides. Because most home health aides do not carry primary responsibility for the delivery of high-tech home health care services, it is understandable that they would have some difficulty in defining high-tech intervention.

Some staff also indicate that they are not required to participate in training related to high-tech services (predominantly home health aides and professionals other than nurses such as occupational, speech, and physical therapists and social workers). However, many home health aides are in the home more frequently than skilled nurses or therapists and may at times be called on to troubleshoot in relation to equipment or complicated treatment routines. For example, if the caregiver wishes to leave the home when the aide is present for respite or other responsibilities, it may be expected that the aide would then monitor the patient's care needs and treatment. In fact, the research at the local level confirms that many home health aides are assisting regularly in the delivery or monitoring of high-tech services as are professionals other than nurses. These staff perceive themselves to be engaged in high-tech related activities considerably more often than the executive directors in the national survey would have us believe. It appears that executive directors are not fully aware of actual staff experience in this regard.

This inevitable and perhaps unanticipated spread of responsibility by staff other than nurses into the area of high-tech service provision is worrisome if it is occurring without the benefits of continual upgrades in their practice knowledge base. And, this gap in their in-service training is apparently present, as the national survey data confirm that only one in every two home health aides and professional staff other than nurses are participating in specialized agency training as compared to nine of every 10 nurses. If these staff have not received training in the particular treatments to which they are exposed, the patient may be left in a precarious situation. It is important for agencies to be aware of this dilemma and to provide essential training to all staff who may be called on to both provide high-tech care directly as well as provide ancillary assistance such as monitoring such services. At a minimum, the training should consist of teaching similar to that provided to families.

The issue of training arises again when staff are asked to discuss the challenges associated with providing high-tech home health care services. Lack of adequate numbers of trained staff is one of the top mentioned challenges according to staff. It seems clear that they are expressing their own concern with the training needs of home care personnel, both their own needs and those of their colleagues. This is also important when we consider the problems that patients have had with services. These problems are attributed to staff changes and the transition to a new staff person. In these cases, training is essential to ensure a smooth transition that is minimally upsetting to patients.

Staff Burnout and the Rise in High-Tech Service Requests

Both executive directors and staff report that high-tech service delivery is on the rise. This is consistent with the literature (Estes et al., 1993;

Mehlman & Youngner, 1991). Yet, the experiences of direct service staff in the area of high-tech care is uneven to say the least. Some staff have no high-tech patients on their caseload while others have all high-tech patients. The fact that some staff may be handling all high-tech patients could lead to burnout, if in fact these are very complicated cases. Almost all staff feel that high-tech services require more training than traditional home care services. Again, we see a strong need for training related to high-tech services both for those staff who have fully saturated high-tech caseloads and those who have very little contact with high-tech patients. An additional reason for training staff is that they are responsible for teaching the patient and informal caregivers how to perform certain self-care tasks related to the treatment. If staff are not trained properly it is likely that they will not be able to teach patients and their families adequately.

Data suggest that staff do not perceive themselves to be involved very often in the planning of high-tech services at the agency. Maximizing the involvement of personnel in agency planning has its advantages and should be seriously considered by agency directors. This may be an important strategy for building allegiance and commitment among both professionals and paraprofessionals in a field of service that has traditionally been beset with high turnover and burnout rates. Engaging more field staff in the planning function will also put to good use their direct and often intimate knowledge of the status and needs of the consumer population.

HIGH-TECH HOME HEALTH CARE
ADMISSIONS CRITERIA

Considerable unevenness remains in terms of those agencies that have established special admissions criteria for high-tech patients (Kaye & Davitt, 1995b). As is the case for other organizational policies (see discussion on policies pertaining to life-sustaining treatment and advance directives below), it appears that certain types of agencies are more likely to have special admissions criteria for prospective patients requesting high-tech services. Hospice providers are less likely to have such criteria. This may be due to the nature of the service provided by such agencies. Although the patient may be receiving high-tech services, the emphasis is on palliative care, maintaining the patient in a comfortable setting until the patient dies. The fact that hospice providers only serve terminal patients in the end stage of their illness may be a sufficient criterion in and of itself (Kaye & Davitt, 1998).

What is perhaps most interesting about the issue of admission criteria policy is the number of agencies that lack such criteria in the first place. Agencies may be providing service to all types of patients regardless of diagnosis or treatment modality. This triggers questions regarding quality of service, training needs of staff, and the capacity of agencies to respond to all care needs and to provide all types of treatments. It also raises questions pertaining to agency liability. At what point is the agency responsible for ensuring that a particular patient's care needs can be adequately met? Likewise, if an agency does not have set criteria for staff to follow, how then are admissions decisions made?

For those agencies that do have special admissions criteria, the most popular choices are the need for an available caregiver and a safe home environment. Clearly, this indicates the concern providers have for the complex nature of high-tech patient care. Given the frailty of this patient population, agencies are legitimately concerned that patients may not be able to handle their own care needs and therefore will need caregivers that are available when staff are not there. Likewise, many home environments may not be suitable to support the complex equipment or procedures needed by the patient. For example, patients' homes may not have adequate power supplies to handle complex electrical equipment, or patients' homes may be unsanitary or lacking adequate space, utilities, and so forth.

The ability of patients to learn to handle their own care is frequently cited as an admissions criterion by agencies as well. High-tech patients in particular tend to have heavier care needs of greater duration and intensity. Rarely are enough resources available to maintain 24-hour staff presence in the home. Unfortunately, many high-tech patients receive treatment around the clock (e.g., total parenteral nutrition feedings and infusion therapy). Limitations on the amount of service that can be provided to the patient increase the need for the patient to become an active participant in the provision of treatment.

BENEFITS AND CHALLENGES
OF HIGH-TECH CARE

While not without its drawbacks, provision of high-tech care appears to be largely a positive experience for both agency administrators and direct service staff. Both clearly feel that there is great benefit to being home while recuperating from an illness or surgery. They feel that being at home is a more pleasant experience for patients, which, in turn, reduces their stress and increases their comfort. Although cost savings was mentioned by some as a benefit of high-tech interventions, the actual cost savings that are realized during the delivery of high-tech services at home is questionable. This debate has been presented in the literature (Dombi, 1992; Haddad, 1992). It would seem that staff in particular are more concerned about patient improvement during the course of high-tech care provision than they are about the potential for cost savings to the system. Ironically, when asked to list the drawbacks to high-tech care in the home, both agency directors and staff were most concerned with stress on the family and cost factors.

The nature of high-tech home health care encourages considerable sharing in the responsibility of care among formal and informal caregivers. This sense of partnership in the responsibility of care may be emphasized more during the course of providing home health care services than any other health or social service intervention. On the one hand, such an emphasis may be seen as helping to prevent the disintegration of family ties during an impaired relative's time of need. On the other hand, such responsibility placed on friends and relatives can serve to seriously test the integrity of the bond that exists between patients and their loved ones. Both agency directors and local agency staff perceive the heavy care needs of the high-tech patient coupled with the limited availability of reimbursement for such care as having placed much of the burden for daily care on family and other caregivers. Because staff are generally not on-site 24 hours each day, much of the burden of responsibility rests with informal supports to monitor and provide patient care. Staff are well aware of this and appear to be concerned that the consequence of this responsibility is more likely to breakdown than bolster patient-caregiver bonds of affection.

The uncertainty surrounding new treatments being provided in the home creates anxiety for staff as to whether their services will be reimbursed by Medicare or private third-party insurers. These concerns must be addressed by agency administration to ensure that the agency remains fiscally solvent, while still providing quality care. It has been clearly documented in the literature that denials by Medicare are a well-known part of the home health game. It is sometimes very difficult for agencies to be certain that patients' care needs will be covered under Medicare. This is especially problematic when the service is new to the home health arena. The fact that patients are, on the average, receiving services for less than one year and less than three visits per week in this research attests to the limits of third-party reimbursement in assuring that patients receive services for a sufficient period of time.

The majority of patients who requested additional services desired additional hours of the same service rather than new services. Furthermore, more patients feel that they need additional home health aide hours than skilled nursing hours. Again, the limits of Medicare appear to be impacting on the type, amount, and duration of services provided. Nevertheless, patients are very much satisfied with the services they are receiving. Or perhaps it is more accurate to translate this satisfaction into a sense of personal relief that they are receiving additional increments of support in their home, albeit limited, which enable them to more easily forestall decisions concerning institutional forms of care.

In comparison, patients are less concerned with cost factors or reimbursement problems. They are more likely to worry about stress felt by their caregivers (especially when receiving skilled nursing services), receiving adequate hours of the service from home health aides in particular, and increased risk involved in receiving professional services at home. Patients understand their level of dependence on the formal system as well as informal supports. They are aware of the risks involved in receiving services at home where a caregiver (formal or informal) may not be present 24 hours per day. Even though the patient may not directly relate these concerns to reimbursement issues, ultimately staff and patients are worried about the same thing—the need for additional services in the home.

Informal support is usually provided by daughters and then by spouses according to both staff and patients in this research. This is consistent with the research on informal caregivers (Brody, 1990; Kaye, 1997a; Kaye & Applegate, 1990; U.S. Department of Labor, 1998). Most of the informal support provided is personal care. Again, this should come as no surprise given the limits on reimbursement for custodial care. However, some caregivers are clearly providing or assisting with complicated medical care, especially for high-tech patients. Teaching family members to care for high-tech patients can be more difficult and time-consuming than teaching the self-care tasks of traditional home care patients. Monitoring artificial nutrition and hydration can be very complicated and intimidating to the layperson. This requires not only clear instructions on equipment and modality, but also reassurance and sensitivity to the anxiety and concerns of caregivers. This may mean additional time is required of staff to teach patient care or additional staff hours are needed in the home to actually monitor patient care while the family becomes comfortable with the routine.

Infusion therapy, including a range of specific treatments, are the services staff feel they deliver most effectively. It is interesting to note that staff are less likely to list the less invasive, high-tech services that use specialized equipment, such as cardiac monitors, transcutaneous electronic nerve stimulation, and so forth. This may be due to a lack of usage of such technology by these agencies or may be based on an anxiety related to the equipment. Staff are also hesitant to discuss those services that they feel the agency is less effective in delivering. Only 24 staff were willing to answer this question. Ventilator care was the most frequently mentioned service that is less effectively delivered. However, infusion therapy was the second most frequently cited service in this regard. This is somewhat ironic given the high numbers of staff who think this is their most effectively delivered service. However, the confusion here may be due to the general nature of the term infusion therapy. When staff offer this response, they may in fact have a particular type of infusion therapy in mind. It should also be noted that infusion therapy was cited as the most anxiety-provoking service for patients.

LEGAL AND ETHICAL ISSUES IN SERVING VULNERABLE POPULATIONS

Consideration of the legal and ethical dimensions of providing high technology care to older adults, the disabled, and other vulnerable populations in their own homes is destined to be an issue of central importance in the years ahead (Kaye & Davitt, 1995a). In fact, findings from this research suggest that the legal and ethical dimension of care is surfacing with increased frequency for administrators and their direct service staff in all categories of home health care agencies, whether or not high-tech services are offered. Such discussions between staff and patient are particularly common when issues pertaining to the patient's right to die and delegation of authority arise. And, these discussions can arise regardless of the age of the patient.

It should be noted at the outset that law and ethics are difficult to distinguish; indeed they are often used interchangeably in daily discourse. The two concepts do differ, however, and this is clearest when we focus on enforceability. Put simply, while both law and ethics express norms, law imposes obligations that are enforceable in a court of law. On the other hand, ethical norms tend to be enforced within the context of a particular profession's code of ethics or by reference to social norms or morality. While the discussion that follows focuses primarily on the legal dimension of home health care, the ethical aspects will be apparent.

Employer and Employee Duty to the Patient

Employees of organizations providing high-tech home health care are assumed to act responsibly and competently according to employer guidelines and generally accepted standards of care (Davitt & Kaye, 1995). If the employee incorrectly instructs the patient in the use of high-tech equipment or fails to properly install or operate such equipment, the employee may be found personally liable for any injury that results from the improper conduct. The key consideration therefore becomes whether employees properly discharge their duties in accordance with generally accepted standards. It is important to remember, however, that employers also may be found negligent under some circumstances, owing to their failure to properly instruct or supervise all employees who provide home health care. Finally, it should be noted that employee versus employer liability is not mutually exclusive; an employee may be found liable along with the employer.

Once again, the central importance of an agency establishing sound policies and procedures pertaining to accepted standards of practice in high-tech care as well as providing adequate opportunities for ongoing training and monitoring of staff performance has to be stressed. The employer must properly hire, train, supervise, and monitor the performance of all employees. All supervisory personnel also must monitor employee conduct. Consequently, a home health care agency should institute regular reviews of the conditions of employment and service for all employees. This review should extend to all independent contractors with whom the agency has a business relationship. Such contractors are responsible for their own employees, but the home health care agency should carefully monitor independent contractors to insure they do not expose the agency to legal liability.

An employee of a home health care agency includes, for purposes of legal liability, all paid staff, all students, all volunteers, and anyone else who is working—or is assumed to be working—under the direction of the employer on any activity that affects client care. Courts have held agencies liable for failures in this regard. See, for example, *Roach v. Kelly*

Health Care 742 P2d 1190 (1987). Agency responsibilities are also found in relevant state or federal regulations.

The Employer's Duty to Employees

The home health care agency owes a duty to employees to protect them from injury as they carry out their responsibilities on the agency's behalf. In the normal course of employment, for example, an employee may be injured in the client's home, in the operation of equipment, or in travel to or from the client's home. Staff may also experience some form of harassment (from clients or agency staff), or may contract a contagious disease. The key consideration is whether the employee's injury is job related; it must be associated with or follow from the employee's usual responsibilities.

Liability for Placement and Operation of High-Tech Equipment

As technology becomes more complex, agencies providing high-tech home health care may be legally vulnerable as a result of a number of situations (Safe Medical Devices Act of 1990). The following is a non-exhaustive, illustrative list.

1. Malfunctioning equipment that injures a client, who in turn may seek a legal remedy for actual injury or potential future lost earnings (see later discussion of product liability).
2. Inadequate instruction or supervision of staff or client in operation of equipment.
3. Inadequate monitoring of equipment or improper repair of malfunctioning equipment.
4. Inappropriate term of equipment placement (i.e., equipment is in the home for too long or too brief a period).
5. Unclear or inadequate service contract (between client and agency, or between client and some independent contractor with whom the agency has a business relationship).
6. Improper behavior of independent contractors in relation to any activity that affects client care.

The ethical dimension of malpractice focuses on questions that confront the health care agency and its employees who provide direct care. These questions include:

1. Who is the client?
2. What happens when client and agency interests conflict?
3. What is the dispute resolution process for resolving agency-client conflict?
4. What happens when staff disagree about client care, and how are client interests protected under these circumstances?
5. What is the relationship between funding care and providing care?

Conditions Related to Product Liability Law

To underscore the importance of the proper installation, operation, and inspection of high-tech equipment as part of providing home-based care, Haddad and Kapp (1991) offer the following analysis:

> It should be remembered that the modern home care agency is considered, for legal purposes, to act as both a professional service provider and the seller of a product. The sufficiency of its professional services is judged according to a negligence standard, that is, whether those services were of a quality that would be acceptable to other reasonable, prudent home care agencies. In terms of its role as a seller (or rental agent) of a piece of equipment, the home care agency is judged according to a different (from malpractice or professional negligence) standard, namely, according to the principles of *products liability*. Under products liability law, the seller of a product is legally liable for injuries caused to the purchaser if the product malfunctions as a result of inherent defects, even if there was no fault on the part of the seller. The manufacturer of the equipment and other companies in the chain of supply may also be held accountable, even without fault. Beyond liability for inherent defects, the home care agency may be held liable under a negligence standard for its errors or omissions in operating or installing the equipment or in training the client or caregiver to use it (p. 180–181).

Client Confidentiality

As a general principle, home care agencies are obligated to treat as confidential any information they obtain within the context of the agency-client relationship (U.S. Congress Office of Technology Assessment, 1993). This principle is expressed not only in common law but also in relevant licensure statutes and federal regulations. This obligation is inherent in the relationship, and the client need not explicitly request such protection. Thus, unauthorized release of any information may open the agency to liability. There are recognized exceptions to the general principle, however, such as when agencies must share client information with other service providers responsible for client care. There also may be instances when agencies may be obligated to divulge certain confidential communications (Rennert, 1991).

The ethical dimension of confidentiality raises questions about the conditions under which client-agency communications can be divulged to a third party. The following questions should be considered:

1. Who is the client?
2. Can clients refuse treatment, and what is the process for ensuring that such refusals really represent the client's decision?
3. What is the scope of confidentiality?
4. What are client expectations about confidentiality, and what happens when they conflict with agency expectations?
5. How are the requirements and limits of confidentiality explained to clients, and how does the agency conclude that the client comprehends these requirements?

Informed Consent, Client Competency, and Living Wills

The receipt of health care, including home care services, assumes a match between client and service. Does the client consent to care, and is this consent sufficiently informed as to enable us to conclude that the client is acting voluntarily? Courts will want to see that the client was given material information (i.e., information that a reasonably prudent patient would determine to be relevant to decide whether to consent to care) (American Civil Liberties Union, 1989).

Informed consent implies competency or the capacity to make decisions. The requirement is no less important when the client is incapacitated, although it is satisfied somewhat differently. The incapacitated may include infants, children, the mentally ill, the mentally handicapped, the comatose, and so forth. Both legal and ethical issues converge in the attempt to provide care to these particularly vulnerable populations. Home care agencies should institute, at the very least, procedures whereby they can identify: (a) when a client is incapacitated; (b) how to designate an incapacitated client's needs; and (c) the steps they will take to ensure that the care given to incapacitated clients remains relevant (American Bar Association, 1987; Regan, 1990).

Patient Rights and Advance Directives

Two forms of advance directives are living wills and durable powers of attorney for health care. Living wills are written documents that express the patients' wishes regarding treatment in the event they cannot make their own decisions (American Bar Association, 1991). A related legal instrument is the durable power of attorney for health care, which effectively enables clients to express how an agent will carry out their wishes should they become incapacitated. In addition to maintaining substantial familiarity with various types of advance directives, agency staff should remain aware of their own state laws regarding life-sustaining treatment decisions.

Perhaps the key ethical consideration revolves around identifying conflicts of interest and establishing a process that identifies and resolves these conflicts. This certainly represents a major administrative challenge for today's home health care agency.

Since enactment of the Patient Self-Determination Act (PSDA) in 1991, it would be safe to assume that agencies should have developed policies related to life-sustaining treatment decisions and advance directives (Davitt & Kaye, 1996; Kaye & Davitt, 1998). The PSDA requires health care providers, including home health agencies to: (a) maintain written policies and procedures regarding state law on advance directives; (b) inform patients upon admission of their rights under state law to direct their medical treatment and to execute an advance directive; (c) inform patients of agency policy on advance directives; (d) document the existence of an advance directive in the medical chart; and (e) educate agency staff and the community about advance directives (Patient Self-Determination Act of the Omnibus Budget Reconciliation Act 1990 42USC Section 1395 cc (a) (1) and 1902, 42USC Section 1396a (a) for Medicare and Medicaid, respectively [May, 1992, supp.]).

Given this mandate, it is disturbing to learn that 31% of the agencies participating in the national survey still did not have a policy on advance directives and treatment decisions. Granted, the survey research reported in this book was carried out approximately 5 years ago. However, home care organizations had already been operating approximately 3 years under the new legal mandate. Are agencies in greater conformity with the law today? Will they be 5 years from now? We are not convinced that conformity has dramatically increased during the past several years, especially because such practices are not systematically audited by a public oversight body.

This research confirms that for those agencies that do have policies, there is great variation both in the actual policies and the types of agencies that have them. Not surprisingly, hospital-based agencies have developed policies most often. Obviously these agencies benefit from the hospital auspice, with previously established legal support and expertise in the analysis of responsibility around the provision of medical care. However, hospice providers do not have established policies as often as nonhospice providers. Given the nature of hospice service and its emphasis on palliative care, the need for such formal policies may be reduced. Regardless of the experience or focus of individual home health care providers, the law still requires that agencies have such policies and that they explain them to all their patients.

Variations in actual policies and procedures can be expected to some degree because agencies work under different state laws and regulations. However, the variation uncovered in this survey is much greater then anticipated. Several agencies appear to lack procedures for determining whether a patient has an advance directive, something that is required by the PSDA. This is unfortunate because it appears that the original goal of the PSDA—to promote greater consumer awareness and understanding of advance directives—is not being met (at least not in the home care setting). This failure to satisfy the federal mandate is further highlighted by the low number of agencies providing either staff training or community education on advance directives.

On the other hand, several agencies have clearly developed comprehensive policies and procedures to ensure that a particular patient's wishes are followed in the event of incapacity. For example, several agencies have developed simple, straightforward procedures to flag charts when the patient has an advance directive, including using red or orange stickers on the chart or file or using similar stickers in the home such as on the telephone. These same agencies tend to maintain a copy of the patient's advance directive both on the chart and in the home (e.g., in a file near the telephone). These procedures ensure that all staff who enter the home will be able to determine immediately the patient's wishes, even when the patient is incapacitated. Such procedures may be especially important for high-tech providers because their patients may be more likely to experience serious and urgent complications in the home.

Paralleling the absence of industry-wide establishment of policies and procedures around life-sustaining treatment and advance directives is the substantial number of agencies that do not have policies on how to handle a patient who has questionable decision-making capacity. The low number of hospice providers with such policies (less than half) is especially curious. Without such policies, agencies are left to their own discretion on how to handle ethical dilemmas, which may arise in making treatment decisions. Not surprisingly, agencies that have policies on advance directives are more likely to have policies on patient decision-making capacity. Apparently those agencies that have implemented treatment-related policies are likely to have approached the challenge with an eye toward its multiple dimensions and implications.

Patients' Knowledge of Their Rights and Informed Consent

Staff and patients surveyed in the local analysis tend to concur on their perceptions related to patient rights and informed consent. Both agree that patients are adequately informed of their rights as patients. The concern around patient rights is generated around their awareness of their right to execute advance directives and their general knowledge about advance directives. Fewer patients were aware of their right to execute an advance directive than other patient rights. Also, very few patients have actually executed such a document. These findings parallel those emerging from the national data in which it appears that there may be some gaps in patient rights education provided by agencies. It can be expected that many patients will be hesitant to raise these issues with staff. Research has demonstrated that patients expect providers to address these kinds of issues and actually wait for providers to initiate these discussions. However, if staff are not even providing minimal information about such advance care documents, which is indicated in the national data by the failure of agencies to develop thorough and appropriate policies on advance directives, patients will remain uninformed and unprotected.

FUTURE DIRECTIONS IN HIGH-TECH INNOVATION IN HOME HEALTH

Exciting times lie ahead for the field of home health care. In no small part that excitement will be fueled by continued and impressive developments in the high-tech sector. It is predicted that particularly active growth will be seen in several distinct categories of home-delivered high-tech innovation that have not yet made significant headway in the home health sector even though the technology has now been available for a number of years. These include telehealth, robotics, and smart-house applications.

Telemedicine, Telehealth, and Home Care

Among the more fascinating of technological innovations is the potential of extending telemedicine capacity to the home. While the extension of telemedicine technology to the home seems logical, exploration of the possibilities in the home health care market remains relatively rare. That is predicted to change in the not too distant future. Telemedicine refers to the electronic transfer of health care information between two (or more) locations and can be divided into four general application categories: (a) experimental applications such as the surgeon's smart glove; (b) interactive video; (c) transmission of medical images such as X-rays and the use of telemetry and still video; and (d) electronic transfer of medical records, faxes, on-line text references, and e-mail.

According to a study by consultant Arthur D. Little, the ability of the medical community, insurers, and employers to use the nation's widespread telecommunications network could cut the U. S. health care bill by as much as $36 billion (Shoor, 1994).

Over the past several years, funded telemedicine projects have identified and substantiated numerous benefits, both medical and financial, to patients and the health care community. Previously underserved populations in remote communities and low-income inner city neighborhoods have improved access to specialized medical care; small rural hospitals can partner with more sophisticated urban hospitals for real-time medical image interpretation, diagnostic support, and specialized medical services; and correctional facility inmates can receive specialty consultations by medical center physicians. Not only does telemedicine reduce the often critical time consumed by patient or provider travel, it reduces the economic burden as well.

Despite the conceivable advantages of telemedicine and its technological feasibility, the path to widespread use is not without obstacles in the government-policy arena (Telemedlaw, 1997). A prime roadblock has been the refusal of the Health Care Finance Administration to allow Medicare and Medicaid reimbursement to health care providers for videoconferencing-based telemedicine services. Private insurers have followed suit.

There are signs that the government may be altering its position. Medicare provisions in the Balanced Budget Act of 1997 allow reimbursement for physicians and other providers including social workers who provide professional consultation via telecommunications networks to Medicare beneficiaries. The provisions of the legislation took effect in January 1999. The Act also requires that the Department of Health and Human Services research the possibility of providing Medicare teleconsults for homebound beneficiaries who would otherwise face serious hardship if they were transferred to a long-stay institution (NASW News, 1998).

A truly national or regional implementation plan is hindered by the requirement of physicians to practice with state-specific licenses, thus barring them from practicing telemedicine across state borders. The delay of government policy makers to support telemedicine initiatives will likely postpone, but not prevent, the achievement of telemedicine's potential.

The extension of telemedicine[2] to the home is a logical progression given the current home health care market. The trend toward provision of medical services in the home as an alternative to expensive hospitalization or nursing home care, in conjunction with declining computer costs per unit of power, support the application of telemedicine to home health care as a means of providing care at significantly lower cost. Not only does the introduction of telemedicine into the home allow home care staff to potentially treat more patients in a given period of time, but it may improve the quality of patient care by allowing:

- More frequent interactions with medical personnel;
- Round-the-clock coverage;
- Fewer missed home care visits resulting from obstacles to travel or inclement weather;
- Immediate access to vital signs for emergency, as well as routine, assessment; and
- Preventive care that could reduce hospitalizations, skilled nursing facility stays, emergency room visits, and unnecessary doctors' office visits and house calls (Kaye, 1997b).

Warner (1996a, 1996b) suggests that the use of telehealth in the home setting should promote patient autonomy as well, given that such technology enables persons to maintain their independence in the community. She suggests not only nurse and physicians can put such equipment to good use during the course of delivering home health services but physical and speech therapists and social work care managers can as well. Participating in interactive electronic home visits, capturing vital sign information data without visiting the home, scheduling daily activities, remotely managing the overall care plan, and even conducting individual therapy all can be accomplished using telehealth in home care (Levenson, 1997; Warner, 1996a).

A prospective productivity and cost analysis of a telemedicine home care system suggests that significant increases in productivity and savings are possible compared to a traditional model of service delivery (Kaye, 1997b). Kaye's analysis indicates that increases in productivity accruing from the implementation of televisits can enhance agency operations in three possible ways: (a) an increase in the total number of patients served; (b) an increase in the average number of visits of all types per patient; and (c) a decrease in the number of agency staff or full-time equivalents.

As compared to traditional home health care, televisits make 24-hour accessibility a reality and should be able to increase response time through the elimination of travel. These efficiencies may reduce the number of emergency room visits, the majority of which are known to be nonurgent (McCaig, 1994). Additionally, a number of physician's office visits or house calls for concerns related to medication or vital signs might be reduced as well, being replaced by a prompt, after-hours televisit.

The successful implementation of telemedicine in home health care on a wide-spread basis faces a series of challenges. These challenges, taken together, are considered to be normally occurring developments in the evolution of emergent technology in the human services. All are seen to impact potentially the end user in terms of likely service cost and quality. They include the following.

1. Hesitancy by the Health Care Financing Administration and third-party payors to recognize teleconferencing-based medical services as reimbursable entities.
2. Resistance among some physicians and other medical personnel to utilize such technology because they sense a threat or feel a lack of comfort using the equipment.
3. Hesitancy and a lack of comfort on the part of some home health care consumers, especially the geriatric population, in using the equipment.
4. Perceptions by some home health care providers and consumers of a degree of emotional disconnection and decrements in personal rapport brought on by the use of telemedicine technology.
5. The potential loss of the supplemental therapeutic benefits that would normally have been realized when nurses made in-person visits to homebound, isolated patients.

6. Inconsistencies in the technology itself, including variation in quality from provider to provider, variation in the cost of procuring and maintaining systems, variable reliability, and differences in useful life span prior to obsolescence.
7. Overreliance on laboratory experimentation and thus contrived service demonstrations rather than the real world experiences of consumers in using telemedicine in home health care.

It is to be expected that a period of full roll-out and more naturalistic yet systematic research and evaluation will be critical in ultimately determining with full accuracy the multiple benefits to accrue from telemedicine systems in home health care (Kaye, 1997b).

Home Robotics

Robots perform both simple and complex tasks, functions, and acts normally ascribed to humans. They are mechanisms guided by automatic controls displaying what appears to be human intelligence. The application of robotics in medicine is a hot topic. Robotic devices display the capacity to reduce the cost of health care, contribute to research and development, and increase the accuracy and efficiency of selected clinical procedures. Their application has been particularly robust in the areas of microsurgery, rehabilitation, and patient transfer. Robot assistants for persons with disabilities, robotic laboratories, telesurgery, and robotic devices for amputees are some of the more common application examples and to greater or lesser degrees have considerable potential for importation into the home of the home care patient. Some of the same drawbacks impacting the telehealth and smart house industry apply in the case of robotics, including issues of cost, quality, and availability. Even so, when properly developed, robotics have the capacity to assist homebound persons in performing their activities of daily living. Voice-activated personal robots are already available and can assist impaired older people and other disabled persons with such functions as lifting, bathing, and feeding (Haber, 1986; Kaye & Davitt, 1995c).

Smart-House Technology

Smart-house or home automation technology continues to hold considerable, though not yet realized, promise in relationship to the needs of homebound or otherwise incapacitated persons restricted in their functional and instrumental capacities. Home-control technology generally encompasses computer-controlled environmental systems for the home that have security and surveillance, telephone equipment and communications, energy efficiency, and entertainment applications. Smart-house technology includes but is not limited to the capacity to provide:

1. Zoned temperature control;
2. Water heater control;
3. Automatic control of small appliances;
4. Remote control of both indoor and outdoor home lighting;
5. Remote video monitoring and video transmission including time lapse video cassette recorders;
6. Glass break and motion sensors and instantaneous alerting of authorities to intruders;
7. Pet care automation (automatic feeders and water bowls, doors, litterboxes, containment, repellers, bark control);
8. Electronic door strikes and deadbolts;
9. Automatic watering systems;
10. Motorized heating and cooling registers;
11. Motorized drapery, window, and door controls;
12. Remote video and audio controls (volume, speakers, frequencies); and
13. Wireless intercoms, phone systems, automatic dial alarms, and door answering.

To date smart-house technological capabilities have been applied more commonly to the tele-office and home-office environment and the homes of the well-to-do rather than in the residences of older and disabled people in need of assistance. Bill Gates, chairman and chief executive officer of Microsoft Corporation, among others, has included the topic in his visionary account of what lies ahead on the home front (Gates, 1997).

Drawbacks in this technology at this stage in its evolution include: (a) inadequate standards in home automation equipment creating compatibility problems between different devices; (b) the prohibitive cost of much home automation technology; and (c) varying availability of adequate expertise in the home automation technology industry (professional expertise is not yet widely available, and qualified service personnel can be difficult to secure) (Jacobson, 1997).

While the concept of smart-house technology has been with us for a number of years, it has not been implemented in a widespread manner for the reasons cited above. Therefore, its application admittedly remains rather novel. Even so, one can expect the cost of the technology to significantly decline over time and its availability to become increasingly widespread and reliable.

The technology described above and similar such innovations will find their way into the homes of the functionally impaired, community-residing older population more and more commonly. This is already the case for personal emergency response systems, which are fast becoming a common staple of this population. It will, we believe, be the case for other innovation as well. The home care organization is positioned quite strategically to serve as a central distribution point of the technology and therefore in making it more easily accessible to the older adult.

FUTURE TRENDS IN HIGH-TECH HOME HEALTH

Just as the home care sector is now being challenged with a series of growth and development issues, so will the industry be challenged by an additional set of developments and issues impacting its continued evolution in the years ahead. This volume closes by reviewing these emerging trends.

Consumer-Directed Home Care Services

Consumerism will be an increasingly powerful factor in the organization and delivery of home health services in the years ahead. The older people of tomorrow, the *new aged* if you will, are going to enter into old age not only with greater resources but with higher expectations, greater political and strategic sophistication, and greater experience maneuvering through the quagmire of health and human services as well. They will be exceedingly vocal and influential. The demands they place on health care institutions generally, and the home health sector specifically, will be heightened. One manifestation of their activism and sophistication will be their call for consumer direction and influence in the organization of the services they require in old age (Scala & Mayberry, 1997; Scala, Mayberry, & Kunkel, 1996; Woodruff & Applebaum, 1996).

Consumer direction speaks to the idea of services being consumer centered or consumer driven as reflected in the incorporation of greater consumer choice and control into the planning, administration, management, delivery, and evaluation of services. Consumer-directed home care services of the future will embody the empowerment of service beneficiaries (both older service recipients and their families and caregivers) and the belief that such individuals are able to make informed decisions about the shape and form of the health care services they receive.

Evidence of the growing popularity of consumer direction in elder health and long-term care services is considerable. It includes: the establishment of the National Institute on Consumer-Directed Long-Term Care Services (funded by the U.S. Administration on Aging and the Office of the Assistant Secretary for Planning and Evaluation of the U.S. Department of Health and Human Services), funding opportunities in the area of consumer direction by the Robert Wood Johnson Foundation, and rapid growth in the consumer-directed Medicaid Personal Care Services Optional Benefit in which more than 30 states now participate (Doty, Kasper, & Litvak, 1996). A 1996 survey conducted by the National Council on the Aging (NCOA) identified 103 consumer-directed home and community-based service programs throughout the United States serving, for the most part, consumers of all ages (Cameron, 1996). The number of such programs will grow dramatically in the years ahead.

Geriatric Care Management and Managed Care

It should come as no surprise that home care is predicted to be increasingly influenced by the managed care paradigm in the future. Managed care organizations, through their review techniques and procedures, can be expected to press both high-tech and traditional home health agencies to become more cost efficient and effective. Agencies will need to explicitly document their effectiveness and find more equitable and accountable ways of managing scarce resources (Corwin, 1998). For-profit, managed care, and similar such organizational entities will continue to stake more and more claims in the home health sector.

Accompanying the spread of a managed care mindset in home health will be the central yet modified function to be played by both agency-based and independent geriatric care managers. These professionals (usually social workers or nurses) can be expected to be called to the fore more frequently given the movement away from heavy reliance on utilization review and toward other methods of cost containment that emphasize case management, triaging, and strict adherence to formal practice guidelines.

While geriatric care managers will be utilized more frequently in the home health sector in the future, they will be expected to go about their jobs in somewhat different fashion. Specifically, they will be required to engage in more time-limited intervention and be exceedingly strategic, systematic, and focused in their approach to practice as they adhere to preestablished intervention protocols. Corwin (1998) outlines a number of principles that will guide their practice including:

1. Emphasis on client competencies, strengths, and resources as the starting point of the intervention process.
2. Shifting of service delivery from a single long-term involvement to an intermittent, as-needed, service approach.
3. Use of interventions that are biphasic or triphasic in execution such that presenting problems are dealt with immediately.
4. Close attention to a client's definition of and engagement in the resolution of their problems and needs.
5. Performance of accurate, rapid assessments.
6. Clear and specific focusing of the work to be performed.
7. Flexible use of time based on client need.
8. Emphasis on client empowerment.

Put simply, care managers will be required to return to the more traditional essence of gerontological service intervention (e.g., assessment, case planning, service contracting, service monitoring, reassessment) (Kaye, 1998). In the managed care home health environment, their challenge will actually be to perform these traditional functions and practice competencies in increasingly cost-effective and efficient fashion in their work with older home health care consumers.

HOME HEALTH POLICIES AND THE POLITICS OF THE FUTURE

Although high-tech care has allowed many patients to recover at home in a more comfortable and familiar environment, it is not always the appropriate answer for every patient. In fact, many policy analysts have cautioned that home care has become exceedingly medicalized in recent years;

a process that can at times undermine the benefits accruing to in-home care. Efforts to help patients who suffer from chronic conditions that are not high tech in nature or do not even require skilled nursing care have frequently taken second seat to more medicalized forms of care. Therefore, patients who require less skilled services are less able to have their needs met in their homes because these services are generally not reimbursable under private and public insurance programs. A continued focus on high-tech or high-skill care may make it increasingly difficult for individuals with chronic conditions to find the help they need to remain in their homes. This may increase the burden of caregiving for families, an issue that is especially problematic in an era of two-earner couples and single-parent households. An important policy question is who will be available to care for older or disabled relatives when most adults are working.

Recent revisions in Medicare and Medicaid have highlighted the tendency to view home health care as a medical service only. Concern with increased utilization of nonskilled services has contributed to the demand for reforms in both the Medicare and Medicaid home health care benefit. However, the recent round of reforms represents a double-edged sword. The reforms are most likely to lead to dramatic cutbacks in the amount and duration of services available to individual clients. This may be problematic in several ways. First, certain regions or communities may have severely limited alternatives to home health care. For example, nursing home bed shortages in many cities and states may mean that patients will be discharged from acute care settings without adequate services to meet their needs. This leads directly to the second problem, caregiver burden. Although many families will consciously choose not to place a loved one in an institutional setting (regardless of the availability of that option), others may be forced to provide care because they have no alternative. This may prove an overwhelming burden to families with multiple demanding responsibilities, including employment outside of the home and intergenerational family obligations. These trends could lead to an increased incidence of elder neglect. Which brings us to the third problem, the potential to compromise the safety and security of patients discharged from acute care settings.

The ironic twist in this policy shift results in a robbing Peter to pay Paul type of conundrum. As the increase in home care utilization resulted from the development of the prospective payment system (PPS) in acute care, the creation of the PPS in home care may simply lead to a new shift in the locus of care. Cutbacks and limitations initiated through the Balanced

Budget Act of 1997 (BBA) may, in fact, increase the use of institutional care, including subacute and long-term care facilities.

The field of home care may experience other trends in the near future due to ramifications of the BBA. It is likely that the field will experience an increase in agency mergers, as have occurred in other health care settings. Smaller providers and non-profit providers may decline in numbers. This may affect clients directly in relation to quality of care and access to home health care. Mergers are likely to reduce competition in any given market, potentially impacting negatively on quality of care. If one large provider monopolizes a market, consumers will have little option to seek services elsewhere, which is the ultimate consumer advocacy tool. In addition, it will be more difficult for licensing bodies to revoke operating privileges for quality of care violations when the agency is the only shop in town.

Likewise certain types of patients may have reduced access to home health care due to restrictions on the amount and duration of services and the method used to determine agency reimbursement rates. High-tech patients in particular may be less able to access home care services. The complexity and intensity of care needed in such cases may discourage providers from admitting high-tech patients in general or specific types of high-tech patients. In addition, changes in reimbursement determinations may discourage new providers from entering the high-tech market, thereby reducing competition and limiting the availability of such providers. Agencies may be less willing to expand their available services; choosing not to offer novel or experimental treatments that could increase their cost ratio. Such treatments may not be reimbursed or may prove more expensive to administer in the home setting than reimbursement standards will allow.

Policy analysts also fear that rural patients may lose access to necessary home care services. Expenses for travel, time, and emergency interventions in rural areas can be much higher than in more densely populated areas. In these situations patients may also have little access to other long-term care options, such as nursing home or subacute care. This raises serious concerns regarding the potential for dangerous conditions for such patients, especially if hospitals continue to pressure families to accept discharge to home without an adequate care plan.

The need for research that monitors these changes is obvious. It will be important to demonstrate very concretely any negative effects of the changes in reimbursement policies. Research should consider both the direct and indirect effects on patients, as well as the effects on agencies.

EPILOGUE

The home health care industry has emerged full bloom. This sector of the health and human services is rapidly developing a powerful contingent of special interest and advocacy groups and organizations that can seemingly mobilize at a moment's notice. As recently as February 1998 a vigorous protest erupted in the halls of Congress over proposed cuts in home care. In a matter of days, Congress was inundated with letters from both home care providers and beneficiaries. The effort was spearheaded by the National Association for Home Care, the major trade association representing the interests of more than 6,000 home care agencies, hospices, and home care aide organizations.

Additional evidence of home care's arrival is not difficult to locate. Expenditures for home health services through government programs, private insurance companies, and out-of-pocket payments are mushrooming. Research and demonstration projects on various and sundry topics in home and community-based care are underway, funded through a wide variety of public and private sources of support. We now have a National Home Care Month, National Hospice Month, and National Home Care Aide Week, all used to educate the public about the nature of this popular service entity. The World Homecare and Hospice Organization (WHHO) represents a growing network of global leaders and organizations representative of home care providers, home care associations, public and private sector agencies, hospices, and personal services practitioners. The WHHO has been organized to serve as an international clearinghouse and forum for communication, business development, and information and technology sharing.

Technologically enhanced care delivered in the home is also destined to become increasingly commonplace in the years ahead. The powerful trend toward high-tech care provision in the home health industry, highlighted by the findings arising from research reported in this volume, is going to transform necessarily the way in which home health care services are organized and delivered to functionally impaired older people and other vulnerable populations residing in the community.

While the importation of technology into the home health sector may serve to reduce our overdependence on institutional solutions to dependency at the same time that it elevates the status of this field of service to levels never before realized, it will also surely challenge our abilities to provide home-centered care in an effective and efficient manner. The fiscal survival of the home health organization and the personal welfare of our most vulnerable citizens may lie in the balance.

A critical measure of our success in meeting these challenges may ultimately be our ability to attract skilled service professionals to the field who can not only organize and deliver high-tech services in competent fashion but can communicate with clarity the nature and intent of the changing home care interventive scenario to the potential consumer population as well as the larger public. Unfortunately, such services remain clouded in mystery to considerable degree despite the public's preference for home-based solutions to their dependent care needs and our increased capacity to care for individuals in the familiar surroundings of their homes. Many caregivers and their elders continue to lack even the most basic information about community home care services. This analysis has sought to address this awareness gap through constructive dissemination of much needed information about technologically enhanced in-home services to home health care agencies and the publics they may eventually serve. We hope we have been reasonably successful in this effort and encourage others to make similar such efforts in the future.

NOTES

1. The conclusions and interpretation of study findings presented in the first section of this chapter (as well as selected data presented in section II, chapters 3 through 7) draws on material found in an earlier series of articles published by the authors including Kaye, L. W. and Davitt, J. K. (1998). Comparison of the high-tech service delivery experiences of hospice and nonhospice home health providers. *The Hospice Journal, 13,* 1–20; Davitt, J. K. and Kaye, L. W. (1996). Supporting patient autonomy: Decision making in home health care. *Social Work, 41,* 41–50; Davitt, J. K. and Kaye, L. W. (1995). High-tech home health care: Administrative and staff perspectives. *Home Health Care Services Quarterly, 15,* 49–66; Kaye, L. W. and Davitt, J. K. (1995a). Assessing the legal and ethical dimensions of delivering high-tech home health care. *Journal of Ethics, Law, and Aging, 1,* 37–54; Kaye, L. W., and Davitt, J. K. (1995b). Provider and consumer profiles of traditional and high-tech home health care: The issue of differential access. *Health & Social Work, 20,* 262–271; and Kaye, L. W. and Davitt, J. K. (1995c). The importation of high technology services into the home. *Journal of Gerontological Social Work, 24,* 67–94.
2. The term telehealth may well be more accurate terminology in describing telemedicine applications in home health care given the likelihood that professions other than medicine (such as nursing) will be major participants in its implementation.

References

Agency for Health Care Policy and Research. (1997). Washington, DC: AHCPR. Available: www.ahcpr.gov.

Agency for Health Care Policy and Research, Center for Cost and Financing Studies. (1997). *National medical expenditure survey, March 1997.* Washington, DC: U.S. Government Printing Office.

American Bar Association. (1987). *Exploring ethical issues in meeting the legal needs of the elderly.* Washington, DC: Author.

American Bar Association. (1991). *Court-related needs of the elderly and persons with disabilities.* Washington, DC: Author.

American Civil Liberties Union. (1989). *The rights of older persons.* Carbondale, IL: University of Illinois Press.

American Law Report. (1996). Annotation, physician's duty to instruct nurse or attendant. *ALR3rd, 63,* 1022–1027.

American Law Report. (1997a). Annotation, physician's joint liability when independent negligence of physician causes indivisible injury. *ALR5th, 9,* 768–773.

American Law Report. (1997b). Annotation, liability of health maintenance organizations for negligence of member physicians. *ALR5th, 51,* 296–299.

American Law Report. (1997c). Annotation, propriety of, and liability related to, issuance or enforcement of do not resuscitate (dnr) orders. *ALR5th, 46,* 793–811.

American Nursing Association. (1997). Telehealth—issues for nursing. *American Nursing Association Policy Series.* Washington, DC: Author. Available: www.ana.org/readroom/tele2.htm

Appelbaum, P. S., Lidz, C. W., & Meisel, A. (1987). *Informed consent.* New York: Oxford University Press.

Applebaum, R. (1997). The emergence of community-based long-term care. *The Public Policy and Aging Report, 8* (2), 3–5.

Ardoin v. Hartford Accident and Indemnity Co., 350 So.2d 205 (La. App. 1977).

Arno, P. S., Bonuck, K. A., & Padgug, R. (1994). The economic impact of high-technology home care. *The Hastings Center Report, 24,* S15–19.

Arras, J. D., & Dubler, N. N. (1994). Bringing the hospital home: Ethical and social implications of high-tech home care. *Hastings Center Report, 24*(5), s19–s28.

Bankert by Bankert v. U.S., 937 F. Supp. 1169 (D. Md. 1996).

Barber v. Reinking, 411 P.2d 861 (1966).

Barton, W. E., & Barton, G. M. (1984). *Ethics and law in mental health administration.* New York: Author.

Benjamin, A. E. (1993). An historical perspective on home care policy. *The Millbank Quarterly, 71,* 129–165.

Besdine, R. W. (1985). Decisions to withhold treatment from nursing home residents. In M. B. Kapp, H. E. Pies, Jr., & A. E. Doudera (Eds.), *Legal and ethical aspects of health care for the elderly,* (pp. 268–276). Ann Arbor, MI: Health Administration Press.

Binney, E. A., & Estes, C. L. (1990). Setting the wrong limits: Class biases and the biographical standard. In P. Homer, & M. Holstein (Eds.), *A good old age? The paradox of setting limits* (pp. 260–282). New York: Simon and Schuster.

Blackhall, L. J., Murphy, S. T., Frank G., Michel, V., et al. (1995). Ethnicity and attitudes toward patient autonomy. *Journal of the American Medical Association, 274,* 820–825.

Blumenthal, J., & Haynes, J. (1995). Home health care nursing: Liability and risk management for "informed consent" and "the Safe Medical Practices Act" duties. *Journal of Health and Hospital Care, 28,* 286–291.

Blustein, J. (1993). The family in medical decision making. *Hastings Center Report, 23*(3), 6–13.

Boas, E., & Michelsohn, N. (1929). *Challenge of chronic disease.* New York: MacMillan.

Brennan, P. F., Moore, S. M., & Smyth, K. A. (1991). ComputerLink: Electronic support for the home caregiver. *Advances in Nursing Science, 13,* 14–27.

Brent, N. (1997). Risk management in home health care: Focus on patient care liabilities. *Loyola University Law Journal, 20,* 775–795.

Brent, N. J. (1992). Focus on the home healthcare nurse. *Home Healthcare Nurse, 10,* 10–11.

Brody, E. M. (1990). *Women in the middle: Their parent-care years.* New York: Springer.

Burwell, B. (1997). *Medicaid long-term care expenditures.* Lexington, MA: Systemetrics.

Cahil v. HCA Management Co. Inc., 812 F.2d 170 (1987).

California Telemedicine Development Act, 5 Cal. Bus. and Prof. Code, §2135 (1996).

Cameron, K. (November 1996). State demonstrations and initiatives in consumer choice and direction: Findings from the national survey of states. In D. L. Wagner (Chair), *Consumer-directed long-term services,* Symposium conducted at the 1996 annual scientific meeting of the Gerontological Society of America, Washington, DC.

Capone v. Donovan, 480 A.2d 1249 (Pa. Super. 1984).

Carrese, J. A., & Rhodes, L. A. (1995). Western bioethics on the Navajo reservation: Benefit or harm? *Journal of the American Medical Association, 274,* 826–829.

Center for Telemedicine Law. (1997a). *Regulatory update.* Washington, DC: Author.

Center for Telemedicine Law. (1997b). Telemedicine and interstate licensure: Findings and recommendations of the center for telemedicine law licensure task force. *North Dakota Law Review, 73,* 109–131.

Cepelewicz, B. (1997). Legal issues in telemedicine. In A. Kincella (Ed.), Home health care: Wired and ready for telemedicine (221–227). *Information for Tomorrow.*

Chadiha, L. A., Proctor, E. K., & Morrow-Howell, N. (1995). Post-hospital home care for African-American and white elderly. *The Gerontologist, 35,* 233–239.

Cohen, M. A., & Tumlinson, (1997). Understanding state variation in Medicare home health care: The impact of Medicaid program characteristics, state policy, and provider attributes. *Medical Care, 35,* 618–633.

Coile, R. C. (1990). Technology and ethics: Three scenarios for the 1990s. *Quality Review Bulletin, 16,* 202–208.

Collopy, B. A. (1988). Autonomy in long term care: Some crucial distinctions. *The Gerontologist, 28*(Suppl.), 10–17.

Collopy, B. A. (1990a). An introduction to home care: What are the issues? In C. Zuckerman, N. N. Dubler, & B. Collopy (Eds.), *Home health care options: A guide for older persons and concerned families.* New York: Plenum.

Collopy, B. A. (1990b). Ethical dimensions of autonomy in long-term care. *Generations, 14*(Suppl.), 9–12.

Collopy, B. A., Dubler, N., & Zuckerman, C. (1990). The ethics of home care: Autonomy and accommodation. *Hastings Center Report,* March/April, *20*(2), 1–16.

Collopy, B. M. (1992). *The use of restraints in long-term care: The ethical issues.* Washington, DC: American Association of Homes for the Aging.

Commission on Chronic Illness. (1956). *Chronic illness in the United States: Vol. 2 care of the long term patient.* Cambridge, MA: Harvard University Press.

Compton, B. R., & Galaway, B. (1979). *Social work processes.* Homewood, IL: Dorsey.

Conditions of Participation: Home Health Agencies. 42 C.F.R. §484.36 (1997a).

Conditions of Participation: Home Health Agencies. 42 C.F.R. §484.10 (1997b).

Conditions of Participation: Home Health Agencies. 42 C.F.R. §484.18 (1997c).

Congressional Budget Office. (1991). *Policy changes for long term care.* Washington, DC: U.S. Government Printing Office.

Corcoran v. United HealthCare, Inc., 965 F.2d 1321 (5th Cir. 1992), *cert denied,* 113 S.Ct. 812 (1993).

Corrigan v. Methodist Hospital, 869 F. Supp. 1208 (E.D. Pa. 1994).

Corwin, M. D. (1998). Therapeutic techniques for the geriatric care manager in a managed care environment. *Geriatric Care Management Journal, 8,* 6–10.

Coulter, K. (1997). Nurses transition from hospital to home: Bridging the gap. *Journal of Intravenous Nursing, 20,* 89–93.

Crowley, S. L., & Glasheen, L. K. (June 1998). Getting the care you need. *AARP Bulletin, 38,* 12–15.

Crown, W., MacAdam, M., & Sadowsky, E. (1992). Home care workers: A national profile. *Caring Magazine, 11,* 34–38.

Cruzan v. Director, Missouri Department of Health, 110 S.CT. 2841, 2855–56 (1990).

Darlington v. Charleston Community Memorial Hospital, 33 Ill.2d 326 (1965), *cert denied,* 386 U.S. 946 (1966).

Davitt, J. K. (1992). *The patient self-determination act: Promoting autonomy in long term care.* Philadelphia: Northwest Interfaith Movement.

Davitt, J. K. (1996). Promoting cultural pluralism in advance care planning. *Geriatric Care Management Journal, 6* (4), 2–10.

Davitt, J. K., & Kaye, L. W. (1995). High-tech home health care: Administrative and staff perspectives. *Home Health Care Services Quarterly, 15* (4), 49–66.

Davitt, J. K., & Kaye, L. W. (1996). Supporting patient autonomy: Decision making in home health care. *Social Work, 41* (1), 41–50.

deSavorgnani, A. A., Haring, R. C., & Davis, H. (1992). A survey of home care aides: A personal and professional profile. *Caring Magazine, 11,* 28–32.

Diamond, E. L., Jernigan, J. A., Moseley, R. A., Messina, V., & McKeown, R. A. (1989). Decision-making ability and advance directive preferences in nursing home patients and proxies. *The Gerontologist, 29,* 622–626.

Dombi, W. (1992). Chronic intensive home care. *Caring Magazine, 11,* 58–63.

Donaldson v. YWCA, 539 N.W.2d 789 (Minn. 1995).

Doty, P., Kasper, J., & Litvak, S. (1996). Consumer-directed models of personal care: Lessons from Medicaid. *The Milbank Quarterly, 74,* 377–409.

Dubler, N. (1990). Refusals of medical care in the home setting. *Law, Medicine and Health Care, 18,* 227–233.

Duggan v. Bowen, Civil Action No. 87-0383, U.S. District Court for the District of Columbia, 691 F. Supp. 1487; 1988 U.S. Dist. LEXIS 8800, August 1, 1988.

Eastaugh, S. R. (1981). *Medical economics and health finance.* Boston: Auburn.

Emanuel, E. J. (1991). *The Ends of Human Life.* Cambridge, MA: Harvard University Press.

Emanuel, L. L., Barry, M. J., Stoeckle, J. D., Ettelson, L. M., & Emanuel, E. J. (1991). Advance directives for medical care—A case for greater use. *The New England Journal of Medicine, 324,* 889–895.

Erb, J. (1997). Discharge planning. In M. Harris, (Ed.), *Handbook of home health care administration* (427–446). Gaithersberg, MD: Aspen.

Estate of Leach v. Shapiro, 469 N.E.2d 1047 (Ohio App. 1984).

Estes C. L., Swan, J. H., & Associates. (1993). *The long-term care crisis: Elders trapped in the no-care zone.* Newbury Park, CA: Sage.

Ettner, S. L. (1994). The effect of the Medicaid home care benefit on long-term care choices of the elderly. *Economic Inquiry, 32,* 103–127.

Faden, R. R., & Beauchamp, T. L. (1986). *A history and theory of informed consent.* New York: Oxford University Press.

False Claims Act, 31 U.S.C. §3729 (1997).

Farnsworth, M. G. (1989). Evaluation of mental competency. *American Family Physician, 39,* 182–190.

Federal Privacy Act of 1974, 5 U.S.C. §522a(b) (1974).

Fein v. Permanente Medical Group, 695 P.2d 665 (Cal. 1985).

Folkemer, D. (1994). *State use of home and community-based services for the aged under Medicaid: Waiver programs, personal care, frail elderly services and home health services.* Washington, DC: American Association of Retired Persons.

Follmann, J. F. (1963). *Medical care and health insurance: A study in social progress.* Homewood, IL: Richard D. Irwin.

Fox, D. M. (1992). Health policy and changing epidemiology in the United States: Chronic disease in the twentieth century. In C. R. Maulitz (Ed.), *Unnatural causes.* New Brunswick, NJ: Rutgers University Press.

Frankel, J. (1994). Medical malpractice law and health care cost containment: Lessons for reformers from the clash of cultures. *Yale Law Journal, 103,* 1297–1331.

Frankena, W. K. (1973). *Ethics.* Englewood Cliffs, NJ: Prentice Hall.

Freeman, L. (1995). Home-sweet-home care. *Monthly Labor Review, 118,* 3–11.

Friedman, S., & Kaye, L. W. (1979). Home care for the frail elderly: Implications for an interactional relationship. *Journal of Gerontological Social Work, 2,* 109–123.

Frontline workers in long-term care. (1994). *Generations, 18,* 4–86.

Gates, B. (March 5 1997). The road ahead. Available: www.roadahead.com

General Accounting Office. (1996). *Skilled nursing facilities: Approval process for certain service may result in higher Medicare costs.* Washington, DC: U.S. Government Printing Office.

Gilroy, P., Trager, T., & Kinney, T. J. (1982). *Supervision in home care : A manual for supervisors.* Washington, DC: National HomeCaring Council.

Goldberg, H. B., & Schmitz, R. J. (1994). Contemplating home health PPS: Current patterns of Medicare service use. *Health Care Financing Review, 16,* 109–130.

Gostin, L. O. (1995). Informed consent, cultural sensitivity, and respect for persons. *Journal of the American Medical Association, 274,* 844–845.

Grieco, A. J. (1991). Physician's guide to managing home care of older patients. *Geriatrics, 46,* 49–60.

Haber, P. (1986). Technology and aging. *The Gerontologist, 26,* 350–357.

Haddad, A. M. (1992). Ethical problems in home health care. *Journal of Nursing Administration, 22* (3), 46–51.

Haddad, A. M., & Kapp, M. (1991). *Ethical and legal issues in home health care.* Norwalk, CT: Appleton & Lange.

Halamandaris, V. J. (1986/87). A sense of the right thing to do. *Generations, XI,* 4.

Hastings Center. (1994). The technological tether: An introduction to ethical and social issues in high-tech home care. *Hastings Center Report, 24* (Suppl. 5), S1–S28.

Health Care Financing Administration (HCFA). (1996). HCFA statistics. Washington, DC: Author. Available: www.hcfa.gov/stats/hstats96/

High, D. M. (1993). Advance directives and the elderly: A study of intervention strategies to increase use. *The Gerontologist, 33,* 342–349.

Hoffman, D. (1997). The False Claims Act as a remedy to the inadequate provision of nutrition and wound care to nursing home residents. *Advances in Wound Care, 9,* 25–29.

Hospice Association of America. (1997). *Hospice facts and statistics.* Washington, DC: Author.

Hudson, R. B. (1996). Home and community-based care: Recent accomplishments and new challenges. *Journal of Aging and Social Policy, 7,* 53–69.

Hughes, S. L. (1995). Evaluation and quality assurance for in-home services. In L. W. Kaye (Ed.), *New developments in home care services for the elderly: Innovations in policy, program, and practice,* (pp. 117–131). New York: Haworth.

Illich, I. (1976). *Medical nemesis: The expropriation of health.* New York: Pantheon.

In the Matter of Conroy, 486 A.2d 1209 (N.J. 1985).

In the Matter of Farrell, 529 A.2d 404 (N.J. 1987).

Indest, G. (1997). Applying informed consent to the home health care industry. *Home Health Care Management and Practice, 9,* 17–30.

Institute for Health and Aging. (1986). *DRG study.* San Francisco, CA: Author.

Jacobson, J., Weber State University. (March 1997). Home management systems. Available: cc.weber.edu/itfm/hottopic/homebase1/homebase.htm#Definition

Jarrett, M. C. (1933a). *Chronic illness in New York City, vol. 1: The problems of chronic illness.* New York: Columbia University Press.

Jarrett, M. C. (1933b). *Chronic illness in New York City, Vol. 2: The care of the sick by different types of voluntary agencies.* New York: Columbia University Press.

Johnson, S. (1991). Liability issues. In M. Mehlman, & S. Youngner (Eds.), *Delivering high-technology home care* (pp. 125–159). New York: Springer.

Kane, N. M. (1989). The home care crisis of the nineties. *The Gerontologist, 29,* 24–31.

Kane, R. A., Kane, R. L., Illston, L. H., & Eustis, N. N. (1994). Perspectives on home care quality. *Health Care Financing Review, 16,* 69–89.

Kapp, M. B. (1988). Forcing services on at-risk older adults: When doing good is not so good. *Social Work in Health Care, 13* (4), 1–13.

Kapp, M. B. (1990). Evaluating decisionmaking capacity in the elderly: A review of recent literature. *Journal of Elder Abuse & Neglect, 2* (3–4), 15–29.

Kapp, M. B. (1991a). Health care decision making by the elderly: I get by with a little help from my family. *The Gerontologist, 31,* 619–623.

Kapp, M. B. (1991b). Improving choices regarding home care services: Legal impediments and empowerment. *Saint Louis University Public Law Review, 10,* 441–484.

Kapp, M. B. (1992). *Geriatrics and the law.* New York: Springer.

Kapp, M. B. (1995a). Legal and ethical issues in home-based care. In L. W. Kaye (Ed.), *New developments in home care services for the elderly: Innovations in policy, program, and practice,* (pp. 31–45). New York: Haworth.

Kapp, M. B. (1995b). Restraining impaired elders in the home environment: Legal, practical, and policy implications. *Journal of Case Management, 4* (2), 54–59.

Katsetos v. Nolan, 368 A.2d 172 (Conn. 1976).

Kaye, L. W. (1985). Homecare. In A. Monk (Ed.), *Handbook of gerontological services,* (pp. 408–432). New York: Van Nostrand Reinhold.

Kaye, L. W. (1988). Generational equity: Pitting young against old. *New England Journal of Human Services, 8,* 8–11.

Kaye, L. W. (1991). The future of community-based services for the old-old: Technological and ethical challenges. *Home Health Care Services Quarterly, 12,* 57–67.

Kaye, L. W. (1992). *Home health care.* Newbury Park, CA: Sage.

Kaye, L. W. (1995). Marketing techniques for home care programs. In L. W. Kaye (Ed.), *New developments in home care services for the elderly: Innovations in policy, program, and practice,* (pp. 133–156). New York: Haworth.

Kaye, L. W. (1996). Patterns of targeting and encouraging participation of elder consumers in human services marketing. *Health Marketing Quarterly, 13* (3), 27–46.

Kaye, L. W. (1997a). Informal caregiving by older men. In J. I. Kosberg, & L. W. Kaye (Eds.), *Elderly men: Special problems and professional challenges,* (pp. 231–249). New York: Springer.

Kaye, L. W. (1997b). Telemedicine: Extension to home care? *Telemedicine Journal, 3,* 243–246.

Kaye, L. W. (1998). Practicing geriatric care management: Getting back to basics. *Geriatric Care Management Journal, 8,* 2–5.

Kaye, L. W., & Applegate, J. S. (1990). *Men as caregivers to the elderly: Under-standing and aiding unrecognized family support.* Lexington, MA: Lexington Books.

Kaye, L. W., & Davitt, J. K. (1995a). Assessing the legal and ethical dimensions of delivering high-tech home health care. *Journal of Ethics, Law, and Aging, 1,* 37–54.

Kaye, L. W., & Davitt, J. K. (1995b). Provider and consumer profiles of traditional and high-tech home health care: The issue of differential access. *Health & Social Work, 20,* 262–271.

Kaye, L. W., & Davitt, J. K. (1995c). The importation of high-technology services into home care. In L. W. Kaye (Ed.). *New developments in home care services for the elderly: Innovations in policy, program and practice* (pp. 67–94). New York: Haworth Press.

Kaye, L. W., & Davitt, J. K. (1998). Comparison of the high-tech service delivery experiences of hospice and non-hospice home health providers. *The Hospice Journal, 13,* 1–20.

Kaye, L. W., & Reisman, S. I. (1991a). *A comparative analysis of marketing strategies in health and social services for the elderly: Provider and consumer perspectives.* Final report. Bryn Mawr, PA: Bryn Mawr College.

Kaye, L. W., & Reisman, S. I. (1991b). Life prolongation technologies in home care for the frail elderly: Issues for training, policy and research. *Journal of Gerontological Social Work, 16,* 79–91.

Keenan, J. M., & Fanale, J. E. (1989). Home care: Past and present, problems and potential. *Journal of the American Geriatrics Society, 37,* 1076–1083.

Komisar, H. L., & Feder, J. (1998). *The Balanced budget act of 1997: Effects on Medicare's home health benefit and beneficiaries who need long-term care.* Washington, DC: Institute for Health Care Research and Policy, Georgetown University.

Kottak, C. P. (1978). *Anthropology: The exploration of human diversity.* New York: Random House.

Kurlander, S. (1996). The legal side of guidelines. *Home Health Care Dealer/ Supplier, 17,* 159–161.

LaPuma, J., Orentlicher, D., & Moss, R. J. (1991). Advance directives on admission: Clinical implications and analysis of the Patient Self-Determination Act of 1990. *Journal of the American Medical Association, 266,* 402–405.

Larkins, F. R., & Hellige, M. (1992). Adding high-tech home care services to your agency. *Caring Magazine,* September, 18–22.

Lee v. Dewbre, 362 S.W.2d 900 (Tex. Civ. App. 1962).

Levenson, D. (July 1997). Telehealth: Practice-at-a-distance approaches. *NASW News, 42,* (3).

Lewin Group, The. (1998). *Implications of the Medicare home health interim payment system of the 1997 balanced budget act.* Washington, DC: National Association for Home Care.

Liebig, P. S. (1988). The use of high technology for health care at home: Issues and implications. *Medical Instrumentation, 22,* 222–225.

Lindeman, C. A. (1992). Nursing & technology: Moving into the 21st century. *Caring Magazine,* September, 5–17.

Macklin, R., & Callahan, D. (1990). Some examples to consider. In C. Zuckerman, N. N. Dubler, and B. Collopy (Eds.), *Home health care options: A guide for older persons and concerned families.* New York: Plenum.

Magilvy, J. K., Congdon, J. G., and Martinez, R. (1994). Circles of care: Home care. *Advances in Nursing Science, 16,* 22–33.

Magrinat v. Trinity Hospital, 540 N.W.2d 625 (N.D. 1995).

Marks, W. (1992). Physical restraints in the practice of medicine: Current concepts. *Archives of Internal Medicine, 152,* 2203–2206.

Mauser, E., & Miller, N. A. (1994). A profile of home health users in 1992. *Health Care Financing Review, 16,* 17–33.

McAbee, R. R., Grupp, K., & Horn, B. (1991). Home intravenous therapy: Part I—issues. *Home Health Care Services Quarterly, 12,* 59–108.

McCaig, L. F. (1994). National hospital ambulatory medical care survey: 1992. Emergency department summary. *Advance Data from Vital and Health Statistics;* 245. Hyattsville, MD: National Center for Health Statistics.

McLeod, D. (1998). Home-care patients feel unfairly targeted. *AARP Bulletin, 39,* 1, 8–9.

McMenanim, J. (1997). Telemedicine: Technology and the law. *The Defense Research Institute, 39,* 10–18.

Mehlman, M. J., & Youngner, S. J. (1991). *Delivering high technology home care.* New York, NY: Springer.

Michel, V. (1994, Winter). Factoring ethnic and racial differences into bioethics decision making. *Generations, 18,* (4), 23–26.

Miles, S. H., & Irvine, P. (1992). Deaths caused by physical restraints. *The Gerontologist, 32,* 762–766.

Miller, B. (1987). Gender and control among spouses of the cognitively impaired: A research note. *The Gerontologist, 27,* 447–453.

Moody, H. R. (1988). From informed consent to negotiated consent. *The Gerontologist, 28* (Suppl.), 64–70.

Moody, H. R. (1992). *Ethics in an aging society.* Baltimore: The Johns Hopkins University Press.

Moon, M., Gage, B., & Evans, A. (1997). *An examination of key Medicare provisions in the balanced budget act of 1997.* Washington, DC: The Urban Institute.

Nathanson, M. (1995). *Home health care answer book: Legal issues for providers.* Gaithersberg, MD: Aspen.

National Association of Social Workers News. (1998, April). Home health care cuts trigger alarm. *NASW News, 43,* 6.

National Association of Social Workers News. Medicare pays 'telehealth'. (1998, January). *NASW News, 43,* 6.

National Association for Home Care. (1996). *Basic statistics about home care 1996.* Washington, DC: Author. Available: http://www.nahc.org/Consumer /hcstats.html

National Association for Home Care. (1997). *Basic statistics about home care.* Washington, DC: Author.

National Association for Home Care. (1998a). *Problems with the January 5 surety bond regulations.* Washington, DC: Author.

National Association for Home Care. (1998b). *Regulatory update.* Washington, DC: Author.

National Center for Health Services Research and Health Care Technology Assessment. (1988). Research agenda on home health care. *NCHSR Program Note.* Washington, DC: U.S. Government Printing Office.

Office of Technology Assessment. (1984). *Technology and aging in America.* Washington, DC: U.S. Government Printing Office.

Office of Technology Assessment. (1987). Life-sustaining technologies and the elderly. *OTS Report Brief.* Washington, DC: U.S. Government Printing Office.

O'Keefe, J. (1996). *Determining the need for long-term care services: An analysis of health and functional eligibility criteria in Medicaid home and community based waiver programs.* Washington, DC: The American Association of Retired Persons.

Passuth, P. M., & Bengston, V. L. (1988). Sociological theories of aging. In J. E. Birren, & V. L. Bengston (Eds.), *Emergent theories of aging* (pp. 333–355). New York: Springer.

Patient Self-Determination Act, (1990) P.L. 101-508, U.S.C. Sec. 1395c(a)(1) & 1902, 1396a(a) (May, 1992 Supp.).

Payton Health Care v. Campbell, 497 So.2d 1233 (Fla. App. 1986).

Phelps v. Sherwood Medical Industries, 836 F. Supp. 296 (7th Cir. 1987).

Poulin, J., & Thomas, N. D. (1998). Burnout and the geriatric care manager. *Geriatric Care Management Journal, 8,* 25–29.

Powell, C., Mitchell-Pederson, L., Fingerote, E., & Edmund, L. (1989). Freedom from restraints: Consequences of reducing physical restraints in the management of the elderly. *Canadian Medical Association Journal, 141,* 561–564.

President's Commission for the Study of Ethical Problems in Medicine and Biomedical and Behavioral Research. (1982). *Making health care decisions (Vol. 1).* Washington, DC: U.S. Government Printing Office.

Prince v. Urban, 57 Cal. Rptr. 181 (1996).

Prince v. Urban, 57 Cal. Rptr.2d 181 (1996).

Quinn, J. (1995). Case management in home and community care. In L. W. Kaye (Ed.), *New developments in home care services for the elderly: Innovations in policy, program, and practice,* (pp. 233–248). New York: Haworth Press.

Reamer, F. G. (1982). *Ethical dilemmas in social service.* New York: Columbia University Press.

Reamer, F. G. (1987). Ethics committees in social work. *Social Work, 32,* 188–192.

Regan, J. (1990). *The Aged Client and the Law,* New York: Columbia University Press.

Regan, P. (1995). *Legislating privacy: Technology, social values, and public policy.* Chapel Hill, NC: University of North Carolina Press.

Reid, J. (1996). *A telemedicine primer: Understanding the issues.* Billings, MT: Innovative Medical Communications.

Reker, G. T., & Wong, P. (1988). Aging as an individual process: Toward a theory of personal meaning. In J. Birren, & V. L Bengston (Eds.). *Emergent theories of aging.* New York: Springer.

Rennert, T. (1991). *AIDS/HIV and confidentiality: Model policy and procedures.* Washington, DC: American Bar Association, Commission on the Mentally Disabled, and Center on Children and the Law.

Reverby, S. (1987). *Ordered to care: The dilemma of American nursing, 1850–1945.* New York: Cambridge University Press.

Rice, B. (1997). Will telemedicine get you sued? *Medical Economics, 20,* 56–69.

Rivlin, A., & Wiener, J. (1988). *Caring for the disabled elderly.* Washington, DC: Brookings Institution.

Roach v. Kelley Health Care, 742 P.2d 1190 (Or. App. 1987).

Robinson, B. E., Sucholeike, R., & Schocken, D. D. (1993). Sudden death and resisted mechanical restraint: A case report. *Journal of the American Geriatrics Society, 41,* 424–425.

Rosenzweig, E. P. (1995). Trends in home care entitlement and benefits. In L. W. Kaye (Ed.), *New developments in home care services for the elderly: Innovation in policy, program, and practice,* (pp. 9–29). New York: Haworth Press.

Ruddick, W. (1994). Transforming homes and hospitals. *Hastings Center Report, 24,* S11–14.

Sabatino, C. P. (1993). Surely the wizard will help us, Toto? Implementing the Patient Self-Determination Act. *Hastings Center Report, 23* (1), 12–16.

Safe Medical Devices Act of 1990, 21 U.S.C. Sec. 301.

Sanders, J. (1996). Telemedicine: Capabilities, growth projections and attending issues surrounding its use. *Journal of Pharmacy and Law, 6,* 3–16.

Sankar, A. (1984). "Its just old age": Old age as a diagnosis in American and Chinese medicine. In D. Kertzer, & J. Keith (Eds.). *Age and anthropological theory.* Ithaca, NY: Cornell University.

Scala, M. A., & Mayberry, P. S. (July 1997). *Consumer-directed home services: Issues and models* (In-house paper). Oxford, OH: Scripps Gerontology Center, Miami University.

Scala, M. A., Mayberry, P. S., & Kunkel, S. R. (1996). Consumer-directed home care: Client profiles and service challenges. *Journal of Case Management, 5,* 91–98.

Schlenker, R. E., Shaughnessy, P. W., & Hittle, D. F. (1995). Patient-level cost of home health care under capitated and fee-for-service payment. *Inquiry, 32,* 252–270.

Schloendorff v. Society of New York Hospital, 211 N.Y. 124 (1914).

Schmid, H., & Hasenfeld, Y. (1993, March). Organizational dilemmas in the provision of home-care services. *Social Service Review,* 41–53.

Schor, J. (1994). *Patient, agency and area characteristics associated with regional variation in the use of Medicare home health services.* Princeton, NJ: Mathematica Policy Research.

Sermchief v. Gonzales, 660 S.W.2d 683 (Mo. Banc 1983).

Shoor, R. (1994). Long-distance medicine. *Business and Health, 12,* 39–46.

Smith, S. (1992). Advanced states. *Nursing Times, 88,* 31–32.

Smyer, M. A. (1993, Winter/Spring). Aging and decision-making capacity. *Generations,* 51–56.

Stevens, R., & Stevens, R. (1974). *Welfare medicine in America.* New York: The Free Press.

Stipp v. Kim, 874 F. Supp. 663 (E.D. Pa. 1995).

Telemedlaw. (1997). *California case to offer insight into telemedicine jurisdiction issues? Telemedlaw.* Raleigh, NC: Author.

Thompson, M. (1997). Fatal neglect. *TIME,* 34–38.

Tymchuk, A. J., Ouslander, J. G., Rahbar, B., & Fitten, J. (1988). Medical decision-making among elderly people in long-term care. *The Gerontologist, 28* (Suppl.), 59–63.

U.S. Census Bureau. (1995, May). *Sixty-five plus in the United States.* Statistical brief. Washington, DC: U.S. Government Printing Office.

U.S. Congress Office of Technology Assessment (1993). *Protecting privacy in computerized medical information.* Washington, DC: Author.

U.S. Department of Labor, Women's Bureau. (1998, May). *Facts on working women: Work and elder care.* No. 98-1. Washington, DC: Author.

U.S. Public Health Service. (1955). *A study of selected home care programs.* Washington, DC: U.S. Department of Health, Education and Welfare.

Wallace, S. P., Campbell, K, & Chih-Yin, L-T. (1994). Structural barriers to the use of formal in-home services by elderly Latinos. *Journals of Gerontology, 49,* S253–263.

Wallace, S. P., Levy-Storms, L., & Ferguson, L. R. (1995). Access to paid inhome assistance among disabled elderly people: Do Latinos differ from non-Latino Whites? *American Journal of Public Health, 85,* 970–975.

Warner, I. (1996a). Introduction to telehealth home care. *Home Healthcare Nurse, 14,* 791–796.

Warner, I. (1996b). Telemedicine applications for geriatric care management. *Geriatric Care Management Journal, 6,* 20–23.

Warner, I. (1998). Telemedicine in home care: The current state of practice. *Home Health Care Management and Practice, 10,* 62–71.

Warner, I., & Albert, R. (1997). Avoiding legal landmines in home health care nursing. *Home Health Care Management and Practice, 9,* 8–16.

Warner, I., & Beller, A. (1997). Electronic home visits to improve care and decrease costs. In M. Harris (Ed.), *Handbook of home health care administration.* Gaithersberg, MD: Aspen.

Weber, C. M., Kellogg, F. R., Berrien, R., Wible, J., Bohnet, N., Maja, T., & Ong, I. (1997). Quality management in home health care. In P. W. Brickner, F. R. Kellogg, A. J. Lechich, R. Lipsman, & L. K. Sharer (Eds.), *Geriatric home health care: The collaboration of physicians, nurses, and social workers.* (pp. 275–296). New York: Springer.

Weinberg, J., & Brod, M. (1995). Advance medical directives: Policy, perspectives and practical experiences. *Journal of Ethics, Law, and Aging, 1,* 15–36.

Weissert, W., & Silberman, S. (1996). Health care on the information highway: The politics of telemedicine. *Telemedicine Journal, 2,* 1–15.

Wetle, T., Levkoff, S., Cwikel, J., & Rosen, A. (1988). Nursing home resident participation in medical decisions: Perceptions and preferences. *The Gerontologist, 28* (June Suppl.), 32–37.

Whalen v. Roe, 429 U.S. 589 (1977).

Wickline v. State, 228 Cal. Rptr. 661 (Ct. App. 1986).

Williams, B. (1994). Comparison of services among different types of home health agencies. *Medical Care, 32,* 1134–1152.

Williams, M. E. (1995). Geriatric medicine on the information superhighway: Opportunity or road kill? *Journal of the American Geriatrics Society, 43,* 184–186.

Wilson v. Blue Cross of Southern California, 271 Cal. Rptr. 876 (Ct. App. 1990).

Witkin, B. R., & Altschuld, J. W. (1995). *Planning and conducting needs assessments: A practical guide.* Thousand Oaks, CA: Sage.

Woodruff, L., & Applebaum, R. (1996). Assuring the quality of in-home supportive services: A consumer perspective. *Journal of Aging Studies, 10,* 157–169.

Worcester, M. I., Loustau, A., & O'Connor, K. (1990). Tailoring teaching to the elderly in home care. In *Facilitating self care practices in the elderly* (pp. 69–120). New York: Haworth.

World Health Organization. (1997). *World health report 1997.* Geneva, Switzerland: Author.

Young, H., & Waters, R. (1995). Licensure barriers to the interstate use of telemedicine. In *Fox Newsletter.* Washington, DC: Fox Newsletter. Available: www.arentfox.com/telemed/licensenimplic.html

Zola, I. K. (1987). Some health care for older adults with disabilities. *Aging Network News, IV,* 6–7.

Study Methodology Details

INTRODUCTION

The procedures and techniques employed in performing the national survey and local field study of high technology applications in home health care organizations are reviewed here. Practical recommendations for minimizing methodological problems when conducting agency-based research are also presented. This information will be of particular interest to those readers attuned to technical issues of research and statistical methodology.

THE NATIONAL SURVEY

Areas of Investigation

The research sought to assemble a specialized national data base on technology-enhanced home care. It encompassed the collection of data by means of: (a) a comprehensive review of research and program reports on technological applications in the delivery of in-home services to older and disabled people, and (b) a national survey of the experiences of home health care agencies in providing technology-enhanced care in the patient's home.

The national survey focused on a series of issues, all of which centered around a pivotal concern for this research: *What role does technology play in the organization and delivery of home health care services?* Specific issues addressed in the survey included:

1. The range and type of technology-enhanced home care services and equipment provided.
2. The organizational characteristics of home care agencies that engage in the delivery of technology-enhanced services and equipment.
3. The characteristic profiles of persons receiving technology-enhanced home care.
4. The influence of technology-enhanced home care on home health care organizational structure and function.
5. The degree to which home care agencies are confronted with various legal, moral, and ethical issues that have arisen during the course of delivering technology-enhanced home care.
6. The extent to which home care personnel are equipped to respond to the technological and accompanying legal and ethical dimensions of home care.
7. The extent to which formal mechanisms have been put in place to address the legal, informational, and ethical demands of high-tech home care.
8. The relationship between type of home care services provided and provider and consumer perceptions of service quality and adequacy.

Throughout the course of this study, technology-enhanced home care or high-tech home care was operationally defined as those in-home methods of diagnosis, treatment, and rehabilitation that are physically embodied in specialized equipment and related supplies and services. Conversely, traditional home care services were defined as those interventions not requiring specialized equipment, treatment, or supplies to be performed.

The central research issues and the specific variables that were measured are outlined in greater detail below.

1. The Characteristics of Home Health Care Agencies Providing Technology-Enhanced Services/Equipment
    a. Auspice classification (Visiting Nurse Association, official, proprietary, private/not-for-profit, hospital, other)
    b. Medicare-certification status
    c. Home care or hospice status

   d. Sources of revenue

   e. Geographic boundaries of service provision

   f. Age of the organization

   g. Level of service effort

      i) Number of patients served

      ii) Number of home visits

   h. Budgetary patterns

      i) Revenues and costs

      ii) Profit levels (where applicable)

   i. Staffing patterns

      i) Number of full-time and part-time staff

      ii) Proportion of professional and support staff

      iii) Proportion of field and office staff

      iv) Education and training requirements of staff

   j. Marketing and recruitment patterns

      i) Sources of referral

      ii) Methods and techniques of marketing

      iii) Ability to attract patients

      iv) Ability to attract personnel

      v) Ability to attract external funding support

2. The Characteristic Profiles of Persons Receiving Technology-Enhanced Home Care

   a. Racial or ethnic status

   b. Age

   c. Gender

   d. Marital status

   e. Living arrangements

   f. Functional status (physical and mental)

   g. Range and intensity of help needed

   h. Terminal health status

   i. Financial status

   j. Method of payment

3. The Range and Type of Technology-Enhanced Home Care Services and Equipment Provided

   a. Frequency and length of time of traditional in-home service provision

      i) use of personal care (bathing, grooming, dressing, cooking, ambulation assistance)

      ii) use of case management

      iii) use of social counseling
      iv) use of manual monitoring of vital signs
      v) use of traditional physical, occupational, and speech therapies
      vi) use of manual recording and storage of patient data

b. Frequency and length of time of high-tech or nontraditional service provision
      i) use of parenteral and enteral nutrition programs
      ii) use of home antibiotic infusion and chemotherapy
      iii) use of respiratory therapy, equipment, and gas
      iv) use of renal dialysis supplies and services
      v) use of incontinence products
      vi) use of ostomy products
      vii) use of pressure sore products
      viii) use of apnea monitors
      ix) use of transcutaneous electronic nerve stimulation
      x) use of durable medical products
      xi) use of electronic recording and storage of patient data
      xii) use of personal emergency response systems (PERS)
      xiii) use of robotics
      xiv) use of telecommunications or closed-circuit television

4. The Degree to Which Home Care Agencies Face Legal, Moral, and Ethical Issues When Delivering Technology-Enhanced Home Care
  a. Frequency of decisions to forego life-sustaining treatment
  b. Frequency of do not resuscitate (DNR) orders
  c. Frequency of do not hospitalize (DNH) orders
  d. Frequency of do not treat (DNT) orders
  e. Frequency of living wills
  f. Frequency of durable powers of attorney (DPA)
  g. Frequency of proxy assignments
  h. Frequency of public or private guardianships
  i. Frequency of public or private limited guardianships or conservatorships
  j. Frequency of decisions determining patient competence
  k. Frequency of surrogate decision making or substituted judgment
  l. Frequency of issues of patient autonomy and choice
  m. Frequency of malpractice and vicarious liability cases
  n. Frequency of issues of right to privacy, informed consent, and confidentiality

5. The Extent to Which Formal Mechanisms Have Been Put in Place to Address the Legal, Informational, and Ethical Demands of High-Tech Home Care
   a. Use of special topic in-house training and education regimens for staff, patients, and family members
   b. Use of special theme staff meetings
   c. Use of special supervisory sessions
   d. Use of special staff, family, and patient meetings
   e. Use of legal or ethics committees
   f. Use of legal or ethics consultants
   g. Use of external continuing education or training programs
   h. Use of special policy, procedures, and guidelines for technology-enhanced practice
   i. Use of special information management tools for documenting technology-enhanced practice
   j. Use of ombudsman programs
   k. Use of other technical resources

6. The Quality and Adequacy of Technology-Enhanced Home Care Services
   a. Measures of success of providing high-tech home care (size of patient population, agency revenue levels, patient satisfaction levels, level of staff morale)
   b. Most effective and least effective high-tech home care services or equipment
   c. Adequacy of nonhuman resources (funds, facilities, equipment) set aside for technology-enhanced home care
   d. Adequacy of human resources (degree of knowledge and skill of home care personnel) to respond to technological, informational, and ethical features of home care
   e. Major challenges associated with organizing current high-tech home care initiatives
   f. Degree to which patients are informed about service-related legal rights
   g. Future services planned in the area of high-tech home care

Data Sources and Sampling Strategy

The national survey collected data from the executive directors of a national sample of 650 home health care agencies situated throughout the

United States. A 5%, stratified, systematic random sample of such agencies was drawn from the National Association for Home Care's (NAHC) *1991 National HomeCare & Hospice Directory.* This listing, which is updated annually, represents the most comprehensive compilation of such programs now available. Approximately 13,000 agencies were listed at the time of this research including 5,800 Medicare-certified agencies, some 5,500 home care agencies that do not participate in Medicare, and approximately 1,200 free-standing hospices that provide terminal care in the client's home. NAHC is the trade association representing the nation's home health care agencies, hospices, and homemaker-home health aide organizations. NAHC was founded in 1982, is situated in Washington, DC, and represents the merger of the National Association of Home Health Agencies and the Council of Home Health Agencies/Community Health Services, an entity that was part of the National League for Nursing.

The NAHC Directory lists all categories of home care agencies broken down by geographic location including: Visiting Nurse Associations (VNAs); official (governmental or public) agencies; proprietary or free-standing for-profit agencies; private/not-for-profit agencies (PNPs); and hospital-based agencies. Stratified, systematic sampling procedures insured representation by both Medicare-certified and noncertified programs as well as all categories of home care agencies across all states.

Data Collection Procedures and Instrumentation

Executive directors of each of the 650 sampled agencies received a six-page structured research questionnaire containing 45 open-ended and closed-ended questions that focused on the issues outlined above in the Areas of Investigation section. The questionnaire was accompanied by a letter of explanation from the research team as well as a letter of endorsement from Val Halamandaris, President of the National Association for Home Care. This instrument was pilot tested in late 1992 with a small panel of home health care agency directors representative of the various categories of home care agency auspice and Medicare-certification status as well as research staff at the National Association for Home Care. The pilot test resulted in relatively minor though helpful refinements to the questionnaire.

Executive directors, who received the first wave mailing of questionnaires in early 1993, were instructed to base their responses on their agencies' experiences in providing both general and high-tech home health care services. All directors were also asked to send any program materials that described the range of services offered by their agencies as well as various procedures and policies enacted by their organizations in the areas of personnel training, advance directives, and admissions.

The executive director survey instrument included necessary assurances of confidentiality and an explanation of the study's intent. Respondents were advised of the voluntary nature of the survey and of a coding system that would be used by the researchers for tracking purposes.

Efforts at maximizing survey responses were carried out by sending first, second, and third mail reminders to all those failing to respond to the initial mailing. Each follow-up request was made approximately 2 to 3 weeks subsequent to the preceding request during the first quarter of 1993. Each request (including the initial mailing) included a carefully worded rationale as to why a prompt response was essential not only for insuring the success of the study but also for ultimately providing agency directors (like themselves) with sound advice and proven methods for providing quality high-technology home care services for older adults. As an additional incentive, all agency directors were informed that they would receive complimentary copies of the study products—two practical guidebooks (one for providers and one for consumers) and an executive summary of the study's results—if they participated.

Because the response rate remained below 30% after the third mail reminder, special personal appeals by telephone to all nonresponding agency directors were carried out during the second quarter of 1993. A total of 382 agencies were contacted by telephone. This special effort resulted in the response rate increasing from well below 30% to a final response rate of 33%. The telephone survey also allowed the researchers to make informed determinations of those agencies that were no longer operating, did not provide home health care services or did not serve older people, had changed addresses, or constituted duplicate listings in the directory. This procedure resulted in a final adjusted potential participating sample of 467, with 154 home health care agencies choosing eventually to complete the survey instrument.

Comparative Analysis of Participating and Nonparticipating Home Health Care Agencies

The telephone follow-up procedure also allowed for the identification of nonrespondents, making possible a determination as to whether study respondents could be considered representative of the larger sample of home health care agencies. A brief battery of profile data questions were administered during the telephone interviews to those executive directors who declined to participate in the research project (the questions probed each agency's corporate status, auspice, type of community served, years in operation, and whether the agency provides high-tech home health care services). These profile data, obtained from 182 executive directors who provide home care services, enabled an unusually thorough statistical comparison to be made between respondent and nonrespondent pools.

To determine the extent to which nonparticipants might differ from those organizations agreeing to participate in the study, comparative analysis of the profiles of the 154 participating and 182 contacted nonparticipating agencies was performed. Both similarities and differences were observed. The two groups did not differ significantly in terms of the length of time they have been providing home health care services in the community. Nor did they vary in terms of the likelihood that they currently provided high technology, home-based services at the time of the research. On the other hand, the corporate status and auspice of the two groups as well as the community areas served did differ in significant ways. Specifically, nonparticipating home care agencies were considerably more likely to be for-profit, proprietary agencies and less likely to be not-for-profit agencies. Nonparticipants were also significantly more likely to serve a mixture of urban, suburban, and rural settings and less likely to serve primarily urban settings.

This analysis suggests that participants cannot be considered to have characteristics that completely parallel those of nonparticipants. It appears that our data, when treated in the aggregate, will likely better gauge the experiences of the not-for-profit and public home health care sectors, including those that focus on serving strictly urban communities. Even so, it is worth noting that our data set is no more likely to tap the experiences of home health care agencies that have entered the field of high-tech care than those who have not. Nor is our data set comprised of agencies any more or less experienced in providing home health care services than those agencies not included in our analysis. Given these similarities and differences, analyses presented in this volume will, whenever possible, disaggregate the participating sample by corporate status, auspice, and community catchment area. These procedures aim to control for the possible undue influence of these organizational variables in the participating sample's service delivery experience.

Research Analysis

Quantitative computer analysis of national home care agency director survey data was performed. Descriptive statistics and measures of association were employed where appropriate on the national data base, including chi-square, Pearson correlation coefficients, t tests, analyses of variance, and one-way and multivariate analyses. Key study variables, including home care agency auspice, corporate status, size of staff and budget, level of service effort, years operating, type of community served, whether hospice services are offered, and whether high-tech services are offered, were considered in the analysis of agency experience. Given the relative differences in representation in the respondent group compared to the nonrespondent group, special emphasis in the national analysis was placed on the consideration of variation in experience across agencies varying in their auspice, corporate status, and type of geographic area served.

The Study Indices

Three composite measures of agency experience were constructed during this research. The Legal-Ethical Issues Index (LEII) measures the extent to which home health care agencies have dealt with a range of legal and ethical issues pertaining to the provision of technology-enhanced care in the home. This 12-item index is scored on a 4-point scale in which 0 = never, 1 = rarely, 2 = sometimes, and 3 = often. The items included in the LEII are:

1. Decisions by patients to forego life-sustaining treatment.
2. Decisions by families to forego life-sustaining treatment.
3. Use of living wills.
4. Use of durable powers of attorney for health care.
5. Interaction with guardians (public or private).
6. Limited guardianships or conservatorships.
7. Problems with obtaining informed consent.
8. Decisions determining patient competence.
9. Surrogate decision making or substituted judgment.
10. Issues of patient's right to privacy and confidentiality.
11. Conflicts between family's wishes and patient's wishes.
12. Conflicts between surrogate's (guardian or durable power of attorney) and patient's wishes.

The index mean and standard deviation are 1.4 and 0.5, respectively. The standardized item alpha (a measure of internal consistency or reliability of index items) for the LEII, based on 143 cases is 0.81.

The Legal-Ethical Mechanisms Index (LEMI) measures the extent to which home health care agencies have adopted a range of organizational mechanisms, rules, and procedures for dealing with the legal and ethical demands of delivering high-tech care in the home. This 11-item index is scored on an 11-point scale where 0 = no formal mechanisms used to deal with such issues and 11 = all 11 formal mechanisms used. The score is therefore equivalent to the number of formal strategies adopted by home care agencies to deal with the legal and ethical demands of high-tech service delivery. The higher the score on the LEMI, the more comprehensive the agency response has been. The items included in the LEMI are:

1. In-service training for staff.
2. External continuing education or training for staff.
3. Education programs for patients and their families.
4. Special theme staff meetings.
5. Supervisory sessions.
6. Care plan conferences with staff, patients, and family.
7. Legal counsel or consultants.
8. Ethics committee or ethicists.
9. Special policies, procedures, or guidelines for high-tech service delivery.
10. Special information or management systems for documenting high-tech delivery.
11. Use of external resources such as the ombudsman program, and so forth.

The index mean and standard deviation are 6.6 and 1.9, respectively. The standardized item alpha, based on 113 cases, for the LEMI is 0.52

The third composite measure developed for this analysis is the Technological Services Index (TSI). The TSI measures the extent to which a range of services and equipment potentially offered through home health care agencies are considered to be technology enhanced. This 21-item index is scored on a 21-point scale in which 0 = no services or equipment considered to be high tech and 21 = all 21 services and equipment considered to be high-tech. The scoring is equivalent to the number of different services or equipment felt to be technology-enhanced by agency respondents. The higher the score on the TSI, the more comprehensive a range of perceived technology-enhanced services and equipment by respondents. The items included in the TSI are:

1. Parenteral or enteral nutrition or hydration.
2. Chemotherapy (infusion).
3. Antibiotics (infusion).
4. Pain control or palliative measures.
5. Renal dialysis.
6. Blood component infusion.
7. Ventilator care.
8. Tracheostomy care.
9. Oxygen patient care.
10. Apnea monitors.
11. Cardiac telemetry.
12. Personal emergency response systems.
13. Incontinence care.
14. Ostomy care.
15. Pressure sore care.
16. Electronic monitoring and recording of vital signs.
17. Transcutaneous electronic nerve stimulation.
18. Bone growth stimulation.
19. Telecommunications or closed circuit television.
20. Self-instruction computer.
21. Robotics.

The index mean and standard deviation are 9.3 and 4.6, respectively. The standardized item alpha for the TSI, based on 151 cases, is 0.87.

The Study Factors

In addition to the construction of the three indices described above, a special factor analysis was carried out on items comprising the LEII. Three factors were extracted and rotated using the varimax procedure. Items defining each factor were selected based on loadings of .40 or higher. If the same item loaded at .40 or higher on more than one factor it was used to define that factor that it loaded highest on. Factor I, labeled Patient Rights, is defined by six items—problems with obtaining informed consent, decisions determining patient competence, surrogate decision making or substituted judgment, issues of patient's right to privacy and confidentiality, conflicts between family's wishes and patient's wishes, and conflicts between surrogate's (guardian or durable power of attorney) and patient's wishes. Item loadings range from .47 to .71. Factor I has an eigenvalue of 3.97 and accounts for 33.1% of the variance.

The second factor, labeled Right to Die, is defined by three items—decisions by patients to forego life-sustaining treatment, decisions by families to forego life-sustaining treatment, and use of living wills. This factor has item loadings ranging from .57 to .92, an eigenvalue of 1.82, and accounts for 15.2% of the variance.

The third and final factor, labeled Delegation of Authority, is also defined by three items—use of durable powers of attorney for health care, interaction with guardians (public or private), and limited guardianships or conservatorships. This factor has item loadings ranging from .65 to .74. It has an eigenvalue of 1.24 and accounts for 10.3% of the variance.

Cronbach alphas for the three factors are .73, .80, and .66, respectively. Factor I has a mean score of 1.1 and a standard deviation of .6 based on 145 cases. Factor II has a mean score of 1.7 and a standard deviation of .8 based on 147 cases. Factor III has a mean score of 1.5 and a standard deviation of .6 based on 146 cases. The potential score range for each factor is 0 to 3 where a higher score indicates more frequent agency experience facing the issue area (specific values are 0 = never, 1 = rarely, 2 = sometimes, and 3 = often).

THE LOCAL FIELD STUDY

Areas of Investigation

This phase of the research compiled data on the experience of agency staff and older home health care clients. It provided the opportunity to compare perspectives concerning the delivery and consumption of high-tech home care services. These data were collected during a series of face-to-face interviews with staff and patients. A subset of the national survey questions were adapted for use in the interviews. In general, staff were asked to discuss the challenges associated with delivering high-tech services or serving high-tech patients. Patients were asked to comment on their personal experience receiving home health care services.

Data Sources and Sampling Strategy

Data for the local field study were collected in interviews with agency staff and patients. Four agencies in Southeastern Pennsylvania and Northern Delaware were selected to participate in the research. These agencies represent the broad range of organizational auspices of home health care agencies, including hospital based, VNA, freestanding proprietary, and freestanding non-profit. All agencies were Medicare certified.

Each agency designated a contact person to work on the research project. The agency contact first provided researchers with a complete list of agency staff by position. A systematic, stratified random sample was then drawn from this active staff list. This process ensured representation of all staff types in the research, including: registered nurses; licensed practical nurses; physical, speech, and occupational therapists; medical social workers; and home health aides. Randomly selected staff were invited by the agency contact person to participate in the research. The contact person then provided researchers with a list of staff who agreed to participate in the research. Staff who refused to participate or who left the agency prior to interviewing were replaced using the same sampling methods described above.

Staff were interviewed by trained interviewers from the Bryn Mawr College Graduate School of Social Work and Social Research, using a structured protocol designed by the research team. The protocol consisted of 44 open- and closed-ended questions covering the same issues investigated in the national survey. The tool was pretested with staff from a local home health care agency not participating in the research. Feedback from the pretest was incorporated into the design of the final protocol.

Interviewers contacted staff directly to schedule each interview at a convenient time and location for the staff. Staff were allowed to choose the location, either at the office, at their home, or in a public setting. Signed consent forms were obtained from all participants either by the agency contact person or by the interviewer. Interviewers provided staff with an explanation of the study's intent and assured them that all information would remain confidential. A coding system was used to track completed interviews and to monitor completion rates for each agency. Interviewees were informed about this coding system as well as the voluntary nature of the interview. A total of 92 staff were interviewed, representing a 75% response rate overall.

Obtaining patient permission to participate in the research was somewhat more complicated than with staff. This was because all participating agencies chose to make the initial request to patients themselves and to obtain written consent from the patient, rather than having the researchers contact patients. The agency contact persons provided researchers with a list of active patients by code number. Patient code numbers were used to ensure anonymity until the patient agreed to participate. A random sample was then drawn from this list, which was returned to each agency contact person. Agency direct care staff explained the research to individual patients and asked them to sign a consent form that was designed by the research team. Once consent was obtained, a patient list was then compiled by the contact person and forwarded to the research coordinator.

Patient record reviews were conducted by the research coordinator at each agency prior to assigning patients to be interviewed. Demographic information about the patient and his or her medical diagnosis and care was obtained directly from each chart using a standardized protocol. This reduced the amount of required questions on the interview protocol and ensured accurate and consistent medical data for each patient. Patients were then assigned to interviewers. The next step consisted of a telephone call to the patient from the interviewer to arrange the interview time. All patients were interviewed in their homes at their convenience.

Patients had several opportunities to refuse to participate. They could refuse during the initial request by agency staff, during the telephone call by the interviewer, or when the interviewer actually arrived for the interview. Given the procedures, this stage of data collection took time and several patients died, entered a nursing home or hospital, or were otherwise discharged from agency service before the interviews could be conducted. This increased the need for continual resampling of patient lists to replace patients who refused or were discharged (for whatever reason). It also decreased the overall response rate because many patients had to be replaced, and this increased the amount of time necessary to complete all patient interviews.

A coding system was also used with patients to track completed interviews and agency totals. Patients were interviewed by trained interviewers who, prior to commencing each interview, explained the intent of the study, its voluntary nature, and confidentiality. A total of 67 patients were interviewed for a 53.6% response rate overall.

Research Analysis

Quantitative computer analysis was conducted on data from both the staff and patient protocols. Descriptive statistics and measures of association were employed where appropriate, including frequency distributions, chi-square, and Pearson correlation coefficients. Open-ended responses underwent content analyses. Key study variables included: staff demographic profiles; patient demographic profiles; services provided and received; quality of service; patient understanding of their rights; staff understanding of patient rights; effective service delivery; and benefits, drawbacks, and challenges to high-tech services.

ISSUES AND RECOMMENDATIONS IN CONDUCTING HOME HEALTH AND RELATED RESEARCH

The authors experienced many methodological challenges over the course of this research project that strongly impacted the study group response rates. Home health agencies and their clients are a very difficult target population to study. The following section identifies the issues and offers suggestions on how to conduct similar research with home health agencies and avoid the concomitant pitfalls.

The National Mail Survey

When conducting a mail survey of home health agencies it is essential to have a reliable, up-to-date directory or compilation of agencies in the geographic location targeted. Entries in this list or directory should be thoroughly researched and categorized in terms of the type of services they provide. In this research, we found that many of the agencies listed did not actually provide direct, hands-on, home health care services. Some were community service agencies, others were government agencies that funded programs, and still others were subcontractors or registry services. This uncertainty about service provision impacted the response rate because many of the agencies could not respond to our survey.

To increase response rates with targeted home health care agencies, thoughtful methodological strategies and incentives must be built in to promote completion of the survey questionnaire. Such strategies and incentives include:

- Keeping the survey as short as possible; Anything that takes more than 15 minutes to complete will be thrown away!
- Being prepared to mail the survey more than once and to use reminder notices.
- Using personal contacts to increase the response rate (telephone or in person; research staff or local contacts that might have more leverage).
- Assuring agencies that individual responses will not be shared, especially not with their competitors (the field of home care is highly competitive and agencies can be expected to be protective of certain aspects of their experience).
- Providing concrete benefits for those who complete the survey, such as practical guidebooks, copies of research results, money, and so forth.

The Local Agency Study

We experienced some degree of difficulty with completing a sufficient number of local interviews with both patients and staff. Several coordination factors may have helped to increase the response rate for the interviews. First, meet with the agency contact person and other designated staff expected to play a role in the research from the outset and not just the executive director. This will reduce the likelihood of the agency committing to more than it can deliver. Develop the mutually agreed upon coordination plan with the contact person prior to designing interview protocols. You should use agency contacts to assist in the development of those protocols. Although it may seem like more work for research staff initially, this groundwork will actually reduce their responsibilities later in the research. Also, staff are in many cases excited about working on research, as long as the researchers are realistic in terms of their requirements and time frames and actively seek feedback from agency personnel in terms of preferred procedure.

You may want to consider using more agencies with fewer interviews performed at each agency site than originally planned. Recruiting patients and staff (but especially patients) for such research can be extremely time-consuming. By asking each agency to recruit fewer staff and patients, one reduces the burden on the agency contact person and may therefore reduce the amount of time spent on drawing additional samples due to potential subjects declining to participate. Unfortunately, this process may increase the amount of coordination effort required of the research staff. However, it is likely to be well worth the extra effort in terms of higher numbers of subjects participating ultimately in your research. Finally, be certain that your needs have been clearly communicated to the contact person so there is no confusion later in the research process.

Sources for More Information on High-Tech Home Health Care

PROFESSIONAL JOURNALS/NEWSLETTERS

Activities, Adaptation & Aging
Haworth Press
10 Alice St.
Binghampton, PA 13904-1580
Ph#: (607)722-5857 or
    (800)342-9676
Fax: (607)722-6362
E-mail: *getinfo@haworth.com*
Internet: *www.haworth.com*

Advances in Wound Care
Springhouse Corporation
1111 Bethlehem Pike
Springhouse, PA 19477
Ph#: (215)646-8700, x.272

Aging News Alert
CD Publications
8204 Fenton St.
Silver Spring, MD 20910
Ph#: (301)588-6380
Fax: (301)588-6385
E-mail: *cdpubs@clark.net*

American Geriatrics Society Journal
Williams & Wilkins
351 W. Camden St.
Baltimore, MD 21201-2436
Ph#: (410)528-4068 or (800)222-3790
Fax: (410)528-4452
E-mail: *mricks@wwilkins.com*
Internet: *www.wwilkins.com*

The American Journal of Hospice and
    Palliative Care
Prime National Publishing Corporation
470 Boston Post Rd.
Weston, MA 02193
Ph#: (617)899-2702

The American Journal of Occupational
    Therapy
American Occupational Therapy
    Association
Box 31220
Bethesda, MD 20824-1220
Ph#: (301)652-2682
Fax: (301)652-7711
Internet: *www.aota.org*

American Journal of Public Health
1015 15th St. NW
Washington, DC 20005
Ph#: (202)789-5600

Cancer Nursing
Lippincott-Raven Publishers
227 E. Washington Sq.
Philadelphia, PA 19106
Ph#: (215)238-4200, (800)777-2295
Fax: (215)238-4227
Internet: *www.lrpub.com*

CARING Magazine
National Association for Home Care
228 Seventh Street, SE
Washington, DC 20003
Ph#: (202)547-7424
Fax: (202)547-3540
E-mail: *webmaster@nahc.org*
Internet: *www.nahc.org*

Clinical Gerontologist
Haworth Press, Inc.
10 Alice St.
Binghampton, NY 13904-1580
Ph#: (800)342-9676 or (607) 722-5857
Fax: (607)722-6362
E-mail: *getinfo@haworth.com*

Consumer Choice News
NCOA
409 Third St. SW
Washington, DC 20024
Ph#: (202)479-6670
Fax: (202)479-0735
E-mail: *webmaster@ncoa.org*
Internet:
  *www.ncoa.org/research/demo
  _prjts/ccn_arch/default.htm*

Journal of Ethics, Law and Aging
Springer Publishing Company
536 Broadway
New York, NY 10012
Ph#: (212)431-4370
Fax: (212)941-7842

Generations
American Society on Aging
833 Market St., Suite 511
San Francisco, CA 94103-1824
Ph#: (415)974-9600
Fax: (415)974-0300
E-mail: *info@asa.asaign.org*
Internet:
  *www.sound.com/health/nhic/data
  /hr1000/hr1047.html.*

Geriatric Care Management Journal
National Association of Professional
  Geriatric Care Managers
1604 N. Country Rd.
Tucson, AZ 85716-3102
Ph#: (520)881-8008
Fax: (520)325-7925

Geriatric Nursing
Mosby-Year Book, Inc.
118 Westline Industrial Dr.
St. Louis, MO 63146-3318
Ph#: (314)872-8370 or (800)325-4177
Fax: (314)432-1380
Internet:
  www.mosby.com/mosby/periodicals

Geriatrics
Advanstar Communications, Inc.
7500 Old Oak Blvd.
Cleveland, OH 44130
Ph#: (216)826-2839
Fax: (216)891-2726
Internet:
  *www.modernmedicine.com/geri
  /gerindex.html*

The Gerontologist
Gerontological Society of America
1030 15th St. NW, Suite 250
Washington, DC 20005-1503
Ph#: (202)842-1275
Fax: (202)842-1150
E-mail: *geron@geron.org*
Internet: *www.geron.org*

Hastings Center Report
The Hastings Center
Route 9D
Garrison, NY 10524
Ph#: (914)762-8500
Fax: (914)762-2124

Health and Social Work
NASW Press
National Association of Social
  Workers
750 First St. NE, Suite 700
Washington, DC 20002-4241
Ph#: (202)408-8600
Fax: (202)336-8312
Internet: *www.naswpress.org*

Health Care Financing Review
U.S. HCFA
DHHS
7500 Security Blvd.
Baltimore, MD 21244-1850
Ph#: (202)512-1800
Fax: (202)512-2250
E-mail: *lwolf@hcfa.gov*
www.hcfa.gov/pubfroms/ordpub
  .html

Health Marketing Quarterly
Haworth Press
10 Alice St.
Binghampton, PA 13904
Ph#: (607)722-5857 or
  (800)342-9676
Fax: (607)722-6362
E-mail: *getinfo@haworth.com*
Internet: *www.haworth.com*

Homecare Quality Management
American Health Consultants
A Medical Economics Company
P.O. Box 740060
Atlanta, GA 30374

Home Healthcare Nurse
Lippincott-Raven Publishers
227 E. Washington Sq.
Philadelphia, PA 19106
Ph#: (215)238-4200 or
  (800)777-2295
Fax: (215)238-4227
Internet: *www.lrpub.com*

Home Health Care Services
  Quarterly
Haworth Press, Inc.
10 Alice St.
Binghampton, NY 13904-1580
Ph#: (800)342-9676 or
  (607) 722-5857
Fax: (607)722-6362
E-mail: *getinfo@haworth.com*
Internet: *www.haworth.com*

The Hospice Journal
Haworth Press
10 Alice St.
Binghampton, NY 13904-1580
Ph#: (800)342-9676 or
  (607) 722-5857
Fax: (607)722-6362
E-mail: *getinfo@haworth.com*
Internet: *www.haworth.com*

International Journal of Technology
  and Aging
Human Sciences Press, Inc.
72 Fifth Ave.
New York, NY 10011-8004
Ph#: (212)243-6000

Journal of Advanced Nursing
Blackwell Science Ltd.
Osbey Mead
Oxford, OX2 OEL, England
Ph#: 44-1865-206206
Fax: 44-1865-721205
E-mail: *journals.cs@blacksci.co.uk*
Internet: *www.black.co.uk*

Journal of the American Geriatrics Society
The American Geriatrics Society
Williams & Wilkins
351 W. Camden St.
Baltimore, MD 21201-2436
Ph#: (410)528-4068; 800-222-3790
Fax: (410)528-4452
E-mail: *mricks@wwilkins.com*
Internet: *www.wwilkins.com*

The Journal of the American Medical
   Association
American Medical Association
515 N. State St.
Chicago, IL 60610
Ph#: (312)464-5000 or (800)262-2350
Fax: (312)464-4184
Internet: *www.ama-assn.org*

Journal of Applied Gerontology
Sage Publications
2455 Teller Rd.
Thousand Oaks, CA 91320
Ph#: (805)499-0721
Fax: (805)499-0871
E-mail: *libraries@sagepub.com*
Internet:
   *www.sagepub.com.uk/journals
   /usdetails/j0094.htm*

Journal of Case Management
Springer Publishing Company
536 Broadway
New York, NY 10012
Ph#: (212)431-4370
Fax: (212)941-7842

Journal of Developmental and Physical
   Disabilities
Plenum Publishing Corp.
233 Spring St.
New York, NY 10013-1578
Ph#: (212)620-8000 or (800)221-9369
Fax: (212)463-0742; TELEX 23-421139
E-mail: *info@plenum.com*
Internet: *www.plenum.com*

Journal of Gerontological Social
   Work
Haworth Press, Inc.
10 Alice St.
Binghampton, NY 13904-1580
Ph#: (800)342-9676 or
   (607)722-5857
Fax: (607)722-6362
E-mail: *getinfo@haworth.com*

Journal of Home Health Care
   Practice
Aspen Publishers, Inc.
7201 McKinney Circle
Frederick, MD 21701
Ph#: (800)638-8437

Journal of Musculoskeletal
   Pain
Haworth Press, Inc.
10 Alice St.
Binghampton, NY 13904-1580
Ph#: (800)342-9676 or
   (607)722-5857
Fax: (607)722-6362
E-mail: *getinfo@haworth.com*

Journal of Palliative Care
Center for Bioethics
Clinical Research Institute of
   Montreal
110 Pine Ave. W
Montreal, PQ H2W 1R7,
   Canada
Ph#: (514)987-5617
Fax: (514)987-5695
E-mail:
   marcotc@ircm.umontreal.ca
Internet:
   *www.ircm.umontreal.ca
   /bioethique/francais
   /publications
   /journalofpalliativecare.html*

Journal of Pain and Symptom
   Management
Elsevier Science Inc.
Box 945
New York, NY 10159-0945
Ph#: (212)633-3730
Fax: (212)633-3680
E-mail: *usinfo-f@elsevier.com*
Internet: *www.elsevier.nl*

Journal of Pharmaceutical Care in
   Pain & Symptom Control
Haworth Press, Inc.
10 Alice St.
Binghampton, NY 13904-1580
Ph#: (800)342-9676 or
   (607)722-5857
Fax: (607)722-6362
E-mail: *getinfo@haworth.com*

Journal of Psychosocial Oncology
Haworth Press, Inc.
10 Alice St.
Binghampton, NY 13904-1580
Ph#: (800)342-9676 or
   (607)722-5857
Fax: (607)722-6362
E-mail: *getinfo@haworth.com*

Loss, Grief & Care
Haworth Press, Inc.
10 Alice St.
Binghampton, NY 13904-1580
Ph#: (800)342-9676 or
   (607)722-5857
Fax: (607)722-6362
E-mail: *getinfo@haworth.com*

Managing Elder Care
LRP Publications
747 Dresher Rd.
P.O. Box 980
Horsham, PA 19044-0980
Ph#: (215)784-0860

Nursing Clinics of North America
W.B. Saunders Co.
Curtis Center, 3rd. Fl.
Independence Sq. W.
Philadelphia, PA 19106-3399
Ph#: (215)238-7800 or (800)874-6418
Fax: (215)238-6445
Internet: *www.wbsaunders.com*

Older Americans Report
Business Publishers, Inc.
951 Pershing Dr.
Silver Spring, MD 20910-4464
Ph#: (800)274-6737
Fax: (310)589-8493
Internet: *www.bpinews.com*

The Public Policy and Aging Report
National Academy on Aging
1275 K St. NW, Suite 350
Washington, DC 20005-4006
Ph#: (202)408-3375

Research in Nursing and Health
John Wiley & Sons, Inc.
605 Third Ave.
New York, NY 10158
Ph#: (212)850-6645
Fax: (212)850-6021
Internet: *www.wiley.co.uk*

Respiratory Care
Merion Publications
650 Park Ave.
Box 61556
King of Prussia, PA 19406
Ph#: (610)265-7812
Fax: (610)265-8971

Social Service Review
University of Chicago Press, Journals
   Division
Box 37005
Chicago, IL 60637
Ph#: (773)753-3347
Fax: (773)753-0811; TELEX 25-4603

E-mail:
subscriptions@journals.uchicago.edu
Internet:
www.journals.uchicago.edu/SSR

Social Work
NASW Press
National Association of Social Workers
750 First St. NE, Suite 700
Washington, DC 20002-4241
Ph#: (202)408-8600
Fax: (202)336-8312
Internet: www.naswpress.org

Social Work in Health Care
Haworth Press, Inc.
10 Alice St.
Binghampton, NY 13904-1580
Ph#: (800)342-9676 or (607)722-5857
Fax: (607)722-6362
E-mail: getinfo@haworth.com

Technology and Disability
Elsevier Science Ireland Ltd.
P.O. Box 85, Limerick, Ireland
Subscriptions to
  Elsevier Science
Regional Sales Office
P.O. Box 211, 1000 AE
Ph#: 353-61-471944
Fax: 353-61-472144

Telemedicine Journal
American Telemedicine
  Association
Mary Ann Liebert, Inc. Publishers
2 Madison Ave.
Larchmont, NY 10538
Ph#: (914)834-3100
Fax: (914)834-3582
E-mail: liebert@pipeline.com
Internet: www.liebertpub.com

GOVERNMENT ORGANIZATIONS

Agency for Health Care Policy and
  Research
AHCPR Clearinghouse
P.O. Box 8547
Silver Spring, MD 20907-8547
Ph#: (800) 358-9295
Fax: (410) 381-3150 (800)358-9295
E-mail: info@ahcpr.gov
Internet: www.ahcpr.gov

Champus
TRICARE Benefit Services
16401 E. Centretech Parkway
Aurora, CO 80011-9043
Ph#: (303)676-3526
E-mail: questions@ochampus.mil

Health Care Financing Administration
DHHS
7500 Security Blvd.

Baltimore, MD 21244-1850
Ph#: (202)512-1800
Fax: (202)512-2250
E-mail: lwolf@hcfa.gov
Internet: www.hcfa.gov/pubfroms
  /ordpub.html

National Aging Information Center
Administration on Aging
Dept. of Health and Human
  Services
330 Independence Ave. SW
Room 4656
Washington, DC 20201
Ph#: (202)619-7501
Fax: (202)401-7620
E-mail: naic@ban-gate.aoa.dhhs
  .gov
Internet: www.aoa.dhhs.gov

National Institute on Aging
National Institutes of Health
Building 31, Rm 5C-35
31 Center Dr. MSC-2292
Bethesda, MD 20892-2292
Ph#: (301)496-0765
Fax: (301)496-2525
Internet: *www.nih.gov/nia*

NATIONAL MINORITY AGING ORGANIZATIONS

Asociacion Nacional Por Personas
  Mayores
3325 Wilshire Blvd., Suite 800
Los Angeles, CA 90010-1724
Ph#: (213)487-1922
Fax: (213)385-2014

Association of Jewish Aging Services
316 Pennsylvania Ave. SE, Suite 402
Washington, DC 20003-1175
Ph#: (202)543-7500
Fax: (202)543-4090

B'Nai B'rith Center for Senior
  Housing and Services
1640 Rhode Island Ave. NW
Washington, DC 209036
Ph#: (202)857-6581
Fax: (202)857-0980

National Caucus and Center on Black
  Aged
1424 K St. NW, Suite 500
Washington, DC 20005
Ph#: (202)637-8400
Fax: (202)347-0895

National Hispanic Council on Aging
2713 Ontario Rd. NW
Washington, DC 20009
Ph#: (202)745-2521
Fax: (202)745-2522
E-mail: *NHCoA@aol.com*

National Resource Center for Older
  Indians, Alaska Natives, and
  Native Hawaiians
University of North Dakota
National Resource Center on Native
  American Aging
P.O. Box 7090
Grand Forks, ND 58202-7090
Ph#: (800)896-7628

Native Elder Health Care Resource
  Center
University of Colorado at Denver
National Center for American &
  Alaskan Native Mental Health
  Research
4455 East 12 Ave., Room 308
Denver, CO 80220
Ph#: (303)372-3232

Project Aliento
Asociacion Nacional Pro Personas
  Mayores
3325 Wilshire Blvd., Suite 800
Los Angeles, CA 90010
Ph#: (213)487-1922

Public Policy and Indian Elders in
  the Media
National Indian Council on Aging
6400 Uptown Blvd. NE, Suite 510W
Albuquerque, NM 87110
Ph#: (505)888-3302

Responding to the Needs of the
  Minority Elderly Project
National Caucus and Center on the
  Black Aged, Inc.
1424 K St. NW, Suite 500
Washington, DC 20005
Ph#: (202)637-8400

NATIONAL RESOURCE CENTERS
FOR LONG-TERM CARE

National Center for Long Term Care
University of Minnesota School of
  Public Health
Institute of Health Services Research
420 Delaware SE
Box 197 Mayo
Minneapolis, MN 55455
Ph#: (612)624-5171

National Center on Elder Abuse
American Public Welfare
  Association
Research and Demonstration
  Department
810 First St. NE, Suite 500
Washington, DC 20002
Ph#: (202)682-0100

National Long Term Care
  Ombudsman Resource Center
National Citizens Coalition for
  Nursing Home Reform
1224 M St., NW
Washington, DC 20005-5183
Ph#: (202)393-2018

National Policy and Resource Center
  on Housing and Long Term Care
University of Southern California
Andrus Gerontology Center
Los Angeles, CA 90089
Ph#: (213)740-1364

National Policy and Resource Center
  on Nutrition and Aging
Department of Dietetics and
  Nutrition, OE 200
Florida International University
Miami, FL 33199
Ph#: (305)348-1517

National Policy and Resource Center
  on Women and Aging
Brandeis University
Heller School—Institute for Health
  Policy
P.O. Box 9110
Waltham, MA 02254
Ph#: (617)736-3863

National Resource Center: Diversity
  and Long Term Care
Brandies University
Heller School—Institute for Health
  Policy
P.O. Box 9110
Waltham, MA 02254
Ph#: (617)736-3930

National Resource Center on Long
  Term Care
National Association of State Units
  on Aging
1225 I St. NW, Suite 725
Washington, DC 20005
Ph#: (202)898-2575

National Rural Long Term Care
  Resource Center
University of Kansas Medial
  Center
Center on Aging
3901 Rainbow Blvd.
Kansas City, KS 66167-7117
Ph#: (913)588-1636

LEGAL ASSISTANCE
FOR THE
ELDERLY SUPPORT CENTERS

Black Elderly Legal Assistance
  Support Project
National Bar Association
1225 11th St., NW
Washington, DC 20001
Ph#: (202)842-3900

Eldercare Initiative in Consumer
  Law Project
National Consumer Law Center,
  Inc.
11 Beacon St.
Boston, MA 02108
Ph#: (617)523-8010

Legal Counsel for the Elderly
American Association of Retired
  Persons
601 E St. NW
Washington, DC 20049
Ph#: (202)434-2120

National Legal Assistance Support
American Bar Association
Commission on Legal Problems
  of the Elderly

1800 M. St. NW
Washington, DC 20036
Ph#: (202)331-2630

National Legal Support for
  Elderly People With Mental
  Disabilities Project
Judge David L. Bazelon Center
  for Mental Health Law
1101 15th St. NW, Suite 1212
Washington, DC 20005-5002
Ph#: (202)467-5730

National Senior Citizens Law
  Center
1815 H St. NW, Suite 700
Washington, DC 20006
Ph#: (202)887-5280
Fax: (202)785-6792
E-mail: *nsclc@nsclc.org*

Pension Rights Center
918 16th St. NW
Suite 704
Washington, DC 20006
Ph#: (202)296-3776

PRIVATE ORGANIZATIONS

American Association of Retired
Persons
601 E. St. NW
Washington, DC 20049
Ph#: (800)424-3410
E-mail: *member@aarp.org*
Internet: *www.aarp.org*

American Society on Aging
833 Market St., Suite 511
San Francisco, CA 94103-1824
Ph#: (415)974-9600
Fax: (415)974-0300

Canadian Home Care Association
17 York St., Suite 401
Ottawa, Ontario Canada K1N 9J6
Ph#: (613) 569-1585
Fax: (613) 569-1604
E-mail: *chca@travel-net.com*
Internet: *www.travel-net.com*
    /~chca/en-mem.html

Center for the Advancement of
Health
2000 Florida Ave. NW,
Suite 210
Washington, DC 20009-1231
Ph#: (202)387-2829
Fax: (202)387-2857
E-mail: *rhebert@cfah.org*
Internet: *www.cfah.org*

Center for Bioethics
University of Pennsylvania
3401 Market St. #320
Philadelphia, PA 19104-3308
Ph#: (215)898-7136
Fax: (215)573-3036
E-mail:
    mcgee@mail.med.upenn.edu
Internet:
    www.med.upenn.edu/bioethics

Centers for Disease Control and
Prevention
1600 Clifton Rd. NE
Atlanta, GA 30333
Ph#: (404) 639-3311
E-mail: *netinfo@cdc.gov*
Internet: *www.cdc.gov*

The Gerontological Society of America
1030 15th St. NW, Suite 250
Washington, DC 20005-1503
Ph#: (202)842-1275
Fax: (202)842-1150
E-mail: *geron@geron.org*
Internet: *www.geron.org*

Home Care Aide Association of America
National Association for Home Care
228 Seventh St. SE
Washington, DC 20003
Ph#: (202)547-7424
Fax: (202)547-3540
E-mail: *webmaster@nahc.org*
Internet: *www.nahc.org*

Hospice Association of America
National Association for Home Care
228 Seventh St. SE
Washington, DC 20003
Ph#: (202)547-7424
Fax: (202)547-3540
E-mail: *webmaster@nahc.org*
Internet: *www.nahc.org*

Hospital Home Care Association
    of America
National Association for Home Care
228 Seventh St. SE
Washington, DC 20003
Ph#: (202)547-7424
Fax: (202)547-3540
E-mail: *webmaster@nahc.org*
Internet: *www.nahc.org*

National Association for Physicians
   in Home Care
National Association for Home
   Care
228 Seventh St. SE
Washington, DC 20003
Ph#: (202)547-7424
Fax: (202)547-3540
E-mail: *webmaster@nahc.org*
Internet: *www.nahc.org*

National Association of Area
   Agencies on Aging
1112 16th St. NW, Suite 100
Washington, DC 20036
Ph#: (202)296-8130
Fax: (202)296-8134

National Association of Social
   Workers
750 First St. NE, Suite 700
Washington, DC 20002-4241
Ph#: (202)408-8600
Fax: (202)336-8312
Internet: *www.naswpress.org*

National Consumers League
(*A Consumer Guide to Home Health
   Care*)
1701 K St. NW
Suite 1200
Washington, DC 20006
Ph#: (202)835-3323

National Gerontological Nursing
   Association
7250 Parkway Dr., Suite 510
Hanover, MD 21076
Ph#: (800)723-0560
Internet:
   www.nursingcenter.com/people
   /nrsorgs/ngna/page1.html

National Hospice Organization
P.O. Box 903
Falls Church, VA 22040-0903

National Mental Health
   Association
Information Center
1021 Prince St.
Alexandria, VA 22314-2971
Ph#: (800)969-6642

Proprietary Home Care
   Association of America
National Association for Home
   Care
228 Seventh St. SE
Washington, DC 20003
Ph#: (202)547-7424
Fax: (202)547-3540
E-mail: *webmaster@nahc.org*
Internet: *www.nahc.org*

National Center for Health
   Statistics
Centers for Disease Control
   and Prevention
1600 Clifton Rd. NE
Atlanta, GA 30333
Ph#: (301)436-8500
E-mail:
   NCHSed@nch10a.em.cdc
   .gov
Internet: *www.cdc.gov/nchswww*

World Homecare and Hospice
   Organization
228 7th St. SE
Washington, DC 20003
Ph#: (202)546-4756
Fax: (202)547-3540
E-mail: *whhocomment@nahc.org*
Internet: *www.nahc.org/WHHO*

RESOURCES FOR LOW VISION

American Federation of the Blind
1615 M St. NW, Suite 250
Washington, DC 20036
Ph#: (202)457-1487
Fax: (202)457-1492

American Foundation for the
   Blind
11 Pennsylvania Plaza, Suite 300
New York, NY 10001
Ph#: (800)232-5463

American Optometric Association
243 N. Lindbergh Blvd.
St. Louis, MO 63141
Ph#: (800)365-2219

Association for Macular Diseases
210 E. 64th St.
New York, NY 10021
Ph#: (212)605-3719

Helen Keller National Center for
   Deaf-Blind Youths and Adults
111 Middle Neck Rd.
Sands Point, NY 11050
Ph#: (516)944-8900

Lighthouse International
111 E. 59th St.
New York, NY 10022-1202
Ph#: (212)821-9482
Fax: (212)821-9705

OTHER ORGANIZATIONS

The American Association
   of Retired Persons
601 E St. NW
Washington, DC 20049
Ph#: (202)434-2000
Fax: (202)434-2320

Alliance for Aging Research
2021 K St. NW, Suite 305
Washington, DC 20006
Ph#: (202)293-2856
Fax: (202)758-8574

The Alzheimer's Association
National Headquarters
919 North Michigan Ave.,
   Suite 1000
Chicago, IL 60611-1676
Ph#: (800)272-3900
Fax: (312)335-1110
E-mail: *info@alz.org*
Internet: *www.alz.org*

American Academy of Pain
   Medicine
4700 W. Lake Ave.
Glenview, IL 60025
Ph#: (847)375-4731
Fax: (847)375-4777
E-mail: *aapm@amctec.com*
Internet: *www.painmed.org/html*

American Association for
   International Aging
1900 L St. NW, Suite 510
Washington, DC 20036
Ph#: (202)833-8893
Fax: (202)833-8762

American Association of Homes
   and Services for the Aging
901 E St. NW, Suite 500
Washington, DC 20004-2037
Ph#: (202)783-2242
Fax: (202)783-2255

American Diabetes Association
National Office
1660 Duke St.
Alexandria, VA 22314
1-800-DIABETES (1-800-342-2383).
E-mail: *pbanks@diabetes.org*
Internet:
   www.diabetes.org/membership

AFL-CIO Department of Employee
   Benefits
815 16th St. NW
Washington, DC 20006
Ph#: (202)637-5000
Fax: (202)637-5058

AFSCME Retiree Program
1625 L St. NW
Washington, DC 20036
Ph#: (202)429-1274
Fax: (202)429-1293

American Geriatrics Society
311 Massachusetts Ave. NE
Washington, DC 20002
Ph#: (202)543-7446
Fax: (202)543-5327

American Heart Association
National Center
7272 Greenville Ave.
Dallas, TX 75231-4596
Ph#: (214)706-1448
Fax: (214)706-1341
E-mail: *ncrp@amhrt.org*
Internet: *www.americanheart.org*

American Medical Women's
   Association
801 N. Fairfax St., Suite 400
Alexandria, VA 22314
Ph#: (703)838-0500
Fax: (703)549-3864
E-mail: *director@amwa-doc.org*
Internet: *www.amwa-doc.org/html*

American Society on Aging
83 Market St. Suite 516
San Francisco, CA 94103-1824
Ph#: (415)974-9600
Fax: (415)974-0300

Eldercare America, Inc.
1141 Loxford Terrace
Silver Spring, MD 20901
Ph#: (301)593-1621
Fax: (301)593-1621

Families USA
1334 G St. NW
Washington, DC 20005
Ph#: (202)628-3030
Fax: (202)347-2417

Gerontological Society of America,
   The
1030 15th St. NW, Suite 250
Washington, DC 20005-1503
Ph#: (202)842-1275
Fax: (202)842-1150

Gray Panthers
2025 Pennsylvania Ave. NW, Suite 821
Washington, DC 20006
Ph#: (202)466-3132
Fax: (202)466-3133

National Asian Pacific Center on Aging
   (NAPCA)
Melbourne Tower, Suite 914
1511 Third Ave.
Seattle, WA 98101-1626
Ph#: (206)624-1221
Fax: (206)624-1023

National Association for Home Care
228 7th St. SE
Washington, DC 20003
Ph#: (202)547-7427
Fax: (202)547-9559
E-mail: *webmaster@nahc.org*
Internet: *www.nahc.org*

National Association of Area Agencies
on Aging
1112 16th St. NW, Suite 100
Washington, DC 20036
Ph#: (202)296-8130
Fax: (202)296-8134

National Association of Meal Programs
1414 Prince St., Suite 202
Alexandria, VA 22314
Ph#: (703)548-5558
Fax: (703)548-8024

National Association of Nutrition and
Aging Services Programs
2675 44th St. SW, Suite 305
Grand Rapids, MI 49509
Ph#: (616)513-9909 or (800)999-6262
Fax: (616)531-3103

National Association of Retired Federal
Employees
1533 New Hampshire Ave., NW
Washington, DC 20036-1279
Ph#: (202)234-0832
Fax: (202)797-9697

National Association of State Units on
Aging
1225 I St. NW, Suite 725
Washington, DC 20005
Ph#: (202)898-2578
Fax: (202)898-2583
E-mail: *staff@nasua.org*

National Committee to Preserve Social
Security and Medicare
2000 K St. NW, Suite 800
Washington, DC 20006
Ph#: (202)822-9459
Fax: (202)822-9612

National Council of Senior Citizens
8403 Colesville Rd., Suite 1200
Silver Spring, MD 20910-3314
Ph#: (301)578-8800
Fax: (301)578-8999

The National Council on the
Aging
409 Third St. SW
Washington, DC 20024
Ph#: (202)479-1200
Fax: (202)479-0735

National Institute on Consumer-
Directed Long-Term Care
Services (NCOA)
409 Third St. SW
Washington, DC 20024
Ph#: (202)479-6670
Internet: *www.ncoa.org/research
/demo_prjts/institute.html*

National Osteoporosis Foundation
1150 17th St. NW, Suite 500
Washington, DC 20036
Ph#: (202)223-2226
Fax: (202)223-2237

National Senior Citizens Law
Center (NSCLC)
1101 14th St. NW, Suite 400
Washington DC 20005
Ph#: (202)289-6976
Fax: (202)289-7224
E-mail: *nsclc@nsclc.org*

Older Women's League
666 Eleventh St. NW,
Suite 700
Washington, DC 20001
Ph#: (202)783-6686
Fax: (202)638-2356

Visiting Nurse Association
of America
11 Beacon St., Suite 910
Boston MA, 02108
Ph#: (800)426-2547
Fax: (617)227-4843
E-mail: *webmaster@vnaa.org*
Internet:
www.vnaa.org/default.html

Currently Available In-Home High-Tech Treatments

INFUSION THERAPIES

Various forms of infusion therapy are now offered in the home. Such therapy may include the use of various access devices, including peripherally inserted catheters, subcutaneous access devices, central lines, implantable ports, and electronic infusion devices (IV pumps). Many agencies provide additional infusion therapies, including diuretics, steroids, albumin, immune globulin, tocolytics, antiemetics, chelation, and growth hormones.

Artificial Nutrition and Hydration

This treatment provides necessary food and water for patients who have problems swallowing, digesting, or absorbing food and water. There are two ways to provide artificial food and water to patients: enteral feeding and parenteral feeding.

Enteral Feeding

Food and water are delivered through a tube inserted in the stomach or intestine. This is commonly known as tube feeding and may use the following types of tubes: gastrostomy (inserted in the stomach), jejunostomy (inserted in the intestine), or nasogastric (inserted in the nose and extending internally into the stomach).

Parenteral Nutrition

Food and water are delivered through an intravenous line. This is sometimes referred to as total parenteral nutrition and is used for people who have problems with digestion and absorption.

Intravenous Pain Management

This type of infusion therapy provides pain medication through an intravenous line. This is generally used with patients who suffer from severe pain, who are recovering from surgery, or who have cancer. In some cases the amount of pain medication can be controlled by an automatic pump that provides adequate doses of painkillers at proper intervals.

Blood Product Infusion (Hemotherapy)

This treatment is provided via an intravenous line and delivers blood products, such as blood platelets or packed cells, directly into the patient's vein.

Intravenous Antibiotics, Antifungals, or Antivirals

This treatment is provided to individuals who have some type of infection. The antibiotics are provided through an intravenous line directly into the patient's vein. This is the most common type of infusion therapy provided in the home.

Intravenous Medications for Cardiac Patients

This may include use of intermittent intravenous inotropic therapy to prevent cardiogenic shock in some patients or for patients with advanced heart failure awaiting transplant. It may also include administration of anticoagulants. Medications may include: dobutamine, milrinone, heparin, and so forth.

Chemotherapy

Chemotherapy is the treatment of disease with chemical agents. Generally this treatment is used with individuals who are suffering from cancer. The chemicals are delivered through an intravenous line. In most cases, chemotherapy uses highly toxic chemicals that must be handled and stored with caution. With home chemotherapy, most agencies require a caregiver to be present because of the potential side effects.

Renal Dialysis

This is a treatment for patients suffering from some type of kidney failure or disease that reduces the kidney's ability to filter the blood. Equipment is used in place of the kidney to cleanse the patient's blood of harmful by-products produced by the body.

Peritoneal Dialysis

This procedure uses a dialysis catheter that is inserted into the abdominal cavity. The cleansing solution is flushed into the abdominal cavity, using the intestines as a filter between the solution and the blood stream. The process thereby removes waste products and excess water from the body.

RESPIRATORY THERAPY

Agencies offer a wide variety of respiratory services in the home, including portable oxygen systems, aerosol therapy, transtracheal oxygen therapy, continuous positive airway pressure (CPAP) and bi-level positive airway pressure (BiPAP) therapies, adult apnea monitoring, and so forth.

Mechanical Ventilation

This treatment is provided to individuals who are unable to breathe on their own. A device called a ventilator (positive or negative pressure) is used to help patients breathe by providing oxygen-rich air and by using pressure to help the patient inhale and exhale this air. There are a variety of ventilators that can be connected to the patient through tubing inserted in the nose, mouth, or trachea (throat). Ventilators may also come with humidifiers to prevent dryness, filters to protect the lungs, and heat controls to maintain body temperature.

PATIENT MONITORING

Heart Monitors (Cardiac Telemetry)

This equipment can monitor and record heart functions on a continual basis. This is usually done through electrodes attached to the patient's chest. Cardiac telemetry machines can monitor heart rate, blood pressure, and pacemaker activity and can run electrocardiograms.

Personal Emergency Response Monitors

This is a type of monitoring device that can signal a control center when the patient needs assistance. Usually the patient wears a wireless device around the neck. It may signal for help with the touch of a button by the patient or, in more advanced models, it can monitor patient activity and signal after a period of inactivity. Most services have a control center staffed 24 hours per day. If an emergency is signaled, the staff at the center call for help. Generally this is used for people who are alone for long periods of time and who have serious medical problems that limit mobility and ability to function independently.

Telehealth

This is the electronic transfer of health-care information between the home care agency and the patient's home by means of video, audio, and communications technology. Telehealth allows for the performance of assessment, monitoring, care management, education, diagnostic, and counseling functions over long distances. This technology may allow home care staff to treat more patients in a given period of time while ensuring that quality patient care is provided by allowing more frequent interactions with medical personnel, round-the-clock coverage, fewer missed home care visits resulting from obstacles to travel or inclement weather, immediate access to vital signs in emergencies, and routine assessment and preventive care.

ELECTRONIC STIMULATION

These treatments deliver an electric or electromagnetic stimulus to the body to generate a physiologic response. They are used for pain relief, muscle contraction, or bone growth stimulation.

Transcutaneous Electronic Nerve Stimulation

This procedure is used to reduce chronic or postsurgical pain by delivering a signal to peripheral nerves. Also noninvasive muscle stimulation can be used to stimulate muscle contraction.

Bone Growth Stimulation

Both invasive and noninvasive forms of electronic stimulation have been used to encourage bone growth in patients with nonunion fractures, congenital pseudarthroses, and failed fusions. Units can be implanted or external.

ASSISTIVE DEVICES

Adaptive Computer Aids

Computers can be used to assist clients in communicating with providers and family, in monitoring patient vital signs, and for rehabilitation of functional. In some cases patients will need assistive devices to use the computer. Such high-tech devices include ultrasonic and infrared beams, large-screen monitors, and compatible software.

Robotics

Although not widely available, the use of robotics is currently being studied in a variety of health care settings. Robotics employs a variety of technologies, including computerization, information systems, artificial intelligence, and engineering technology, integrated within the body of a robot. These machines have the ability to manipulate objects and environments through the use of sensors and computers. These applications have the potential to aid in a variety of daily activities, such as lifting patients, retrieving and delivering objects, feeding patients, mobility assistance, minimally invasive medical diagnosis (e.g., temperature, pressure, and acidity), and therapy conducted with a variety of on-board microsensors.

BEDSORE/PRESSURE SORE CARE

A pressure sore is a condition that develops when individuals are bedridden or have severely limited mobility or poor circulation. A pressure sore begins with reddening of the skin in an area of bony prominence (such as the buttocks, heel, and toes). If untreated, it can eventually lead to skin breakdown, which then creates an open wound on the patient. Treatment for pressure sores includes application of topical antibiotics, turning the patient to prevent further pressure on the wound, and use of air mattresses and computerized beds that turn the patient automatically. The treatment depends on the severity of the bedsore.

Index

('n' indicates a note; 't' indicates a table)